GOD'S MIGHTY HAND
PROVIDENTIAL OCCURRENCES IN WORLD HISTORY
VOLUME 1

By
Richard "Little Bear" Wheeler

Published By
Mantle Ministries Press
228 Still Ridge Bulverde, Texas 78163

CONTENTS

PREFACE

"One generation shall praise thy works to another, and shall declare thy mighty acts. I will speak of the glorious honour of thy majesty, and of thy wondrous works. And [men] shall speak of the might of thy terrible acts: and I will declare thy greatness. They shall abundantly utter the memory of thy great goodness, and shall sing of thy righteousness." (Psalm 145:4-7)

As a Christian historian, I am intrigued that most historical writers do an excellent job researching events and recording facts, yet altogether miss the truth that God's mighty hand forged the chain of events people call "history." This is because they are not born-again Christians, and their perspective is earthly, not heavenly. The Bible calls the unbeliever a "natural man," and, therefore, spiritually blind: *"But the natural man receiveth not the things of the Spirit of God: for they are foolishness unto him: neither can he know [them], because they are spiritually discerned"* (I Corinthians 2:14). A Christian, however, believes nothing ever happens by "coincidence" or without design. The Bible declares, *"In him we live and move, and have our being"* (Acts 17:28). Jesus himself told the governor of Judea, Pontius Pilate, that he had *"...no power...except given to him from above"* (John 19:11). The everlasting wisdom of Proverbs 16:9 reveals that, *"A man's heart deviseth his way: but the LORD directeth his steps."* Clearly, God oversees the events of history.

Unfortunately, we Christians receive the bulk of our history lessons from secular historians. The accounts in this book were compiled from various letters, journals, diaries, and previously out-of-print Christian works. As you read them, you will probably ask yourself, "Why wasn't this taught to me in school or recorded in my textbooks?" The answer is sobering and obvious.

For decades, secular historians and teachers either have been ignorant of God's intervention in history, or they have intentionally banned this truth from their writings and classrooms. For example, if you are able to find the account of Moses in a secular history book, you will most likely notice that the story lacks miracles. Frequently the name of Moses will be altogether absent from modern accounts of the time of Moses. Strange? Not really. It is only natural that secular historians remove what they themselves do not believe. Yet Moses was a real person who lived, and struggled to understand life. And he recognized the power of God in history when he wrote the following: *"O Lord God, thou hast begun to shew thy servant thy greatness, and thy mighty hand: for what God is there in heaven or in earth, that can do according to thy works, and according to thy might?"* (Deuteronomy 3:22-24).

God's Mighty Hand (Providential Occurrences in World History) has been written primarily to reveal God's intervention in the affairs of people outside the Bible throughout the ages. Books like this are extremely important because they fulfill the Scriptural admonition of Psalm 78:4 *"We will not hide them from [our fathers'] children, showing to the generation to come the praises of the LORD, and his strength, and his wonderful works that he hath done."* The true stories of history give God the glory due His name. Their re-telling helps build the faith we need in difficult times. These stories also give us hope and assurance that God is in control and that all will be well in the end. Although most of us will not be mentioned in mankind's history books, everyone has significance in God's plan for this world. Even men like General Washington, President Lincoln, David Livingstone, Winston Churchill and most of their distinguished contemporaries did not believe they were significant players in the God's overall plan. All they recognized in their lifetimes was their own call to meet the challenge of serving God and humanity with their dedicated abilities. Yet history shows they moved mountains by God's power and providence.

I hope you will reflect on the wonder of God's mighty hand directing these world affairs long ago. When you are finished, remember to be on the alert to recognize God's handiwork in the historical events developing in your own lifetime. God, one day, may reveal to you how the thread of your very own everyday existence is woven into the profound and intricate tapestry of His perfect plan.

I have purposely written this original collection of narratives for family devotional reading. Therefore, footnotes and references have been omitted. I encourage you and your children to research the details of these and similar stories as the Lord leads you to discover more about His-story.

In His Providential Care,
Richard "Little Bear" Wheeler

JUST A SHEPHERD 984 B.C.

Long before David was king of Israel, God's mighty hand was at work in his life—a life seemingly unimportant until God stepped into it. David was the youngest of the eight sons of Jesse, which means he faced the same problems kids do today dealing with older brothers and sisters. And, sadly, even his father tended to forget he was there. The Bible says when God's prophet Samuel came looking for the boy God would select as the next king of Israel, Jesse did not even call David to appear before him. But Samuel knew one of Jesse's sons was missing. He said to Jesse, "These aren't all your children, are they?"

"No," Jesse said. "The youngest is taking care of the sheep."

"Send for him," Samuel said. "We'll wait till he gets here."

David belonged to the tribe of Judah. And, as we have seen in the Bible verse above, he spent much of his boyhood caring for his family's sheep. He not only fed and watered them, but also guarded them from thieves and wild animals. He was well known in the area for his bravery. In fact, he had killed both a lion and a bear in defense of the flock. Being a shepherd is lonely work. David spent many long hours meditating on the things he had heard about God. His experience and his faith taught him to trust in Jehovah, the God of his fathers.

During David's youth, the peace of Israel was threatened by powerful neighboring people called the Philistines. They lived along the Mediterranean coast from Joppa in the north to Gaza in the south. Among the Philistines was a tribe of people called Rephaims, who were giants. One of them, named Goliath, was particularly troublesome to Israel.

Goliath was not just big; he was positively huge, standing at least nine and one half feet tall. If the ancient Hebrew standard of measuring (called a cubit) is used, then Goliath was thirteen feet, four inches tall! Either size is a challenge for any man, let alone a young boy. Goliath wore a bronze helmet, bronze breastplate, and other armor weighing about 270 pounds. His spear weighed another 25 pounds and his sword was 10 pounds. Altogether, the fully-armed Goliath weighed about as much as any three NFL linebackers combined, tipping the scale at about 800 pounds! Just imagine him walking onto the battlefield and defying the army and the God of Israel—which is exactly what he did, day after day, for 40 consecutive days.

He was definitely a formidable threat. The soldiers in King Saul's army, including David's three oldest brothers, were afraid of Goliath. He intimidated them with his size and his constant taunting. But David was not afraid. David's father had sent him to the battle scene with food for his brothers. His oldest brother, Eliab, teased him about being there. "Why are you here, boy? Where'd you leave that handful of sheep you take care of?" he said sarcastically. "You're just here to play soldier!" But when Goliath took the field to challenge God, David said to King Saul, "Have no fear! I will fight this Philistine!" Saul, however, had his doubts about David's abilities. After all, he was only a boy, and a small one, at that. But David had seen the mighty hand of God at work in the past, and knew God would not fail the one who came against Goliath in the strength of the Lord.

Though Goliath was heavily armed, young David refused the weapons and armor Saul offered. Instead, he took just 5 stones from the nearby stream. Carefully fitting one in his leather sling (which was something like a slingshot), he ran toward Goliath shouting, *"Thou comest to me with a sword, and with a spear, and with a shield: but I come to thee in the name of the LORD of hosts, the God of the armies of Israel, whom thou hast defied. This day will the LORD deliver thee into mine hand; and I will smite thee, and take thine head from thee; and I will give the carcases of the host of the Philistines this day unto the fowls of the air, and to the wild beasts of the earth; that all the earth may know that there is a God in Israel"* (I Sam...17:45-46).

David sent the first stone flying from his sling. And that was all it took. It hit Goliath right in the center of his forehead, killing him instantly.

In 984 B.C., when David was king of Israel, the Philistines rose up against Israel again. When the Philistine army moved into the Valley of Rephaim southwest of Jerusalem, in an attempt to crush King David's stronghold, David called the men of Israel to fight them. Watching from a hill overlooking the battlefield, David realized it would be impossible for his little army to defeat the forces arrayed against it. It would take an act of God. He called his commanders, chiefs and priests together for prayer. The Lord answered their prayers saying, "Do not advance against them in the front, but circle around behind them, and sneak up on them behind those mulberry trees. When you hear the sound of the wind in the tops of the mulberry trees, attack them! For then I, the Lord, will go out before you, at the head of your army, to defeat the Philistines." David ordered his army to do just as the Lord commanded. A supernatural army, sent by God, appeared. A mighty and fearsome sound was heard in the trees around the valley. The army of Israel defeated the frightened Philistine army, ending many years of hostilities. David learned from his experiences that attempting to do battle with only human strength is foolish, and will ultimately lead to defeat. But a battle fought in the name and strength of the Lord will always lead to victory. When you trust in the Lord, mercy will surround you, and the Lord Himself will be your fortress against your enemies in battle.

This song, written by J. Harvey Daily (1881-1964), a renowned Texas preacher among the Primitive Baptist churches, sums up the mighty hand of God as experienced in the Bible narrative of David and Goliath:

When Moses and the Israelites from Egypt's land did flee, Behind them were proud Pharaoh's host, in front of them the sea; God raised the waters like a wall and opened up the way. And the God that lived in the olden times is just the same today.

When David and Goliath met, the wrong against the

right; The giant armed with human strength and David with God's might, God sent a stone by David's sling, the giant low did lay, And the God that lived in the olden times is just the same today.

When Daniel faithful to his God would not bow down to men, And by his enemies was hurled into the lions' den; God shut the lion's mouths, we read, and robbed them of their prey. And the God that lived in the olden times is just the same today.

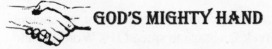

THE BOY WHO WOULD BE KING 336 B.C.

Daniel wrote the Old Testament book that bears his name while in captivity in Babylon, sometime between 605 and 530 B.C. It is truly an amazing book for, by God's mighty hand, Daniel was given prophetic visions of every major world power that would rise and fall until Christ would set up His kingdom rule here on Earth.

In Daniel 11, he predicted the fall of the Persian Empire and the rise of Alexander the Great, who led the Greek conquest of the known world, while spreading the influence of the Greek/Hellenistic culture and language. Daniel's prediction was written and delivered approximately three hundred years before Alexander was even born! What other book can claim such credibility? None! The claims of all other major religions and sects fall short using this prophetic test. Not one of their writings has the power of accurately and completely fulfilled predictions, 100 percent of the time. The Bible stands alone as a unique book. Indeed, God's book. Let's look at the story of Alexander the Great and see the mighty hand of God at work.

Alexander the Great ruled from 336-323 B.C. At that time, near the end of the Old Testament era, Greece had risen to the status of a world power. The Greeks exerted great influence on the Jewish people, particularly during the period between the Old and New Testaments. Greek culture also paved the way for the expansion of Christianity in the first century A.D. Under the leadership of this great military conqueror, the influence of the Greek Empire was extended throughout Asia Minor to Egypt and the borders of India. Alexander's conquests and his passion to spread Greek culture contributed to the advancement of Greek ideas throughout the ancient world. This adoption of Greek ideas by the rest of the world was known as Hellenism.

So thoroughly did Greek ideas penetrate the other nations, that the Greek language became the dominant language of the ancient world. God used the Greek language to spread His Word far and wide. The Septuagint, a Greek translation of the Old Testament, was commissioned to be copied and circulated by Ruler Ptolemy II during the third century B.C. This enabled a widely dispersed population to have access to part of God's word in the new common language.

Since Greek was the universal language due to the influence of Alexander the Great, the apostle Paul could communicate easily with the various nations and provinces he visited during his missionary journeys. Paul visited such major cities as Philippi, Thessalonica, Athens and Corinth, all of which retained distinct Greek cultural ideas, although they were ruled by the Romans in Paul's time. He showed a deep understanding of Greek thought and was able to communicate the Gospel so the Greek mind could understand deep spiritual matters.

In the Old Testament, Greece is referred to as Javan. In the New Testament, the word "Greeks" refers to all people who have been influenced by Greek culture and who are not Jews. The term "Grecians" refers to Greek-speaking Jews who lived in areas outside Palestine. Converts to Christianity included people from both these groups.

What is truly awe-inspiring about God is His ability to raise up people, even unbelievers, to accomplish His divine purpose. In the New Testament book of Galatians (chapter 4, verse 4), Paul refers to God sending His Son, Jesus Christ, to redeem us "in the fullness of time." God was able to turn Alexander the Great's exploits, to Hellenize the world, into a much greater eternal influence, to convert multitudes among all races by using the simple tool of the Greek language, which also came on the scene just when God wanted it too—in the fullness of time.

"God that made the world and all things therein, seeing that he is Lord of heaven and earth, dwelleth not in temples made with hands; Neither is worshipped with men's hands, as though he needed any thing, seeing he giveth to all life, and breath, and all

things; And hath made of one blood all nations of men for to dwell on all the face of the earth, and hath determined the times before appointed, and the bounds of their habitation; That they should seek the Lord, if haply they might feel after him, and find him, though he be not far from every one of us: For in him we live, and move, and have our being; as certain also of your own poets have said, For we are also his offspring"(Acts 17:24-28).

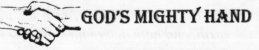

THE SIGN IN THE SKY 272 A.D.

The small cluster of women washing clothes beside the stream were exchanging news. One excitedly said, "Have you heard Christians are no longer being persecuted?" "What is happening? Is it true we can now worship without fear of being arrested?" said another." "Yes, I personally read the edict of toleration signed by Emperor Constantine myself while in the marketplace two days ago!" One of the Christian women said, "I do not trust Constantine. I do not know that much about him to trust him completely. As for our family, we will still worship at Pastor Archippus' house until we see the results of these new events."

Flavius Valerius Constantinus, or Constantine, was born into a military family at Nis, in the region of present-day Serbia. His father, Constantius Chlorus, rapidly advanced in the military system as a commander, like so many Roman military leaders. Due to his success in battles, Constantius became popular with the people and naturally gravitated to higher positions of power.

In 305 A.D., Constantine rose to the position of co-emperor of Rome. Following in his father's steps, Constantine showed military talent in the East; he later joined his father in Britain in 306. He was popular with the troops, who proclaimed him emperor when Constantius died later the same year. Over the next two decades, however, Constantine had to fight his rivals for the throne, and he did not finally establish himself as sole ruler "Constantine the Great," until 324.

In 312, on the eve of a battle against his rival Maxentius, Constantine feared defeat and invoked the gods of Rome for victory. While reviewing the gods and calling on their names, he added the name of the Christians' God, Jesus the Christ. He later recorded that as he prayed to the Christians' God, Christ, he promised God that if he would gain victory over Maxentius during battle that he would become a follower of Christ. In addition, he promised to do all in his power to make Rome a Christian republic. Supposedly, as he prayed, he received a vision of Christ who appeared to him and told him to inscribe the first two letters of His name (XP in Greek) on the shields of his troops. The next day he is said to have had a vision of a cross superimposed in front of the bright sun, and the words "in this sign you will be the victor."

Constantine providentially defeated Maxentius at the Battle of the Milvian Bridge near Rome. The Senate hailed the victor as savior of the Roman people. Thus, Constantine, who had been a pagan solar worshiper, now looked upon the Christian Deity as an instrument of victory. Persecution of the Christians was ended when the co-emperors, Constantine and Licinus, issued the Edict of Milan in 313 A.D. This Edict mandated toleration of Christians in the Roman Empire, which ended three hundred years of Christian persecution. Because Constantine and Rome now favored the Christian religion, the Roman Church was then given legal rights to receive large financial donations for building churches throughout the empire, usually on the same site as pagan temples.

You may wonder how God's mighty hand was in control of these events, and what historical significance they played for the future of the world? I personally do not believe Constantine became a truly converted Christian because his lifestyle did not dramatically change. He did some serious damage to the true Church of Christ which leads me to believe that in reality Satan was behind the scenes trying to weaken the true Church of Christ. For centuries Christians were killed in every imaginable manner in order to stop the spreading of the Gospel of Christ; all to no avail. As the number of martyrs increased, the more victorious the Church became and continued to flourish. I am sure that Satan, frustrated, could not figure a way to stop Christianity until Constantine came along. The old adage here, "If you can't lick them, join them." With Constantine making Christianity the accepted religion of Rome, the true Church of Christ was damaged. The cost of being a Christian was no longer the issue. Weakness, sinfulness, and other destructive influences crept into the Church. Now, the pseudo "angel of light," Satan, got his foot in the door of the organized Church. Unfortunately, this Satanic influence continues with the Church at large to this very day, and will remain until Christ comes to separate the "wheat from the tares," and "the sheep from the goats."

Now, for the positive providential influences of Constantine's actions: The often-quoted verse fits perfectly here. *Romans 8:28 "And we know that all things work together for good to them that love God, to them who are the called according to His purpose."* What Constantine did by creating a "Christian" empire was to secure Christianity in the huge Western World. Had Christianity not been secured, God only knows what ungodly religious sects would today dominate the Western World and perhaps even America. It allowed for Christianity to spread uninhibited throughout the known world with the license of Roman approval. Since Rome specialized in roads that traversed the empire for the soldiers to keep peace, the Christians could use the same roads to carry on the Great Commission, and spread the love of Christ. What soon developed was the age-old struggle between the true Church and the false church. But the fact remains of the true Church that the "gates of hell cannot prevail against it." By trying to join the Church, Satan unwittingly provided the beachhead for Christianity to spread throughout the world. Christ will return to earth at the scheduled time to establish the true Church and to separate the "wheat from the tares." God always wins. His hand is mighty to perform His deeds and good pleasure.

IT'S IN THE CLOVER 435 A.D.

March 17 is a well-known date on which we celebrate Saint Patrick's Day, but what do we know of the man for whom this date is commemorated? Actually, little is known of St. Patrick's early life, but we do know that he was born in Scotland around 387 A.D. and given the name Malwyn. Born into a wealthy family, his father, Calphurius, served as a magistrate appointed by Rome for his community. Although Patrick was raised with Christian principles, he had not come to the full revelation of his need to trust Christ by faith for salvation.

When he was sixteen, he was providentially kidnapped by Irish marauders and sold to a Druid chief in what is now Antrim, Ireland, where he was forced to keep sheep. During his six years of slavery, he learned the Irish language and culture. Little did he realize, at the time, that the Lord's mighty hand was working in his life to accomplish a glorious deed for the advancement of His Kingdom, as you will soon learn. As with Joseph of old, captive in Egypt, what man meant for evil, God meant for good.

During Patrick's captivity, he heard and received the gospel story of Jesus Christ. He wrote about his conversion saying, "I was sixteen years old and knew not the true God and was carried away captive to Ireland, but in that strange land the Lord opened my unbelieving eyes. I called my sins to mind, and was converted with my whole heart to the Lord my God, who regarded my low estate, had pity on my youth and ignorance, and consoled me as a father consoles his children. Well, everyday I used to look after the sheep and I used to pray often during the day while watching sheep; the love of God and fear of Him increased more and more in me and my faith began to grow and my spirit stirred up, so that in one day I would pray as many as a hundred times and nearly as many at night. Even when I was staying in the woods or on the mountains, I used to rise before dawn for prayer, in snow and frost and rain, and I felt no ill effect and there was no slackness in me. As I now realize, it was because the Spirit was glowing in me."

After six years, Patrick saw a chance for escape, made his way to the coast and boarded a ship to his homeland. Imagine the joy his family felt when they saw their long lost son return at age twenty-two. Holding fast to his love for the Lord, Patrick sought ways to learn more about Him. He studied the Holy Scriptures on his own, as well as with various faithful traveling monks whenever possible. Realizing that he needed to know more than he could learn in the British Isles, he went to France and entered the monastery of St. Martin at Tours. During his eighteen years of study there, he became a priest and was later promoted to the position of bishop. Ever zealous for Christ and the cross, he shared his faith with all who would listen.

One night, Patrick was inspired by the Holy Spirit in a vision to return to the pagans who had earlier kidnapped him. He described the incident: "I saw a man who was called 'Victorious' coming as if from Ireland, with innumerable Scrolls, and I read what they said, 'The voice of the Irish,' and while I was reading I heard a voice, 'Please, come and walk with us again."

Patrick recognized that the Lord had sent the vision and was calling him to be a priest to Ireland in the same way He had called Samuel of old to be a priest to Israel. Providentially, Patrick's years in Ireland had prepared him for this work; his experiences enabled him to communicate with the people in their own language and relate to their culture. He understood the power the pagan Druid religion held over the people, but he also knew that the power of God could break that control.

In 431 A.D., Pope Celestin I renamed Malwyn, "Patricius," (Latin for "of noble birth") and commissioned him to go to Ireland. You could well imagine how the Druid priests in Ireland set up strong opposition to Patrick's plans, but Patrick was not intimidated. He spoke openly, not only about salvation, but also against slavery and pagan practices, such as infant sacrifice. Being renounced, stoned, and beaten several times, he counted himself privileged to suffer for Christ. His steadfast determination and love for the souls of the Irish people gained many converts. Even though he and his followers were chained and sentenced to death, God's mighty hand intervened, saving their lives time and time again.

For thirty years, Patrick served the Lord using creative ways to gather crowds together to hear the Word of God. Sometimes he would send a recent convert to beat a large drum throughout his village. Recognizing their neighbor, they would gather in curiosity. Patrick would then step forward and begin to preach the Gospel to them.

The power of the Druid religion over the Irish people was expressed through the Druid priests and the Druid king, King Tara. He was a huge, awe-inspiring man dressed in animal-skin clothing who struck fear into the hearts of the simple peasants. Patrick's job could not be complete until the king's demonic power over the people was broken. Knowing that Christ gave His followers power over the realm of darkness, Patrick prayed for an opportunity to break this bondage.

This opportunity came when King Tara decreed that no lights were to be lit on a certain night. In holy boldness, Patrick ignited a huge bonfire on the highest hill in the area; he wanted to show the people not to fear man, but only to fear God.

The king came to the hill and demanded to know who defied his authority. Patrick stepped forward and said, "O, King, this fire, which has been lighted in indifference to your royal edict, will blaze forever in this land unless it be extinguished this very night."

Intimidated by the power of Patrick, the king backed away, and the fire was not extinguished, nor was the Gospel message. The Gospel spread throughout Ireland with power and might. In time, Ireland became known as the most evangelical nation in the world. Many throughout the then known world traveled there to receive Biblical instruction.

One concept the Irish found difficult to understand was the Trinity: Father, Son, and Holy Spirit, three in one. Once while preaching to a large crowd and trying to explain the reality of the Holy Spirit, a frustrated Patrick bowed his head and prayed in front of the gathered crowd. "Lord, these are Your people. I cannot show them the Trinity. Please help me."

When Patrick opened his eyes, the Holy Spirit directed his attention to a three-leaf clover. Holding up the plucked clover, he said, "Trinity is like this clover; one stem, three leaves." The people's eyes were opened. Having grasped the understanding of that divinely inspired object lesson of the Trinity, they embraced Christianity in droves. Over the years of Patrick's ministry in Ireland, many thousands were baptized and some two hundred churches were established. Truly, God's hand was at work in preparing Ireland for the Gospel.

In his youth when it seemed to Patrick that tragedy had befallen him at the hands of malicious pirates, Patrick yielded his life to God for His use in adverse circumstances. He was then able to make a great difference in the world. God delights in doing the unusual and impossible to show the power of His mighty hand. God had arranged for Patrick's kidnapping at the age of sixteen in order to establish a beachhead for Christianity and to stop the advances of paganism throughout Europe. As a result of Patrick's ministry, converts were discipled and the Church in Ireland was established. Through faithful Christian monks, the Church painstakingly preserved the Scriptures, opened Bible seminaries, and sent missionaries throughout Europe to evangelize and claim heathen territories for the advancement of the Kingdom of Christ.

" Many, O LORD my God, are thy wonderful works which thou hast done, and thy thoughts which are to us-ward: they cannot be reckoned up in order unto thee: if I would declare and speak of them, they are more than can be numbered" (Psalm 40:5).

THE INFLUENCE OF A GODLY WIFE 496 A.D.

Do you ever doubt that prayer changes people and events? This story tells how the prayers of a Godly wife influenced her royal husband, and changed the face of what is today Western Europe.

Western Europe, once called Gaul, was part of the ancient Roman Empire. Gaul included the territories now known as France, Belgium, the Southern Netherlands, Switzerland, Northern Italy, and Germany west of the Rhine River. It was heavily populated by Celtic people—ancestors of the Irish and Welsh peoples—who had been conquered by Julius Caesar's Roman armies around 50 B.C. Rome's dominion lasted for about 500 years. When the Roman civilization crumbled, barbarian tribes regained power over Western Europe. These loosely-aligned tribes often fought with one another to gain more land and power. Gaul, also, was in constant turmoil with fighting factions, and disputes among pagan religions. In the midst of these conditions, the Lord moved to show the power of His mighty hand.

By 496 A.D., King Clovis was rising to power in Gaul. The only threat to his success was the rebellious Franks, a confederation of German-speaking peoples living on the East bank of the lower Rhine River. It was there that the Franks fought the Alemanni, one of the fiercest of the Germanic tribes in Gaul. When King Clovis sent his troops into battle, they lost ground to the Alemanni's steadily advancing troops. Clovis realized that unless something supernatural happened, all his dreams of a united empire would be lost on the field of battle.

King Clovis' wife, Clothilde, had converted to Christianity during their marriage. She lovingly shared her faith with her husband whenever she felt he would listen. The king, however, resisted embracing her Christian God. Clothilde was left with only one resource: prayer. But what a powerful resource! She prayed that circumstances would draw her husband to faith in Christ. Those circumstances came when King Clovis was stopped by the Alemanni. In utter despair, Clovis cried out to the God of his wife. In humility he prayed, "Most Mighty God, whom my Queen Clothilde worships and adores with all her heart and soul, I pledge my perpetual service to your faith. Please give me now the victory over my enemies." When he looked up, he saw a marvelous sight. His army, which had been retreating, had turned and had begun to fight with supernatural valor and strength. At the same time, the Alemanni soldiers were gripped with a spirit of fear and gave up the ground that had been won just moments before. The Alemanni king was killed, and his soldiers lost heart as news of the king's death spread through their ranks. Soon a flag of surrender was raised. King Clovis, overcome with awe at the power of God, gave the command to receive the banner of surrender from the enemy troops.

Later at the victory banquet, the air was charged with wonder and excitement. His soldiers, and the people of the realm who knew him best all had the same question: what had happened to King Clovis? He seemed a changed man! With his wife at his side, the king stood to his feet, and with a humble voice said:

> *"Lords of the Franks, it seems to me highly profitable that ye should know, first of all, that the gods we formerly worshiped are false and powerless. There is only one God and one power over man. Know of a surety that this same God, the one whom our queen embraces, is my God now. He it was who delivered us when all was lost on the battle field. He gave us victory and now the kingdom of the Franks is united. Lift, therefore, your hearts in just hope and ask the Sovereign Defender that He give you all that which you desire, that He save your souls and give us victory over our enemies."*

With one accord, his people embraced the Christian faith, and

3000 soldiers, led by their king, rose and were baptized in the river as new believers in Christ. Wives and children were also moved by the miraculous victory over their enemies on the field of battle and at the conversion of their husbands, fathers, and king. They, too, accepted Christ and were baptized. The presiding bishop laid his hand on the kneeling Clovis, whose eyes were brimming with tears. He said, "Bow down thine head, fierce king. Adore that which once thou hast spurned; spurn that which thou hast in the past adored in sin."

The outcome of that one battle had a tremendous effect upon history. Christianity, in Roman Catholic form, became the foremost faith of Europe. This power was used by the Lord to keep the Moslem religion from gaining a stronghold in Europe. Over the next few years, the Lord gave Clovis victories over the pagan Visigoths and Burgundians. By 507, most of Gaul, Western Germany, and the areas now called Holland and Belgium were under Clovis's rule. However, corruption in the Roman Catholic Church which King Clovis was forced to endure would continue until a more Biblical pattern was established by Wycliffe, Huss, and other reformers, like Luther, who were yet to step onto the stage of human history.

"Behold, thou shalt call a nation that thou knowest not, and nations that knew not thee shall run unto thee because of the LORD thy God, and for the Holy One of Israel; for he hath glorified thee. Seek ye the LORD while he may be found, call ye upon him while he is near: Let the wicked forsake his way, and the unrighteous man his thoughts: and let him return unto the LORD, and he will have mercy upon him; and to our God, for he will abundantly pardon. For my thoughts are not your thoughts, neither are your ways my ways, saith the LORD. For as the heavens are higher than the earth, so are my ways higher than your ways, and my thoughts than your thoughts. For as the rain cometh down, and the snow from heaven, and returneth not thither, but watereth the earth, and maketh it bring forth and bud, that it may give seed to the sower, and bread to the eater: So shall my word be that goeth forth out of my mouth: it shall not

return unto me void, but it shall accomplish that which I please, and it shall prosper in the thing whereto I sent it" (Isaiah 55:5-11).

FOLLOW THE LEADER 800 A.D.

"O clap your hands, all ye people; shout unto God with the voice of triumph. For the LORD most high is terrible; he is a great King over all the earth. He shall subdue the people under us, and the nations under our feet. He shall choose our inheritance for us, the excellency of Jacob whom he loved. Selah. God is gone up with a shout, the LORD with the sound of a trumpet. Sing praises to God, sing praises: sing praises unto our King, sing praises. For God is the King of all the earth: sing ye praises with understanding. God reigneth over the heathen: God sitteth upon the throne of his holiness. The princes of the people are gathered together, even the people of the God of Abraham: for the shields of the earth belong unto God: he is greatly exalted" (Psalm 47:1-9).

After Emperor Constantine had brought the Roman Empire under his control in 323 B.C., he moved the capital city from Rome to the ancient Greek city of Byzantium. This city was in the East (on the Bosporus Sea), while Rome was in the West (on the Mediterranean Sea). Eventually, this caused a split in the Roman Empire. Rome began to disintegrate, losing its power over the people. This disintegration mainly occurred as a result of Emperor Theodosius I (A.D. 379-395) dividing the empire between his two sons. The division turned out to be permanent. It was also a blessing in disguise. Never again was the old Roman Empire governed as a single unit with one emperor.

The Eastern Roman Empire, sometimes called Byzantium, lasted for more than a thousand years and secured Roman Catholic Christianity in its region. This might not have occurred without the division of east and west. The Byzantine Empire was able to stem the tide of Moslem influence from entering Europe, and at the same time provide a beachhead for Christianity to grow unopposed.

The Western Roman Empire struggled to maintain its existence in the face of an onslaught of invasions from warring tribes. The Ostogoths, Visgoths, Vandals, Franks, Angles, and Saxons were the ancestors of the German people. The Romans called them "barbarians" because of the primitive sounds of their languages to the Roman ear. Their words sounded as though they were babbling, saying "bar-bar."

These German tribes, while destroying Rome and the Western Empire, were influenced by the Christians who lived among them as they settled their conquered empire. Missionaries were sent to them and some of their pagan ways were stopped. Winning these German pagans to Christ was quite a challenge. They would go on drunken sprees, killing one another, spurred on by their uncontrolled tempers. They had no regard for unwanted babies, nor the aged; both would be left outdoors to die. Various pagan gods of fear and superstition existed among them. So, the empire gradually became a dark, demonic place.

However, the spark of Christianity still burned brightly. There is always hope in darkness. Even a small flicker from the light of Christ can extinguish darkness, and the mighty hand of God will prevail on every side to redeem His people. He never gives up trying to lead mankind to salvation; to light from darkness. When Jesus appeared on earth, He fulfilled the prophecy spoken of Him by Isaiah: *"The people that walked in darkness have seen a great light: they that dwell in the land of the shadow of death, upon them hath the light shined" (Isaiah 9:2).*

As the struggle for light over darkness and right over wrong continued, God raised several leaders whom He used to secure and reclaim the Western Roman Empire for His kingdom. One already referred to in this book was King Clovis. Another, who turned parts of Europe into strongholds for Christianity, was Charlemagne (French for "Charles the Great"). He ruled for seventy-two years (742-814 A.D.).

Charlemagne, a deeply committed Christian, excelled in warfare. For fifty years he fought all over Europe, conquering pagans by sword or by Christian baptism. The choice was theirs. He followed in the tradition of King Clovis, but extended the Christian influence over a broader area. One of his greatest desires was to see the last of the pagan German Saxon tribes either dispelled from the land or converted.

On Easter Day in 774 A.D., a messenger came riding to Charlemagne from the north. His horse was covered with foam as he drew rein at the palace gate. His face was ghastly white, and his voice shook when he was taken before the king. "Sire," he said, "I bring terrible news. Not long ago the Saxons were meeting in their sacred grove to offer human sacrifices to their pagan gods. An Irish missionary, Libuin by name, entered fearlessly among them, halted their ceremonies, and told them of the true God and of our Savior, Christ. They made no effort, at the time, to stop him speaking or to attack him, but merely listened with sullen faces. Then, he went back to his mission on the edge of the Frankish territory, thinking that his words had softened their hearts.

"But the Saxons were only planning a terrible revenge. Last month, they fell upon the mission, putting Libuin to death most cruelly. They tortured and slew your other subjects there, O, King. I alone escaped, and I have ridden day and night to ask your aid in this matter. The Saxons, made more bold by their success, may harry and destroy other Christian villages also."

Charles leaped to his feet. He clutched the handle of the sword which hung at his side. Nothing touched him more deeply than harm to his Church and his Christian people. "By my faith," he cried, "we will march against those Saxon pagans! We will teach them obedience, and to bow their knee to Christ as King."

To our way of thinking, forcing people to receive Christ is horrible. Yet, in those dark days, force was a way of life. The power of the Roman Catholic Church and its appointed emperor was supreme; never to be questioned. Questioning would begin in 500 years with Wycliffe, Huss, Luther, and Tyndale.

Another Saxon rebellion occurred in 782 A.D. A brilliant young leader, Wittekind, led the Saxons in still another revolt.

Churches were burned. Christian missionaries and Saxon converts to the Christian religion were tortured and killed. Only a small Frankish army existed in the territory at the time and it met with a disastrous defeat.

Charlemagne was very angry as he hastened northward. In the town of Verden, he called a meeting of the Saxons and demanded that the leaders of the rebellion be brought before him. "But, sire," one of the Saxons replied, "the leaders and those who helped them have disappeared into the forests. No one can find them now." The king's eyes flashed while in thundering tones he reminded the Saxons of their broken promises. Filled with awe and fear, they watched and listened to the tall, commanding figure. Finally, they agreed to surrender the guilty men who had burned the churches, killed the Christians, and taken part in the revolt. Forty-five hundred men were brought before the king.

Until that time, Charlemagne had tried to treat the Saxons fairly. He was usually more merciful than most monarchs of his day. But when he looked on these guilty warriors, he ordered all of them put to death. This cruel act only made matters worse. The angry Saxons rebelled again and fought more fiercely than ever. They almost got the better of the Franks. In the end, Charlemagne won and added the Saxon lands to his own kingdom. Even Wittekind surrendered and was baptized. Charlemagne became godfather to him, forgave him, loaded him with gifts, and became his friend.

About this same time, Bavaria was also added to the Franks' growing kingdom. Charlemagne then defeated the Avars, a savage people living on the Hungarian plains. He became the ruler of a vast realm which included the lands later called France, Belgium, the Netherlands, parts of Italy and Germany, and other territory farther east. Not since the old Roman Empire, had such a large part of Europe been under the rule of one man. And the people he conquered were baptized into the Christian faith.

As a boy, Charlemagne had dreamed of greatness and serving God, and now those dreams were coming true. But something happened beyond what even Charlemagne could ever imagine, an achievement most leaders would kill for, but something which caused Charlemagne to feel humbled and unworthy.

On Christmas Day in 800 A.D., Charlemagne rode out at the head of a great throng of Frankish and Italian nobles to attend services at St. Peter's Cathedral in Rome. The nobles of the day usually dressed colorfully in silks and cloth of gold, or they wore scarlet and silver tunics. Pope Leo, however, asked Charlemagne to dress like one of the nobles of the old Roman Empire. So he wore Roman sandals instead of Frankish boots. And over his long, plain linen tunic was a white toga, or robe. Because his costume was so simple, he could be seen all the more clearly against the riot of color all about him.

St. Peter's Cathedral was not built in the form of a cross, like many churches and cathedrals of the day. Rather, it was an oblong building like a Roman court. Rows of columns extended down the sides. On these columns were hung purple, gold, and scarlet tapestries. The altar at the far end was covered by a canopy which sparkled with gold. Indeed, the whole church glittered and shone. Music rolled and swelled, seeming to fill the arches of the high ceiling. Before the altar was the tomb of St. Peter.

The pope, priests, bishops, and choir took their places in the chancel (the space around the altar). Charlemagne halted before St. Peter's tomb and then went down the few steps leading into it. There he knelt and prayed while a great hush fell on the huge assembly. When he rose from his knees, he climbed the steps and stood before the altar. The pope took a gold crown which had been resting on the altar and placed it on Charlemagne's head. A mighty shout shook the heavy rafters of the building. "Charlemagne! Charlemagne! the Augustus, crowned of God, the great and peace-loving emperor, long life and victory!" Charlemagne had been crowned supreme ruler: Emperor of the Holy Roman Empire.

When Charlemagne went forth again from the church, he was the most powerful man on earth. He had been given the same title as the mighty Caesar Augustus and other great monarchs, like Constantine, who had once ruled most of the known world. For the first time in more than three hundred years, since the fall of the Roman Empire, there was an emperor in Rome.

But the new emperor was not happy. Einhard, his secretary, who later wrote the story of his life, reported that Charlemagne turned to him after the ceremony was over. "If I had known what Pope Leo intended this day," Charlemagne whispered, "I would never have set foot in yonder building even for the celebration of the Christmas Mass!"

Why wasn't he glad and proud? He had become the most powerful man in Europe. Perhaps, being a simple, honest, and upright person, he doubted the right of the pope to crown him emperor. Or, possibly, he just did not like so much pomp and ceremony in the church where he had come to worship Jesus. Charlemagne was very humble in his religious life. He ruled his country with a firm and sometimes hard, stubborn hand; but he never set himself up to be anything but a simple worshiper before God and His Church. Therein lay much of the secret of his greatness.

Charlemagne was always frustrated with his lack of education. While living in Aachen (present day Belgium and Holland), he solicited the aid of Alcuin, a famous monk and renowned scholar from Britain, to teach him and his family. Soon, Charlemagne and his children learned to read and write (although Charlemagne never fully mastered writing). Through his zeal for education, he pioneered Christian education for the common man of Europe.

Alcuin and Charlemagne set about to have schools built through the entire empire. Alcuin and other proficient scholars began to write poems, various books of learning, and, most importantly, translations of the Bible for the common man to read. God, by His mighty hand, was using Charlemagne to plant the seeds of Reformation throughout a spiritually dark Europe; seeds which would later blossom with the light of God's Word.

"Gather the people together, men, and women, and children, and thy stranger that is within thy gates, that they may hear, and that they may learn, and fear the LORD your God, and observe

to do all the words of this law: And that their children, which have not known any thing, may hear, and learn to fear the LORD your God, as long as ye live in the land whither ye go over Jordan to possess it" (Deuteronomy 31: 12-13).

"YOU DIRTY RAT" 1348 A.D.

One of the worst plagues in history was so devastating it is called the Black Death. Henry Knighton wrote the following eyewitness account of the Black Death in England:

> In this year of 1348, there was a general mortality among men throughout the world. It began first in India, and then appeared in Tharsis, then among the Saracens, and at last among the Christians and Jews, so that in the space of one year, namely, from Easter to Easter, 8000 legions of men, according to widely prevalent rumors in the Court of Rome, died in those remote regions, besides Christians....The dreadful pestilence penetrated the sea coast by Southampton and came to Bristol. There, almost the whole population of the town perished, as if it had been seized by sudden death; for few kept their beds more than two or three days, or even half a day. Then this cruel death spread everywhere around, following the course of the sun. And there died at Leicester in the small parish of St. Leonard more than 380 persons, in the parish of Holy Cross, 400; in the parish of St. Margaret's, Leicester, 700; and so in every parish, a great multitude. Then the Bishop of London sent word throughout his whole diocese giving general power to each and every priest, regular as well as secular, to hear confessions and to give absolution to all persons with full Episcopal authority. Likewise the Pope granted full remission of all sins to anyone receiving absolution when in danger of death, and granted that this power should last until Easter next following, and that everyone might choose whatever confessor he pleased. In the same year there was a great outbreak of a deadly disease among sheep everywhere in the kingdom, so that in one place in a single pasture

more than 5000 sheep died; and they putrefied so that neither bird nor beast would touch them. Everything was low in price because of the fear of death, for very few people took any care of riches or property of any kind. A man could buy a horse that had been worth 40 shillings [$8.80] for 6 shillings [$1.32], a fat ox for 4 shillings [$0.88] ,a cow for 6 shillings [$1.32], a heifer for 8 shillings [$1.76], a fat whether for 4 shillings [$0.88] ,a sheep for 2 shillings [$0.44] ,a lamb for 2 shillings, a large pig for 5 shillings [$1.10], a stone of wool [24 lbs.] was worth 9 shillings, [$1.98]. Sheep and cattle ran at large through the fields and among the crops, and there was none to drive them off or herd them; for lack of care they perished in ditches and hedges in incalculable numbers throughout all districts, and none knew what to do. For there was no memory of death so stern and cruel since the time of Vortigern, King of the Britons, in whose day, as Bede testifies, the living did not suffice to bury the dead. In the following autumn a reaper was not to be had for a lower wage than 8 shillings [$1.76], with his meals; a mower for not less than 10 shillings [$2.20], with meals. Wherefore many crops wasted in the fields for lack of harvesters. But in the year of the pestilence, there was so great an abundance of every kind of grain that almost no one cared for it.

The Scots, hearing of the dreadful plague among the English, suspected that it had come about through the vengeance of God, and, according to the common report, they were accustomed to swear, "be the foul deth of Engelond." Believing that the wrath of God had befallen the English, they assembled in Selkirk forest with the intention of invading the kingdom, when the fierce mortality overtook them, and in a short time about 5,000 perished. As the rest, the strong and the feeble, were preparing to return to their own country, they were followed and attacked by the English, who slew countless numbers of them. Meanwhile the King sent proclamation into all the counties that reapers *and other labourers should not take more than they had been accustomed to take, under the penalty appointed by statute. But the labourers were so lifted up and obstinate that they would not listen to the King's command. If anyone wished to have them he had to give them what they wanted or he would risk losing his fruit and crops. And when it was known to the King that they had not observed his command, and had given greater wages to the labourers, he levied heavy fines upon abbots, priors, knights, greater and lesser, and other great folk and small folk of the realm, of some 100 shillings [$22.00], of some 40 shillings [$8.80], of some 20 shillings [$4.40], from each according to what he could give. And afterwards the King had many labourers arrested, and sent them to prison; many withdrew themselves and went into the forests and woods; and those who were taken were heavily fined. Their ringleaders were made to swear that they would not take daily wages beyond the ancient custom, and then were freed from prison. And in like manner was done with the other craftsmen in the boroughs and villages.... "After the aforesaid pestilence, many buildings, great and small, fell into ruins in every city, borough, and village for lack of inhabitants, likewise many villages and hamlets became desolate, not a house being left in them, all having died who dwelt there; and it was probable that many such villages would never be inhabited again."*

Throughout the ages, when disasters like the Black Plague have occurred, both the living and the dying wonder who is in control. Some blame God, others Satan. To say it is Satan is to contend that God is powerless, and at Satan's mercy. On the other hand, attributing the disasters to God makes Him look cruel, heartless, and unloving.

But in the final analysis, God is either in control of everything or He is in control of nothing at all. Disasters, therefore, are the result of either providence or chance. There is really no other alternative.

When one studies history from a providential perspective, what is eternal appears beyond the crushing presence of the immediate. In every major disaster which has occurred, finite man has turned to an infinite God. Wars, disasters, and calamities often have been the very tool God used to cause prideful, self-sufficient, egocentric men and women to fall on their knees in humble prayer, turning to the God who holds the future in His hands.

Mr. Knighton said nothing in his account to indicate the spiritual climate in England and on the European Continent at the time of the Black Death. Yet during this period approximately twenty million people died—one quarter of the population of Europe. What spiritual fruit did these events have?

John Wycliffe was twenty years old during the Black Death. Within ten years, John Wycliffe would be used of God to shake England from religious fear and superstition. Through him those who lived through "the Death" would begin to learn of a merciful and caring God, who, in the midst of the world's disasters brings life through Christ Jesus our Lord. When Wycliffe taught school at Oxford, people were ready to listen. Having translated the Bible into the common language of the people, he gave them the ability to find passages of comfort and hope on their own, without a priest. In reading passages like Revelation 22:6-7, they would come to know that God's mighty hand is truly in control of all things:

And he said unto me, These sayings are faithful and true: and the Lord God of the holy prophets sent his angel to shew unto his servants the things which must shortly be done. Behold, I come quickly: blessed is he that keepeth the sayings of the prophecy of this book. And I John saw these things, and heard them. And when I had heard and seen, I fell down to worship before the feet of the angel which shewed me these things. Then saith he unto me, See thou do it not: for I am thy fellow servant, and of thy brethren the prophets, and of them which keep the sayings of this book: worship God. And he saith unto me, Seal not the sayings of the prophecy of this book: for the time is at hand. He that is unjust, let him be unjust still: and he which is filthy, let him be filthy still: and he that is righteous, let him be righteous still: and he that is holy, let him be holy still. And, behold, I come quickly; and my reward is with me, to give every man according as his work shall be.

"I am Alpha and Omega, the beginning and the end, the first and the last. Blessed are they that do his commandments, that they may have right to the tree of life, and may enter in through the gates into the city. For without are dogs, and sorcerers, and whoremongers, and murderers, and idolaters, and whosoever loveth and maketh a lie. I Jesus have sent mine angel to testify unto you these things in the churches. I am the root and the offspring of David, and the bright and morning star. And the Spirit and the bride say, Come. And let him that heareth say, Come. And let him that is athirst come. And whosoever will, let him take the water of life freely" (Revelations 22:6-17).

"THE MORNING STAR" 1330 A.D.

John Wycliffe is called "the Morning Star of the Reformation," because he was the very first theologian to take a courageous stand against the wicked practices of the corrupt Roman Church. He lived one hundred forty years before Martin Luther and set into motion events that would have a profound impact on Luther and the other Reformers.

Born in 1330 A.D. in Yorkshire, England, Wycliffe received his doctorate in theology at Balliol College, an extension of Oxford University. He knew the inner workings of the established Roman Church in England, having received an education steeped in their traditions.

Skilled in understanding the Latin Bible, Wycliffe began to hold Bible studies at the university, and was sought after by students hungry for God's Word. There was a revival in the making, and it disturbed the leaders of the Roman Church to no end! How was it that this young upstart could command more attention and a larger following than they themselves could?

To make matters worse, in 1374 Wycliffe came to the aid of King Edward III of England, who was in a power struggle with Pope Gregory XI. The conflict concerned fees paid by the English government to the Roman Church. Both Parliament and the king were reluctant to pay the fees because they were essentially taxes collected by a foreign power. Wycliffe wrote several pamphlets refuting the pope's claims and upholding the rights of Parliament to limit church power over Parliament and king.

The king appointed Wycliffe to represent him in this matter at the Royal Court in Bruges, Belgium. The meeting failed to resolve the dispute, but was instrumental in building a friendship between John Wycliffe and the king's fourth son, John of Gaunt, who also represented Edward.

Two years later, Wycliffe began to teach on the doctrine of

"dominion as founded in grace." This doctrine taught that God conferred grace as a gift, and that it carried authority which could be forfeited when misused. The implications of this teaching were clear to the Roman Church leaders. Wycliffe was asserting that God could reprove the Church for violating Biblical doctrine and, therefore, was capable of losing its God-given grace and its position of authority over the people.

As you might expect, the Church reacted vigorously against this strong rebuke and called Wycliffe to give account before William Courteny, Bishop of London. It did not go well for Wycliffe, and he would have been jailed if not for the friendship and intervention of John of Gaunt.

Wycliffe, experiencing from these near disasters the difficulty in challenging the authority of the Roman Church, could have withdrawn from the battle. Instead he continued to work to hold the Church in England accountable in many areas. He questioned the legality of Rome's demand for English tribute and disavowed both serfdom and welfare. He held that the clergy should strive to imitate evangelical poverty, as did Christ and the disciples while ministering on earth. He repudiated the doctrine of "transubstantiation," the teaching that the priest transforms the communion bread or wafer into the actual body of Christ during the ceremony. These and other teachings alienated Wycliffe from most of the royal court, and also some who had formerly defended him in Parliament. Even John of Gaunt, his former friend and advocate, eventually withdrew, leaving Wycliffe to stand utterly alone.

But John Wycliffe was just getting started! For in 1378, he began a work that was to overshadow everything he had done up to that point, one that would mount the greatest challenge yet to church authorities. He began to translate the Latin Bible into English, for the first time giving the common people of England an opportunity to read the Bible for themselves. Since most people were unable to read, he and his followers also began teaching this vital skill, using the Bible as the basis of education.

The Roman Church in England was furious that the common

people would be able to read the Bible—at a time when even few priests could! It was in this ignorance of what God had actually spoken that the Church held the priests and the people in spiritual slavery.

The effort to translate the Bible and teach literacy was the last straw. The Church stripped Wycliffe of all honors and titles, expelled him from his position at Oxford, and labeled him a heretic. A petition was sent to the pope in Rome advocating his trial and execution.

Having lost the status of his life-long work at the university, and facing a potential death sentence, John Wycliffe retired to the small parish of Lutterworth. But he never gave up his dream. He continued to teach the Bible to whoever would come to learn. His writings and teaching were spread further by the Lollards (a term of derision given by their detractors, meaning "mumblers" in Dutch). They were followers of Wycliffe, itinerant preachers who traveled the countryside like the Apostles.

John Wycliffe died on December 31, 1384, but his influence lived on after him. By the grace of God and His mighty hand, the teachings of Wycliffe spread across to Bohemia (modern Czechoslovakia) and inspired another early Reformer, John Huss, who began to affect the continent of Europe.

Huss led the people of Bohemia to recognize the false doctrines of the Roman Church. For his teachings, Huss was burned at the stake.

The Roman Church continued to blame "that heretic, John Wycliffe," even though he had been dead for thirty-one years! Frustrated church officials became so enraged about the continued spread of "Wycliffism" that they convened the Council of Constance in 1415. There, these desperate men decreed that Wycliffe should be burned at the stake. So, in 1428—forty-four years after his death—his body was disinterred. With great ceremony his enemies burned his body to ashes, cursed them to damnation, and threw them into the river, as a warning to all who held his views.

Church historian Fuller aptly said,

"They burned his bones to ashes, they cast them into the River Swift that runs by. Thus this brook had conveyed his ashes into the River Avon, and into the Severn. The Severn into the mighty ocean, and so the ashes of Wycliffe are the emblem of his doctrine which are now dispersed the world over."

Those spiritual ashes did indeed cover the European continent as you will see in other stories in this book. John Wycliffe was a light of Biblical understanding to people blindly following church dogma. He often stood alone to question years of false church teachings. In doing so, he gave to the common people the seeds of Biblical self-government, and the courage to love and serve God apart from the Roman Church. Is it any wonder that Martin Luther said that he "owed Wycliffe a great debt?"

The Church at Rome vainly thought that by burning his skeleton at the stake they would silence his followers. How foolish to fight against the mighty hand of God in such a futile way, for who can fight God?

Many times men have attempted to destroy the Bible. In 303 A.D., the Roman Emperor Diocletian issued an edict to destroy Christians and their Bibles. The persecution that followed was horrible.

In 1776, Voltaire, the French godless philosopher, announced, "One hundred years from today, there will not be a Bible in the earth except one that is looked upon by an antiquarian curiosity seeker."

One hundred years later, Voltaire was dead and his own house and press were being used to print and store Bibles by the Geneva Bible Society. One hundred years from the day of Voltaire's prediction, the first edition of his works sold for 11 cents in Paris. But the British government paid the Czar of Russia one-half million dollars for an ancient Bible manuscript.

The Bible gives us a glimpse of what God thinks of those who try to stop His Kingdom work:

"Why do the heathen rage, and the people imagine a vain

thing [like burning a skeleton!]? The kings of the earth set themselves, and the rulers take counsel together, against the LORD, and against his anointed, saying, Let us break their bands asunder, and cast away their cords from us. He that sitteth in the heavens shall laugh: the LORD shall have them in derision..." (Psalm 2:1-5).

COOK YOUR GOOSE 1415 A.D.

The Roman Church thought burning Wycliffe's skeleton, and throwing the ashes into the River Swift as a curse, would stop the spread of his teachings.

Those spiritual ashes surely must have fulfilled Fuller's prophecy by landing on the shores of Holland, where Mr. Laurence Coster lived (see Coster story 1423 A.D.). In this story, you will see how those ashes were carried figuratively to Bohemia by a follower of John Wycliffe, who spread his own ashes of truth furthering the Gospel of Christ.

John Huss was born in Husinec, in southern Bohemia (now Bosnia-Herzogovenia) and was educated at the University of Prague. He received his Master of Arts degree in 1396. Two years later, he became a lecturer in theology at the university. In 1401, he was appointed dean of its theological school. The Czech reformist movement that had been initiated by the popular 15th century Bohemian preacher, Jan Milíc, was prevalent at both the University of Prague and Bethlehem Chapel. Huss quickly became involved in it.

Like Wycliffe, Huss vigorously condemned church abuses. Through preaching, he attempted to bring the Church to the people. Every Sabbath, Huss preached at the Bethlehem Chapel in the Czech language instead of the traditional Latin. He taught the people that they could receive Christ personally, apart from church traditions and dogma.

On the doctrinal level, both Wycliffe and Huss believed in predestination, regarded the Bible as the ultimate religious authority, and held that Christ is the true Head of the Church, rather than any inevitably corrupt church official. Thanks to Huss, Bohemia was experiencing an awakening—a mini-reformation—prior to the Reformation to come under Martin Luther. Needless to say, it was not long before Huss got into trouble with Roman Church leaders.

In 1408, the archbishop of Prague ordered John Huss to defend some of his sermons. After his defense, Huss was forbidden to exercise his priestly functions in the diocese. The following year, Alexander V, one of the three rival popes then contending for authority in the Church, issued a bull condemning the teachings of Wycliffe. He ordered all the materials John Huss had printed to be destroyed by a symbolic act of burning them. Receiving a bull was very serious; a bull is a letter or an edict of the pope, published and transmitted to the Roman Catholic churches containing some decree, order, or decision handed down by the pope. It is used chiefly in matters of justice or of receiving special grace and favor. If of a judicial nature, as in the case with John Huss, a lead seal was attached to the letter by a hempen cord, with a bull's head impressed on the lead with images of St. Peter and St. Paul. On the reverse side was the name of the acting pope and the year of his rule.

The Roman Church, not being satisfied with only the public burning of John's works, continued to persecute and hound Huss, calling for his excommunication for insisting to hold and teach the doctrines of John Wycliffe. John Huss was finally excommunicated in 1410. By then, however, he had already gained great popular support. Riots broke out in Prague. Backed by these popular demonstrations, Huss continued to preach, even after the city was laid under interdict in 1412. By the next year, however, many of his influential supporters had fallen from power. Huss fled Prague, finding refuge in the castles of several friendly noblemen. During this time he wrote his most important work, *De Ecclesia.*

In 1414, Huss was summoned to appear at an ecclesiastical judicial hearing historically known as the Council of Constance. This Church council meeting was held in the imperial city of Constance (Konstanz) from 1414 to 1418. The council condemned the doctrines of the English reformer John Wycliffe and those of the Bohemian reformers John Huss and Jerome of Prague, labeling them heretical. Even though Huss had received a pass of safe conduct from Holy Roman Emperor Sigismund, this promise of safety was betrayed. Huss was thrown into a cold, damp, rat-infested prison, for months. While in prison he wrote to his friends and ended the letter with this prayer:

O loving Christ, draw me, a weakling, after Thyself; for if Thou drawest me not, I cannot follow Thee. Grant me a brave spirit that it may be ready. If the flesh is weak, let Thy grace prevent, come in the middle, and follow; for without Thee I can do nothing, without Thee helping I cannot go to a cruel death. Grant me a ready spirit, a fearless heart, a right faith, a firm hope, and a perfect love, that for Thy sake I may lay down my life with patience and Joy.

When finally brought to trial, Huss managed by the grace he prayed for to defend his beliefs successfully. Tragically, like Christ, his had false charges brought against him, by his enemies, misstating the doctrines he had preached. On the final day of trial, Huss saw that some of the men he had accused of leading wicked lives were determined to have him put to death (for they shouted at him when he tried to speak in his own defense). He stood up calmly and, turning to Emperor Sigismund, said, "I came to this Council of my own free will, with a safe conduct from the emperor. I came in full confidence that no violence should be done me, and that I might prove my innocence." Huss then knelt down and prayed in a loud voice. "Lord Jesus Christ, forgive all my enemies, I entreat You, because of Your great mercifulness. You know that they have falsely accused me, brought forth false witness against me, devised false articles against me. Forgive them because of Your immense mercifulness."

The emperor knew Huss had spoken the truth. With one word he could have commanded thousands of men to defend and protect Huss. But, as Pilate did with Christ, the emperor did nothing to save him. While Huss stood gazing steadily, the emperor's face turned scarlet, and the thousands in that great Council of Constance beheld the blush of shame on the cheek of

Sigismund, Holy Roman Emperor.

Called upon to recant and promise not to teach his doctrines, Huss refused categorically. Jerome of Prague, John's dear friend, attempted to defend Huss. For this he, too, was arrested and later burned at the stake.

On July 16, 1415, John Huss was taken to the stake before an assembled crowd of family, friends, and enemies. As the wood was being arranged at Huss's feet, the man who was called upon to do this dastardly deed could not contain himself. Risking his own life, he prophetically declared,

"Today you will roast a lean goose [Huss means 'goose'], but one hundred years from today you will hear a swan sing. Him you will leave unroasted. No trap or net will catch him for you."

True to this word, God's mighty hand prevailed. Over one hundred years later, another German emperor, Charles, was presiding over another great council. When asked why he did not break his word and violate the safe conduct he had given Martin Luther, he said, "I should not like to blush as Sigismund blushed before John Huss." Martin Luther was not burned at the stake. The "goose" of the Reformation had escaped.

Great things happened for Christian liberty in the century after the deaths of Huss and Jerome of Prague. Savonarola preached against the wickedness of Lorenzo de' Medici and other great sinners in Florence, Italy. As with the Lord Jesus, *"The common people heard him gladly"* (Mark 12:37) for a time. But revenge came, swift and sure. He too was burned at the stake. The ashes of Savonarola were thrown into the River Arno, in Italy, as the ashes of Huss and Jerome of Prague had been cast into the Rhine—just as the ashes of their forerunner, Wycliffe, had been cast into the Swift.

Satan tried to stop the Reformation, but to no avail, for who can stop the hand and Word of God? Christ Himself predicted the outcome of those who try to oppose the will of God:

"And I say also unto thee, That thou art Peter, and upon this

rock I will build my church; and the gates of hell shall not prevail against it" (Matthew 16:18).

THE SECRET WOOD CARVER 1423 A.D.

Mankind was created for one purpose: to know God. That means to love Him and reflect His glory in all we do and say. Unfortunately, not everyone agrees with this, nor cares to pursue the knowledge of God, or to recognize His mighty hand in history. History written without the acknowledgment of God is like beholding a skeleton—it has no life, no flesh and blood. Is it any wonder that most young people hate history and file it away as "boring"? History is far from boring when one sees the intricate and unique ways God's hand does some monumental work, often in a quiet way, for those who have "eyes to see and ears to hear."

This is the story of one of those quiet deeds that changed the face of the earth in a monumental way.

Laurence Coster was a Dutchman who lived in the town of Haarlem, in the land of windmills, great dikes, and beautiful farms producing world-famous cheese. By the providence of God, Laurence Coster—a quiet man from this quiet land—was destined to impact millions of lives. Isn't it just like God to choose a sleepy, old, fifteenth-century town to bring about worldwide change? After all, He did the same thing when He chose the small, out-of-the-way town of Bethlehem as the birthplace of Jesus Christ, His Son.

Mr. Coster was in the habit of taking his children for walks along the canals whenever time permitted. There he would teach his children and their friends how to carve wood, much to their delight. One of his specialties was carving the initials of the children on nearby trees. One boy named John took special interest in these forms of carving. He would spend hours learning the skill from his mentor, Mr. Coster.

In 1423, Laurence was inspired to make some small blocks of carved letters and tie them in such a way that they would spell words. He then stamped them on paper, making small pamphlets with little stories and Bible verses. Up until then (except for the Chinese) all printing was done the slow, methodical way: by pen and ink. Mr. Coster's little booklets were sold on a small scale since his operation was more of a hobby than a serious business. His apprentice, young John, naturally jumped for joy at the mentor's little invention. "How simple, yet brilliant!" John said to himself. Soon people were clamoring to buy more of Coster's little books, never knowing they were printed by blocks of wood. Coster kept his invention a secret, and it appeared when he died that his invention had died with him. The books were no longer sold and the people sorely missed him and his books. But God was directing events, because young John knew of the invention, and the secret had not died but had stayed alive with him. One day John's family moved away from Haarlem. They took a boat, sailing slowly up-river past ancient towns and castles. At Strasbourg, France, John's family found their new home. John especially liked walking about the charming old city and visiting the Strasbourg Cathedral. He stared up at the high spire which could be seen above the other buildings in the city. Perhaps it directed his heart and mind to lofty thoughts of how he might someday do something special for the work of Jesus Christ. Such was his devotion to the Lord.

As John grew into manhood, he found he liked working with his hands. Learning various skills, he gravitated to the art of forming stained glass and setting it in lead to be used in churches. He also repaired broken stained glass windows and became a goldsmith. Business was so good that he took on a partner, Andreas Dritzehn. But one interest that never left John's mind was the love of carving letters that he had learned from his friend, Mr. Coster. One day the Lord quickened John's spirit with an idea of forming small lead letters instead of wooden ones. He began to make letters of various sizes, but found that the lead was too soft for heavy stamping. During his spare time he would try developing other forms of metal that would not destroy the edges of his carved letter. In due time, he became frustrated for lack of money to buy the various materials to continue his experiments.

John and his partner concluded they would have to borrow money. Hearing of a wealthy German merchant named Johann Faust, they approached him for the necessary funds to continue the project. Mr. Faust had heard of John's experiments in creating metal letters that could be used for printing. He was so intrigued that he committed large portions of his wealth to continue the project. In 1456, overcoming all difficulties through prayer and perseverance, John, Andreas, and Mr. Faust's son-in-law Peter Schoffer, began to print the Holy Bible. In a relatively short time they produced a beautifully decorated and neatly printed Bible. The Bible was taken to John Faust to see what he thought of the quality. Mr. Faust was overcome with emotion. It was far more beautiful than he had ever expected.

The young lad who learned the skill of carving letters from Mr. Coster was none other than Johann Gutenberg. The beauty of this story is that while John Wycliffe's dead body was being burned at the stake for distributing handwritten copies of portions of the Bible to the citizens of England (see Wycliffe 1378 A.D.), Laurence Coster was forming letters on blocks of wood that inspired his apprentice, Johann Gutenberg, to invent movable type.

Gutenberg's invention contributed to the breakup of the cloister of monastical scribes whose purpose was to hand-copy the Scriptures. The movable type made the Holy Bible available to the common people rather than just the powerful religious and social elite. On the horizon lay Martin Luther, William Tyndale, John Calvin, and countless others waiting to translate and teach the Bible; to set it in movable type, and make it available to people in their own language. This was destined to explode the world with the knowledge of God's mighty hand extended to bring man out of the darkness of the Middle Ages into the light of the Reformation and the Renaissance. People could now understand how to receive salvation apart from the superstitious fear of the Roman Church, which taught salvation by works instead of solely by the merit of Jesus Christ's death and resurrection. Mankind was set free to experience life as God intended from the day He created Adam and Eve. Johann Gutenberg's movable type moved against Satan's kingdom, delivering a major and irreversible defeat!

"How beautiful upon the mountains are the feet of him that bringeth good tidings, that publisheth peace; that bringeth good tidings of good, that publisheth salvation" (Isaiah 52:7).

THE NOBODY BECOMES SOMEBODY 1492 A.D.

There scarcely lives a person who has not heard and known, somewhat, of the name and deeds of Christopher Columbus, that how on the morning of October 12, 1492, he stepped ashore... an island he christened San Salvador (Holy Savior), in recognition of Christ's answers to all his prayers, hopes, dreams, and desires. That single day changed the course of history. The discovery of the Western Hemisphere is one of the pivotal events in world history. It opened up a new world for Europeans and initiated the spread of Western Christian civilization to a new hemisphere.

The mighty hand of God was written all over the voyages of discovery. In so many situations, both in going and coming across the Atlantic for twelve years, coupled with the dangers of explorations of the new world, Columbus would have died many times over had God not proven Himself mighty in Columbus' life. Columbus recognized early in his life that the mighty hand of God lay on him for special service. He recorded his feelings in his journal, which he entitled *Profecias Libro de las* (Book of Prophecies):

"At a very early age I began to sail upon the ocean. For more than forty years, I have sailed everywhere that people go.

"I prayed to the most merciful Lord about my heart's great desire, and He gave me the spirit and the intelligence for the task: seafaring, astronomy, geometry, arithmetic, skill in drafting spherical maps and placing correctly the cities, rivers, mountains, and ports. I also studied cosmology, history, chronology, and philosophy.

"It was the Lord who put into my mind (I could feel His hand upon me) the fact that it would be possible to sail from here to the Indies. All who heard of my project rejected it with laughter, ridiculing me.

"There is no question that the inspiration was from the Holy Spirit, because He comforted me with rays of marvelous illumination from the Holy Scriptures, a strong and clear testimony from the 44 books of the Old Testament, from the four Gospels, and from the 23 Epistles of the blessed Apostles, encouraging me continually to press forward, and without ceasing for a moment, they now encourage me to make haste.

"Our Lord Jesus desired to perform a very obvious miracle in the voyage to the Indies, to comfort me and the whole people of God. I spent seven years in the royal court, discussing the matter with many persons of great reputation and wisdom in all the arts; and in the end they concluded that it was all foolishness, so they gave it up.

"But since things generally came to pass that were predicted by our Savior Jesus Christ, we should also believe that this particular prophecy will come to pass. In support of this, I offer the Gospel text, Matthew 24:25, in which Jesus said that all things would pass away, but not His marvelous Word. He affirmed that it was necessary that all things be fulfilled that were prophesied by Himself and by the prophets.

"I said that I would state my reasons: I hold alone to the sacred and Holy Scriptures, and to the interpretations of prophecy given by certain devout persons.

"It is possible that those who see this book will accuse me of being unlearned in literature, of being a layman and a sailor. I reply with the words of Matthew 11:25: '*Lord, because thou hast hid these things from the wise and prudent, and hath revealed them unto babes.*'

"The Holy Scripture testifies in the Old Testament by our Redeemer Jesus Christ, that the world must come to an end. The signs of when this must happen are given by Matthew, Mark, and Luke. The prophets also predicted many things about it.

"Our Redeemer, Jesus Christ said that before the end of the world, all things must come to pass that had been wri ten by the prophets.

"The prophets wrote in various ways. Isaiah is the one most

praised by Jerome, Augustine, and the other theologians. They all say that Isaiah was not only a prophet, but an evangelist as well. Isaiah goes into great detail in describing future events and in calling all people to our holy catholic faith. Most of the prophecies of Holy Scripture have been fulfilled already....

"I am a most unworthy sinner, but I have cried out to the Lord for grace and mercy, and they have covered me completely. I have found the sweetest consolations since I made it my whole purpose to enjoy His marvelous presence.

"For the execution of the journey to the Indies, I did not make use of intelligence, mathematics, or maps. It is simply the fulfillment of what Isaiah had prophesied. All this is what I desire to write down for you in this book.

"No one should fear to undertake any task in the name of our Savior, if it is just and if the intention is purely for His holy service. The working out of all things has been assigned to each person by our Lord, but it all happens according to His sovereign will even though He gives advice.

"He lacks nothing that it is in the power of men to give Him. Oh, what a gracious Lord, who desires that people should perform for Him those things for which He holds Himself responsible! Day and night, moment by moment, everyone should express to Him his most devoted gratitude.

"I said that some of the prophecies remained yet to be fulfilled. These are great and wonderful things for the earth, and the signs are that the Lord is hastening the end. The fact that the Gospel must still be preached to so many lands in such a short time, this is what convinces me."

It intrigues me to meditate on the possibilities of "what if's." What if Columbus had failed on his voyage in 1492? All of Europe was waiting with bated breath to find out if Columbus would succeed in finding another trade route to the Orient. Had he failed Europe, would have turned her back on such a foolhardy, risky attempt and would have further explored the southern trade route that Bartholomew Diaz discovered in August, 1487.

The implications of this are very profound. Allow me to reveal a not too farfetched possibility. The Moslems at that time were very aggressive in the conversion of the people they conquered. The Moslems were also very dominant in exploring and taking land in the name of Allah. Had Columbus failed in the voyage of discovery to the Orient (New World), and the Moslems succeeded, today from South America to Canada would be primarily Moslem, and the Gospel of Christ suppressed. It is similar to the familiar story, so often seen during the Christmas season, *It's a Wonderful Life,* starring Jimmy Stewart. In the story George Bailey (Stewart) is the town's hero. As the story unfolds he is allowed to see what would have happened had he never been born. The outcome is tragic, for the town's bully, the evil, greedy Mr. Potter (Lionel Barrymore) takes control and the town is consumed in destruction. In like manner had any people other than Christians found these countries, the Gospel of Christ would have suffered major setbacks. Imagine the outcome: few Bible seminaries, little missionary endeavor, and very few Christian churches across our land.

What Columbus did was not open a "trade route" to the Orient, but open a trade route for the Gospel of Jesus Christ to be preached throughout the world. It gave the world the greatest nation that has ever existed, with the possible exception of Israel. America has been used by God to be a beacon in its Godly institutions of family, church, and Biblical law. World War I, and World War II would have had disastrous outcomes had America not been discovered by a Christian and founded on Christian principles set down by our Godly forefathers.

Listed below are some of the Bible passages Columbus listed in his book as his motivation of seeking a new trade route to the Orient. His primary goal was to be used by God to convert the people of China to the Catholic Christian faith. Keep in mind that the only visible witness to Biblical Christianity was the Roman Catholic Church. The much-needed reformation of the Roman Catholic Church was yet approximately twenty-five years away.

"The LORD reigneth, let the earth rejoice; let the multitude of isles be glad thereof" (Psalm 97:1).

"Listen, O isles, unto Me; and hearken, ye people from far; The Lord hath called me from the womb; from the bowels of my mother hath he made mention."(Isaiah 49:1).

"Sing unto the LORD a new song, and his praise from the ends of the earth, ye that go down to the sea, and all that is therein; the isles, and the inhabitants thereof "(Isaiah 42:10).

"I will also give thee for a light to the Gentiles, that thou mayest be my salvation unto the end of the earth"(Isaiah 49:6).

"My righteousness is near; my salvation is gone forth, and mine arms shall judge the people; the isles shall wait upon me, and on mine arm shall they trust" (Isaiah 51:5).

"Surely the isles wait for me, and the ships of Tarshish first, to bring thy sons from far, their silver and their gold with them, unto the name of the Lord thy God, and to the Holy One of Israel, because he hath glorified thee"(Isaiah 60:9).

"I am sought of them that asked not for Me; I am found of them that sought Me not; I said, Behold Me, behold Me, unto a nation that was not called by My name" (Isaiah 65:1).

"Go ye therefore, and teach all nations, baptizing them in the name of the Father and of the Son and of the Holy Ghost: Teaching them to observe all things whatsoever I have commanded you: And, lo, I am with you always, even unto the end of the world" (Matthew 28:19,20).

"But ye shall receive power after that the Holy Ghost is come upon you; and you shall be witnesses unto me both in Jerusalem, and in all Judea, and in Samaria, and unto the uttermost part of the earth" (Acts 1:8).

I would like to list several accounts of the mighty hand of God in the life of Columbus so that you too can praise the Lord for the great things He has done. These accounts are directly from the writings of Columbus' own journal. The Bible teaches that we must remember the mighty deeds of God and teach them to our children, so they will not forget the Lord nor the things He has done.

"Give ear, O my people, to my law: incline your ears to the words of my mouth. I will open my mouth in a parable: I will utter dark sayings of old: [historical stories] Which we have heard and known, and our fathers have told us. We will not hide them from their children, shewing to the generation to come the praises of the LORD, and his strength, and his wonderful works that he hath done" (Psalm 78:1-8).

Account #1 Sunday, 23 September 1492

The crew is still grumbling about the wind. When I get a wind from the southwest or west it is inconstant, and that, along with a flat sea, has led the men to believe that we will never get home. I told them that we are near land and that is why the sea is smooth. Later, when the sea rose up without wind, they were astonished at this sign. I saw this as God, and it was very helpful to me. Such a sign has not appeared since Moses led the Jews out of Egypt, and they, because of this sign, did not lay violent hands on me. God used this miracle to inspire my life.

Account #2 Sunday, 7 October 1492

This morning we saw what appeared to be land to the west, but it was not very distinct. Furthermore, no one wished to make a false claim of discovery, for I had ordered that if anyone make such a claim and, after sailing three days, the claim proved to be false, the 10,000 Maravedies [equal to about $540] reward promised by the Catholic Sovereigns would be forfeited, even if afterwards he actually *did see it. Being warned of this, no one aboard the Santa Maria or Pinta dared call out, "Land, land!" However, after we rendezvoused this morning, I ordered that we assemble at sunrise and sunset because that is when there is the least haze and we can see the farthest. The Nina, which is a better sailer, ran ahead and fired her cannon. She then ran up a flag on her mast to indicate that land had been sighted. Joy turned to dismay as the day progressed, for by evening we had found no land and had to face the reality that it was only an illusion. God did offer us, however, a small token of comfort: many large flocks of birds flew over, coming from the north and flying to the southwest. [These birds were providentially provided to direct their course]. They were more varied in kind than any we had seen before, and they were land birds, either going to sleep ashore or fleeing the winter in the lands whence they came. I know that most of the islands discovered by the Portuguese have been found because of birds. For these reasons I have decided to alter course and turn the prow to the west-southwest. This I did an hour before sunset, and I shall proceed on this course for two days. I added another 15 miles before darkness, making a total of 84 miles by night and by day.*

Account #3 Thursday, 11 October 1492

I saw several things that were indications of land. At one time a large flock of sea birds flew overhead, and a green reed was found floating near the ship. The crew of the Pinta spotted some of the same reeds and some other plants; they also saw what looked like a small board or plank. A stick was recovered that looks man-made, perhaps carved with an iron tool. Those on the Nina saw a little stick covered with barnacles. I am certain that many things were overlooked because of the heavy sea, but even these few made the crew breathe easier; in fact, the men have even become cheerful. As is our custom, vespers were said in the late afternoon, and a special thanksgiving was offered to God for giving us renewed hope through the many signs of land He has provided.

About 10 o'clock at night, while standing on the stern castle, I thought I saw a light to the west. It looked like a little wax candle bobbing up and down. It had the same appearance as a light or torch belonging to fishermen or travelers who alternately raised and lowered it, or perhaps were going from house to house. I am the first to admit that I was so eager to find land that I did not trust my own senses, so I called for Pedro Gutierrez, the representative of the King's household, and asked him to watch for the light. After a few moments, he too saw it. I then summoned Rodrigo Sanchez of Segovia, the comptroller of the fleet, and asked him to watch for the light. He saw nothing, nor did any other member of the crew. It was such an uncertain thing that I did not feel it was adequate proof of land.

The moon, in its third quarter, rose in the east shortly before midnight. I estimate that we were making about 9 knots and had gone some 67 1/2 miles between the beginning of night and 2 o'clock in the morning. Then, at two hours after midnight, the Pinta fired a cannon, my prearranged signal for the sighting of land. I now believe that the light I saw earlier was a sign from God and that it was truly the first positive indication of land. When we caught up with the Pinta, which was always running ahead because she was a swift sailer, I learned that the first man to sight land was Rodrigo de Triana, a seaman from Lepe. I hauled in all sails but the mainsail and lay-to till daylight. At dawn we saw naked people ashore, and I went ashore in a small boat, armed, followed by Martin Alonso Pinzon, captain of the Pinta, and his brother, Vincente Yanez Pinzon, captain of the Nina. I unfurled the royal banner and the captains brought the flags which displayed a large green cross with the letters F and Y at the left and right side of the cross. After a prayer of thanksgiving I ordered the captains of the Pinta and Nina to record and bear witness to the act of laying claim to this land in the name of Spain. To this island I gave the name San Salvador, in honor of our Blessed Lord.

It would be recommended to read the journal or the many writings available today of Columbus, in order to see how many miracles the Lord formed throughout his life. Columbus was born with a destiny to change the course of history. God's mighty hand prevails.

"O come, let us sing unto the LORD: let us make a joyful noise to th rock of our salvation. Let us come before his presence with thanksgiving, and make a joyful noise unto him with psalms. For the LORD is a great God, and a great King above all gods. In his hand are the deep places of the earth: the strength of the hills is his also. The sea is his, and he made it: and his hands formed the dry land. O come, let us worship and bow down: let us kneel before the LORD our maker. For he is our God; and we are the people of his pasture, and the sheep of his hand" (Psalm 95:1-7).

"Then the word of the LORD came unto me, saying, Before I formed thee in the belly I knew thee; and before thou camest forth out of the womb I sanctified thee, and I ordained thee a prophet unto the nations" (Jeremiah 1:4-5).

OPEN THE EYES OF THE KING 1494-1536 A.D.

B y the mighty hand of God's sovereign power, a number of world-changing events took place in a relatively short period of history. Do you suppose this could have been a coincidence?

EXPLORERS

*1450-1500—Bartholomew Diaz is the first Portuguese European to see the stormy Cape of Good Hope at the southern tip of Africa, helping find the southeastern water route between western Europe and Asia.

*1460-1524-Vasco de Gama, a Portuguese navigator, presses farther and farther down the uncharted west coast of Africa in search for a sea route to India, which is discovered in 1479.

*1480-1521—Ferdinand Magellan becomes the first European to sail across the Pacific Ocean. He is the first to discover a route by which ships could sail a complete circle around the world in 1519-1522. Magellan is the Portuguese navigator for whom the Strait of Magellan is named. The strait, located at the southern tip of South America, proves to be the long-sought connection between the Atlantic and Pacific oceans. Magellan proves in his explorations that the Earth is round.

*1492-1504—Christopher Columbus explores the "New World" and discovers America in 1492. Opens an entire continent hitherto unknown.

INVENTORS

*1397-1468—Johann Gutenberg, prominent inventor of moveable type, produces the first printed Bible in1455, which is also the first printed book in Europe.

*1452-1519—Leonardo da Vinci lives and observes human anatomy, constructs designs for flying machines, machine guns, and water turbines.

*1473-1543—Polish astronomer, Nicolaus Copernicus, discovers that the Earth rotates on its axis and that the Earth and the other planets revolve around the sun. In 1530, he finishes his great book *On the Revolutions of the Celestial Spheres*. The Roman Catholic Church opposes his theory, so the book is not published for 13 years. Copernicus receives the first copy as he is dying, on May 24, 1543. The book opens the way for a truly scientific approach to astronomy, and profoundly influences such men as Galileo and Johannes Kepler.

*1500—German locksmith, Peter Henlein creates a small timepiece that fits into a pocket. The personal understanding of time and its use comes into being.

REFORMERS

*1330-1384—John Wycliffe

*1374-1415—John Huss

*1467-1536—Desiderius Erasmus

*1483-1546—Martin Luther-In 1517, starts the Protestant Reformation in Germany and Europe.

*1484-1531—Ulrich Zwingli

*1488-1569—Miles Coverdale

*1490-1527—Michael Sattler

*1491-1547—King Henry VIII-In 1509, he succeeds throne of England. Unwittingly starts the English Reformation.

*1509-1564—John Calvin

*1514-1572—John Knox

During this time period, God began to raise up the English people as His instruments in the salvation of many in England and Europe. An Englishman of particular importance was William Tyndale, whom God used to translate the Bible into English. God ushered Tyndale onto history's stage in 1492, the same year Columbus set sail to discover a trade route to the Orient and discovered a New World instead. The stage was now set for His Word to go through time and space, guided by His mighty hand, to these newly discovered, uncharted lands.

Around 1512, Tyndale went to Magdalene College at Oxford and eventually received his M.A. degree. While attending Cambridge in 1515, he encountered Lutheran ideas. Tyndale probably began to form his Protestant ideas as a result of debates between the Roman Catholic Church officials and students questioning traditional church dogma. These students, undoubtedly, were reacting to the flagrantly ungodly lifestyles of Roman Catholic Church leaders in England, at the time. It was not uncommon to see Catholic parish priests behaving as "common drunkards," or to see the abbeys used as houses of ill repute. In addition, most of the priests were uneducated and could not read the Bible.

In the midst of this corruption, God led Tyndale to translate the Bible so that, as he told the priests, "If God spare my life, ere many years pass, I will cause a boy that driveth a plow to know more of the Scriptures than thou and the pope doest." This prediction did not make William well accepted. He was railed against, and charges were brought before King Henry VIII. To understand better the wonder of God's mighty hand during the life of Tyndale, we must detour into the political arena of his time. We will see how God causes "all things to work together for good" (Romans 8:28).

King Henry VIII was born on June 28, 1491, in Greenwich. He was the second son of Henry VII and Elizabeth of York. Although one of England's strongest monarchs, he was also among the least popular. The first English ruler educated under the influence of the Renaissance, Henry was a gifted scholar, linguist, composer, and musician. As a youth, he was skilled in all manner of athletic games. He was happy and seemed suited for being a good future king. However, in his later life he became coarse, selfish, arrogant, and willful.

When his elder brother, Arthur, died in 1502, Henry became undisputed heir to the throne of England. He succeeded his father in 1509, and soon after married Arthur's young widow, Catherine of Aragon. This marriage secured the peace for the English throne with Spain, the most powerful nation at that time. It also established a stronger rule of the Roman Catholic Church in England.

However, all of this was about to change because of Henry's selfish, godless lust toward a woman. He lost interest in Catherine and pursued a relationship with Anne Boleyn, her lady-in-waiting. This willfully ungodly relationship changed the course of world history.

Henry VIII sent the Archbishop of Canterbury (the highest church official in England), Cardinal Wolsey, to Rome to secure a divorce from Catherine. He suspected their marriage to be cursed by God, because he had married his dead brother's wife. Henry's excuse for the divorce was that Catherine had not given him a living son to be heir to his throne. When Pope Clement VII would not annul his marriage, Henry turned against Wolsey, deprived him of his office of Chancellor, and had him arrested on a charge of treason. Henry then obtained a divorce through Thomas Cranmer, whom he had made archbishop of Canterbury. Soon after, Henry married Anne Boleyn. Henry's defiant act against the pope broke all ties between the English Church and Rome. Appeals to the pope's court were stopped. Henry abolished the pope's authority in England through the Act of Supremacy in 1534, and declared himself to be "Supreme Head of the Church of England." Anyone denying this title would be guilty of treason. Thus was the birth of the Church of England. During all these royal intrigues and under pressure from Cuthbert Tunstall, the Bishop of London, Tyndale fled England in 1524. He would never return. Tyndale sailed for Germany, and in Hamburg began his English Bible translation. Fleeing England, his beloved home, proved to be a blessing in disguise. He had been led to Germany where Gutenberg had invented movable type and set up a printing press. Now, as Tyndale's work was almost completed, copies could be printed more quickly and smuggled throughout England.

His hateful enemy, the Bishop of London, would rue the day he forced Tyndale from the realm. Of course, Satan was quick to try to stop Tyndale's work, using one of his pawns, John

Dobneck, alias Cochlaeus. Cochlaeus ordered a raid on the printing press, which was being readied for the completion of Tyndale's New Testament translation. Tyndale, however, was warned in time. He took his manuscript and fled to Worms. The following year he completed his translation and was selling six thousand initial copies as fast as he could. Needing more money to begin the work of translating the Old Testament, Tyndale hoped the sale of his New Testaments in England would produce the necessary money to continue his translation project. With God's mighty hand at work is it any wonder that the very enemies of Tyndale would indirectly aid his work? William Warham, the new archbishop of Canterbury who replaced Wolsey, came up with the seemingly ingenious idea of buying up all of Tyndale's Bibles in order to keep them off the street markets. But God used this ploy to further the work. It would have taken months for all the Bibles to sell, but when Warham bought all the books, the money immediately went to Tyndale and he began the Old Testament translation without delay! Soon a complete Bible would be printed and ready for sale to the people of England. This is yet another instance where *"God laughs and holds his enemies in derision"* (Psalm 2:4).

In 1536, Tyndale was betrayed, as Christ was, by a supposed friend in whom he had confided. Henry Phillips, a secret agent from England, had arranged for Tyndale to have supper with him. On the way, Tyndale was captured and delivered to the police to be taken to the prison castle of Vilvoorde, near Brussels, in Belgium. There, in that cold, damp, and dreary place, Tyndale learned the secret of abiding in Christ.

On October 6, 1536, after an 18-month confinement, William Tyndale was brought out to face an assembled rabble. His sentence was read, with a warning to all heretics who might defy the established Church of Rome. Through interpreters, Tyndale preached his last sermon, telling the people that the Bible was a gift for all men to possess; that by the Scriptures men could govern themselves; that kings and all in authority were sinners; and that all must come to salvation through Christ only, and not through the established Roman Catholic Church. He declared that Christ is the head of the true Church.

While Tyndale was speaking, those commissioned to burn him were having great difficulty getting the wood to catch fire. As Tyndale continued to speak, his words became a threatening tide against the church officials who wanted to keep the people in ignorance and dependent on them for their salvation, rather than on Christ alone. If the people got wind of what Tyndale taught, the priests would lose power over the people and the people could learn to govern themselves by God's Word. After forty-five minutes of trying to burn him at the stake—while I am sure that angels were blowing out the flames—a guard finally came up behind Tyndale with a cord, pressed his head against the post to which he was tied, and strangled him to death. His last words were very insightful, and spoken as a prayer: "Lord, open the eyes of the King of England that he may see the power of Your holy Word...." In the portals of darkness, the principalities and powers must have celebrated as this threat to their regime was silenced. Yet Christ said, "The gates of hell will not prevail," and indeed they did not. Tyndale's prayer was answered in a most unique way.

Remember that King Henry broke with the Roman Catholic Church to marry Anne Boleyn. To keep peace in the realm, and to secure the independence of the Church of England from Rome, he issued an order to have Miles Coverdale (a former Augustinian friar who now opposed the Roman Catholic Church) circulate copies of the Bible throughout the kingdom. Little did King Henry realize that Coverdale was William Tyndale's friend and collaborator in his Bible translation work. The very Bible translation that cost Tyndale his life under the knowledge of Henry was the Bible that Henry now paid large sums to have freely distributed throughout his realm! With the Bible in the hands of the common people, England was forever changed.

Tyndale's Bible—translated from ancient Greek and Hebrew manuscripts and early versions of Scripture including the Codex Vaticanus, Codex Alexandrinus, and Sinaiticus—became the forerunner of the Great Bible of 1539, the Geneva Bible of 1560, and ultimately the King James Bible of 1611. The English, through the Pilgrims, were destined to become the founders of America. They proved a nation could be founded on God's Word. Through English versions of the Bible, God spread the English language and customs throughout the world as with no other nation. At first, Tyndale's death might have appeared to be in vain, but his death planted the seed of life through the proclaiming of God's Word. Likewise, Christ's death on the cross at first appeared to be a disgraceful defeat—until His triumphant resurrection destroyed the power of sin and death. Mankind and demons may try to stop God's Word in their imaginatively evil ways, yet God always prevails by His mighty hand!

"In thee, O LORD, do I put my trust; let me never be ashamed: deliver me in thy righteousness. Bow down thine ear to me; deliver me speedily: be thou my strong rock, for an house of defense to save me. For thou art my rock and my fortress; therefore for thy name's sake lead me, and guide me. Pull me out of the net that they have laid privily for me: for thou art my strength. Into thine hand I commit my spirit: thou hast redeemed me, O LORD God of truth, I have hated them that regard lying vanities: but I trust in the LORD" (Psalm 31:1-24).

Many times man has attempted to destroy the Bible. In 303 A.D., the Roman Emperor Diocletian issued an edict to destroy Christians and their Bibles. The persecution that followed was brutal.

In 1776, Voltaire, the French philosopher, announced, "One hundred years from today, there will not be a Bible in the earth except one that is looked upon by an antiquarian curiosity seeker."

One hundred years later, Voltaire was dead and his own house and press were being used to print and store Bibles by the Geneva Bible Society. One hundred years from the day of Voltaire's prediction, the first edition of his work sold for 11 cents in Paris. But the British government paid the Czar of Russia one-and-a-half million dollars for and ancient Bible manuscript.

The more the Bible is adhered to in any country, the more freedom that nation has. If a little of the Bible is adhered to, the people have little freedom. If no part of the Bible is adhered to, then the people have no freedom. Thank God that in America the Bible is still the best seller this nation has ever known.

THE 'OLD FOX' GOT AWAY 1517 A.D.

Can you guess which three books Christians cherished above all others during the sixteenth, seventeenth, and eighteenth centuries? Any household who could afford to buy a book was sure to buy these books. The first, you could probably guess, was the Bible. The second, I would venture to guess, you probably would not have known, but you probably have read portions of it and certainly have heard of it: John Buyan's *The Pilgrim's Progress.*

Of the third book hardly a Christian today would have any inkling. Yet it was a book that inspired faith in countless Christians and give them the courage to withstand all manner of trials and tribulations from the world, the flesh, and the devil. This third book is the subject of the intriguing story you are about to read. See how the mighty hand of God preserved the life of a humble man in order to encourage Christians throughout the past four hundred years.

John Fox (or Foxe) was born in Boston, Lincolnshire, in 1517. (This was the very spot where, nearly one hundred years later, the Pilgrims would try to flee England for Holland.) John was deprived of his father at an early age; however, his mother soon remarried. His parents are said to have lived in respectable circumstances.

From an early age, John exhibited talents and an inclination to learning. He was sent to Oxford University in order to cultivate these gifts. During his residence at the university, he became distinguished among his fellow collegians for his keenness of intellect and excellence in his studies. He applied himself with inexhaustible zeal and diligence. These qualities, along with his good-natured temperament, soon gained him the admiration of all. He was chosen to be a fellow of Magdalen College, a distinct honor.

John soon directed his thoughts to a more serious subject, the study of the Scriptures, not common to many students of his day. He applied himself to theology with more fervency than prudence would dictate, since Bible study could arouse suspicion of being a heretic. John, like Reformation leader Martin Luther, began to see the dissolute life-styles of the higher church clergy and found Scriptural inconsistences with popish doctrine. In time, these observations became appalling to him, shaking his faith in the Roman Church.

Before his thirtieth birthday, he had mastered the writings of the Greek and Latin fathers and other learned authors, and he had acquired competency in the Hebrew language. In these studies he frequently spent a considerable part, or even the whole of the night. In order to relax his mind after such intense study, he would resort to a grove near the college, a place much frequented by the students in the evening, because of the privacy and tranquility it offered. In these solitary walks he was often heard to cry heavy sobs and sighs, and with tears to pour forth his prayers to God.

These nightly retreats gave rise to the suspicion of his disinterest in the Roman church. Called to question for his unusual behavior, he boldly stated his opinions and was, by the sentence of the college, convicted, condemned as a heretic, and expelled in disgrace from his honored position.

His friends, highly offended, chose to reject him. Thus forsaken by his own so-called friends, John found a refuge in the house of Sir Thomas Lucy of Warwickshire, who asked him to instruct his children.

While here employed Fox married. With enemies of the Protestant opinion closing in on him, he soon departed to his wife's parents' home in Coventry. John realized that harboring a fugitive was an offense that could result in being burned at the stake, and he decided not to risk putting his wife's family in such a great danger. Therefore, soon afterward John journeyed to London to seek employment, in the latter part of the reign of Henry VIII. Being unknown in the city of London, he had difficulty finding suitable employment. However, it was when he was in distress that God's mighty hand forever changed the course of his life.

One day Mr. Fox was sitting in St. Paul's Cathedral praying, seeking guidance from the Lord. He was exhausted from long fasting, and feeling dejected, for it seemed the doors to future work were all slamming shut. Suddenly a stranger took a seat by his side, courteously saluted him, and thrust a sum of money into his hand. He bade him cheer up his spirits, for in a few days new prospects would present themselves to him. Who this stranger was, John would never know, but he felt perhaps the Lord had sent an "angel unawares."

Three days later, he miraculously received an invitation from the Duchess of Richmond to tutor the children of her brother, the Earl of Surry. The earl and his father, the Duke of Norfolk, were imprisoned for a short time in the Tower of London by the jealous, ungrateful king. The children thus confided to Fox's care were Thomas, who succeeded to the dukedom; Henry, who became Earl of Northampton; and Jane, who became Countess of Westmoreland. In the performance of his duties, he fully satisfied the expectations of the duchess, their aunt.

These cheerful days continued during the latter part of the reign of Henry VIII and the five years of the reign of Protestant King Edward VI. At the unfortunate death of King Edward, Queen Mary came to the crown. A devout Roman Catholic, she placed all power once again into the hands of the Roman Catholic leadership.

At this time, the envy and hatred of many began to be aroused against Mr. Fox, who was still under the protection of his noble former pupil, Thomas, who was now the Duke of Norfolk. In the course of time, Dr. Gardiner, Bishop of Winchester, who hated Protestants, became his most violent enemy. Aware of this enmity and sensing the beginning of dreadful persecutions toward all Protestants, Mr. Fox began to think of leaving London. As soon as the duke knew of his intentions, he tried to persuade him to remain, and his arguments were so powerful and sincere that Mr.

Fox gave up the thought of abandoning his sanctuary for the present.

Ironically, Bishop Gardiner was a friend of the new duke and his family, who were responsible for his rise to the dignity he then enjoyed. He frequently visited the duke to fellowship with and minister to the family. Bishop Gardiner was aware of John Fox's reputation yet had not seen or ever met him personally. During a visit to the duke, the Bishop asked him to introduce his children's tutor, not realizing that the very tutor was his hated enemy.

The duke denied his request, at one time saying he was absent, at another, that he was indisposed. It so happened one day that Mr. Fox, not knowing the bishop was in the house, entered the room where he and the duke and were in conversation. Seeing the bishop, Fox wisely and discretely withdrew through another door. Gardiner asked who that was, and the duke answered in order to protect Fox, "My physician. He is somewhat lacking in courtly manners. I apologize that he left so rudely without the customary courteous greeting."

"I like his countenance and aspect very well," replied the bishop. "And when occasion offers, I will send for him."

The duke took this as a sign from the Lord of impending danger, and now he thought it was high time for Mr. Fox to flee the city, and even the country. He hastily made arrangements for his secret departure. He sent one of his servants to Ipswich to hire a small private ship and to prepare all the necessities for his journey. He also inquired at the house of another servant, who was a farmer, if Mr. Fox might lodge there until the wind for sailing became favorable. When everything was ready, Mr. Fox took leave with heartfelt thanks. He and his wife, who was expecting a child, secretly departed for the awaiting vessel.

The ship had scarcely set sail when a violent storm began. It raged all day and night, and the next day drove them back to the port from which they had departed. During the time that the vessel had been at sea, the Bishop learned of the true identity of the tutor and quickly dispatched an officer. The officer traced John Fox to the farmhouse where he had secured refuge with his family. With a warrant the officer broke into the farmer's house only to discover the "old Fox got away."

Meanwhile, the sea captain desired to return to port for fear of the raging storm. Mr. Fox convinced the captain of the vessel to sail for any place as soon as the wind should shift, only desiring him to proceed, and not to doubt that God would protect them. The mariner reluctantly set sail and within two days landed his passengers safely at Newport.

After spending a few days in Newport, Mr. Fox and his wife set out for Switzerland, where they joined a number of English refugees who had fled from their country to avoid the cruelty of their persecutors. There he began to write his *History of the Acts and Monuments of the Church*. It was first published in Latin at Basle, Switzerland in 1554, and in English in 1563.

In the meantime, with the death of "Bloody Mary," the Protestant Reformed religion began again to flourish in England under Queen Elizabeth, and the Roman Church faction began to decline. A great number of Protestant exiles returned to their native country. Fox was among those who resettled in England. He employed himself in revising and enlarging his admirable martyrology. With prodigious pains and constant study he completed that work in eleven years. For the sake of accuracy, he wrote every line of this vast book with his own hand and transcribed all the records and papers himself.

At length, having served both the Church and the world by the ministry of his pen, and by the immaculate luster of a benevolent, useful, and holy life, he humbly resigned his soul to Christ, on April 18, 1587, at seventy years of age. He was interred in the chapel of St. Giles in Cripplegate, England.

The beauty of the life of John Fox is that in escaping his own sure martyrdom, he was spared by God to write of the martyrdom of hundreds in ages past. His celebrated work, *Fox's Book of Martyrs*, is a condensed version of his *History of the Acts and Monuments of the Church*. These writings have influenced countless Christians throughout the past four hundred years in building their faith.

It has been said that the blood of martyrs is the seed bed of the Church. Although the accounts of the deaths of Christians throughout the ages grips the reader today with sorrow and horror, it is imperative that Christians read accounts of martyrs. Christ warned that in the last days many would once again be martyred for their faith. Are you and your family prepared for such trials that may come in your lifetime? I take great comfort in knowing that our sovereign God is fully aware of our time of death and the manner of our death. To Him the deaths of His saints are precious. I am so thankful that God raised up John Fox to write such an inspirational book that honors the heroes of the Church. The book shows that, as Jesus said, the gates of hell cannot prevail against His true Church.

"Precious in the sight of the Lord is the death of his saints"(Psalm 118:15).

"He shall redeem their soul from deceit and violence, and precious shall their blood be in his sight"(Psalm 72:14).

"For all the saints who from their labors rest, Who Thee by faith before the world confessed, Thy name, O Jesus, be forever blest. Alleluia!"
William W. How, 1864

"DIVINE RIGHT OF KINGS" 1599 A.D.

Oliver Cromwell seemed to be born ahead of his time. Yet by God's wise foreknowledge, He ordained that on precisely April 25, 1599, Oliver would be born, his life destined to change the course of world history forever. God's mighty hand influenced Oliver's life during a critical time in English history, and he became one of the most important leaders of the English Civil War fought between 1640 and 1660. Untrained and inexperienced in military matters, Cromwell relied completely on God for direction and ability, and God did not disappoint that trust.

King Charles I of England had led his nation down the slippery path of absolute monarchism, a form of government in which supreme power is attributed to a crowned sovereign. The "Divine Right of Kings" was now being challenged, but Charles intended to fight to preserve it. Under this ancient way of thinking, the king was believed to have been placed in power by God; therefore, anything he did had the same impact and authority as if God Himself had ordained it personally.

The Magna Carta, reluctantly signed by King John on June 15, 1215, dramatically changed the idea that the king was above the law. In a major departure from the traditional divine right of kings, this historic document stated that, in fact, the king's power was derived from the consent of the governed, over whom he reigned. It was in direct violation of the Magna Carta that King Charles attempted to regain the absolute power formerly held by ancient kings.

To Oliver Cromwell, to the Puritans, and to many others of the English people, the king's attempt to flaunt the Magna Carta was a serious threat to their liberties. King Charles' actions violated the English rule of limited power vested in the monarch, the forerunner of the rule "of the people, by the people, and for the people," which would later be foundational in forming our American republic.

Oliver Cromwell had a exceptional understanding of limited government which most Englishmen did not yet possess. The English were torn between the traditional reign of a powerful king and the sweet taste of self-government with its accompanying liberty. This teetering between two ideologies led to a civil war, in which Cromwell was used by God to steer the English people away from absolute monarchism as a form of rule.

From 1653, until his death in 1658, at the age of 59, Oliver Cromwell, Lord Protector of the Commonwealth of England, Scotland, and Ireland, ruled as a virtual dictator. Cromwell's government successfully maintained peace and stability, providing a measure of religious toleration under which Jews, excluded from England since 1290, were allowed to return to England in 1655. By receiving the Jewish people, the nation invoked on itself the blessing found in the Bible in Genesis 27:29b, ...*May those who curse you be cursed and those who bless you be blessed.* It seems likely that because of Cromwell's desire to allow the Jews the right to worship God in England, the Lord blessed much of what he set his hand to do. Cromwell's vigorous foreign policy and the success of the English army and navy gave England a prestige abroad such as it had not enjoyed since the days of Queen Elizabeth I.

Oliver Cromwell is often portrayed as a religious fanatic, one who used religion to accomplish his desire for power, but this is far from the truth. The following letter, written by Cromwell, reveals his tender side and his complete trust in the Lord in the challenging circumstances of the English Civil War. After the successful battle of Marston Moor, during which Cromwell and his loyal army broke the power of the Royalist army under King Charles I, Oliver wrote to his brother-in-law:

To my loving Brother,
Colonel Valentine Walton:
It's our duty to sympathize in all mercies; and to praise

the Lord together in chastisements or trials, that so we may sorrow together. Truly, England and the Church of God hath had a great favor from the Lord, in this great victory given unto us, such as the like never was since this war began. It had all the evidences of an absolute victory obtained by the Lord's blessing upon the Godly Party principally. We never charged, but we routed the enemy. The Left Wing, which I commanded, being our own house, saving a few Scots in our rear, beat all the Prince's horses. God made them as stubble to our swords. We charged their regiments of foot soldiers with our horse, and routed all we charged. The particulars I cannot relate now; but I believe, of twenty thousand the Prince hath not four thousand left. Give glory, all the glory, to God.

Sir, God hath taken away your eldest son by a cannon-shot. It brake his leg. We were necessitated to have it cut off, whereof he died. Sir, you know my own trials this way [Cromwell's own son had been killed shortly before]: but the Lord supported me with this, that the Lord took him into the happiness we all pant for and live for. There is your precious child full of glory, never to know sin or sorrow anymore. He was a gallant young man, exceedingly gracious. God give you His comfort.

Before his death he was so full of comfort that to Frank Russell and myself he could not express it, "It was so great above the pain." This he said to us. Indeed it was admirable. A little after, he said, one thing lay upon his spirit. I asked him what that was. He told me it was that God had not suffered him to be anymore the executioner of his enemies. At his fall, his horse being killed with the bullet, and as I am informed three horses more, I am told he bid them open to the right and left, that he might see the rogues run. Truly he was exceedingly beloved in the army, of all that knew him. All but a few knew him for he was a precious young man, fit for God.

You have cause to bless the Lord. He is a glorious saint

in Heaven; wherein you ought exceedingly to rejoice. Let this drink up your sorrow; seeing these are not feigned words to comfort you, but the thing is so real and undoubted a truth. You may do all things by the strength of Christ. Seek that, and you shall easily bear your trial. Let this public mercy to the Church of God make you to forget your private sorrow. The Lord be your strength: So prays your truly faithful and loving brother,

OLIVER CROMWELL

Oliver Cromwell was not a perfect ruler, but the Lord used him to teach the English people the danger of the "divine right" mentality. Had Oliver Cromwell not come into his position of power and influence at this critical time in English history, America might not today enjoy the constitutional form of government we have. The tyranny of the old "divine right" of kings had to be destroyed once and for all. By the mighty hand of God, Cromwell's military forces won every major battle fought in the English Civil War against superior royal forces, because God had a plan for the future of America.

I am convinced that, due to Cromwell's anointed leadership, England was forevermore changed. The people of England savored the sweet taste of liberty and would not give it up. That same liberty was later birthed here in America by John Endicott and John Winthrop, leaders of the Massachusetts Bay Company and contemporaries of Oliver Cromwell during the English Civil War. These were the very men God used to impact world history by creating a clear distinction between liberty and despotism. The war over tyranny and oppression, which they successfully fought by the grace of God, is one which will continue to be waged until Christ comes to rule as the only One who truly has the "divine right of kings."

"I saw heaven standing open and there before me was a white horse, whose rider is called Faithful and True. With justice he judges and makes war. His eyes are like blazing fire, and on his head are many crowns. He has a name written on him that no one

knows but he himself. He is dressed in a robe dipped in blood, and his name is the Word of God. The armies of heaven were following him, riding on white horses and dressed in fine linen, white and clean. Out of his mouth comes a sharp sword with which to strike down the nations. 'He will rule them with an iron scepter.'' 'He treads the winepress of the fury of the wrath of God Almighty. On his robe and on his thigh he has this name written: KING OF KINGS AND LORD OF LORDS" (Revelation 19:11-16).

GOD'S MIGHTY HAND

STEPS ORDERED BY GOD 1605 A.D.

It was a glorious day in June 1619. The coastal grasses of Cape Cod swayed in the breeze; sandpipers played "catch me" with waves along the shore; and gulls squawked and fought over morsels of fish in shallow water. Alone and forlorn, an Indian sat and reflected on how so much could go so wrong in one person's life. That Indian was Squanto, and this is his story—an intriguing story dearly loved by schoolchildren throughout America during the Thanksgiving season.

In 1619, Squanto could not have known the significant role he would play in the script of God's drama of life, which He wrote with His mighty hand at the beginning of time.

The date of Squanto's birth is unknown, but we do know that in 1605 he was coaxed by George Weymouth to leave his Pawtuxet Indian tribe in order to sail to England. He was educated according to English manners and customs so the British would have a more complete knowledge of New England from a native's perspective. With a command of the English language, Squanto could serve the English explorers better and tell them of the natural resources in the area. Little did Squanto realize just how mightily the hand of God was going to use him because of this training.

After spending approximately nine years in Great Britain and receiving an English education (which may have included some Bible and the memorization of prayers), he was taken back to North America by Captain John Smith. Shortly after he arrived and while on the way to his village, he and 23 other Indians were captured by Thomas Hunt, an English ship captain and slave trader. Squanto cried out for mercy, but to no avail. He begged to be allowed to return to his village and family—whom he had not seen for many years. Captain Hunt only laughed as he forced the Indians aboard his ship. He then took Squanto and the other

-73-

Indians across the Atlantic Ocean to the slave markets in Spain. Some Catholic monks there took pity on Squanto and bought him in order to spare him the grief of having a slave owner who would probably mistreat him.

During his captivity Squanto applied himself to learning Spanish and serving the monks. In time, he endeared himself to the monks and received Catholic/Christian training from them. When he had learned enough Spanish, he was able to communicate his life's sorrows and his deep desire to return to America to see his family. As far as can be surmised, the monks were so moved by his plight that they decided to set him free so he could return home.

Moved by compassion and the mighty hand of God's providence, the monks arranged for Squanto to go to England. Mr. John Slany housed Squanto while making preparation for his return to America. Squanto was introduced to a Captain Dermer, and it was agreed that by waiting six months for good sailing weather, he could hope to see his beloved homeland once again.

Squanto arrived on the shores of Cape Cod in 1619, just six months before the Pilgrims were destined to arrive on the same shore, providentially led there by God.

After Squanto arrived he went straight to his village. It had been two years since he had been kidnapped by Captain Hunt. Joyfully running up the beach, he called out to his people, but there was no response. He looked everywhere for his people, but the village was gone. All that remained were a few old fire pits and the vestiges of former planting grounds. The grass and reed shelters had long since blown away.

Alone and bewildered on the shore, Squanto perhaps looked to the sky with the question, "Now what?" He may have prayed and questioned any and all gods he knew of, both the "great spirit" and the God of the British as to his plight. Not knowing what to do, he decided to go to a Wampanoag Indian village not far from his former village. The Wampanoag chief, Massasoit, greeted him with wonder, as one would greet one risen from the dead. From Massasoit, Squanto learned that the people of his tribe had died from a mysterious illness, that his former village had "bad spirits," and that no Indian would dare set foot in that evil place. After hearing Squanto's incredible tale of the Old World and all that he experienced in the past eleven to twelve years, Massasoit told Squanto of a significant event that had taken place just a year or so before the entire village was wiped out.

A French captain and his crew were shipwrecked just off Cape Cod. The Pawtuxets, hating all white men because of the wicked deeds of Hunt, the slave trader, had made a vow that "all pale faces must be killed on sight." The destitute French, not knowing of Hunt's wicked deeds in that area, were surrounded by the Pawtuxets and tied up to be tortured before they were killed. The French captain was able to warn the Indians through interpreters that they had nothing to do with Hunt and that they meant the Indians no harm. He entreated the Indians to release them.

The Indians were inexorable, so the French captain warned them that if they harmed him or his men, the Christian God would hold them responsible for the deaths of innocent people and would destroy them. He told them of the white man's God and of the law of "sowing and reaping." The Indians laughed at such "foolish" talk and shortly afterward killed every one of the men.

Massasoit went on to explain that he had learned all of this as he traded with the village people—until they were all wiped out by disease. So many died that the living could not bury the dead. Soon all were dead, and the wolves carried off the last ones. Massasoit said that as far as he knew, Squanto was the only living Pawtuxet.

The forlorn and dejected Squanto was invited by kind Massasoit to live among the Wampanoag people, an invitation which he accepted. Squanto realized that he would have died along with his people, had he not been kidnapped and sold into slavery. But he still did not understand why all of this had happened to him. He must have wondered about the meaning and purpose of life and why things had turned out so badly for him. Little did he know then, but as with Joseph in Egypt, God's mighty hand was working out a far greater plan than he could ever imagine. He was going to be, as Governor William Bradford later wrote, "A special instrument used of God for their good." (To fully understand the significance of this story, read the Pilgrims' account in the next story.)

"And Joseph said unto his brethren, I am Joseph; doth my father yet live? And his brethren could not answer him; for they were troubled at his presence. And Joseph said unto his brethren, Come near to me, I pray you. And they came near. And he said, I am Joseph your brother, whom ye sold into Egypt. Now therefore be not grieved, nor angry with yourselves, that ye sold me hither: for God did send me before you to preserve life. For these two years hath the famine been in the land: and yet there are five years, in the which there shall neither be earing nor harvest. And God sent me before you to preserve you a posterity in the earth, and to save your lives by a great deliverance. So now it was not you that sent me hither, but God: and he hath made me a father to Pharaoh, and lord of all his house, and a ruler throughout all the land of Egypt. . . .

And Joseph said unto them, Fear not: for am I in the place of God? But as for you, ye thought evil against me; but God meant it unto good, to bring to pass, as it is this day, to save much people alive" (Genesis 45:3-8, 50:19-20).

"The steps of a good man are ordered by the LORD: and he delighteth in his way. Though he fall, he shall not be utterly cast down: for the LORD upholdeth him with his hand" (Psalm 37:23-24).

"Behold, I go forward, but he is not there; and backward, but I cannot perceive him: On the left hand, where he doth work, but I cannot behold him: he hideth himself on the right hand, that I cannot see him: But he knoweth the way that I take: when he hath tried me, I shall come forth as gold. My foot hath held his steps, his way have I kept, and not declined. Neither have I gone back from the commandment of his lips; I have esteemed the words of

his mouth more than my necessary food" (Job 23:8-12).

Praise to the Lord,
Who with marvelous wisdom hath made thee;
Decked thee with health,
and with loving hand guided and stayed thee;
How oft in grief Hath not He brought thee relief;
Spreading His wings for to shade thee.
Joachim Neander (1650–1680)

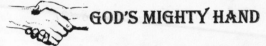

REJECTED OF MAN, CHOSEN OF GOD
PILGRIM'S PART 1 1608 A.D.

The Pilgrims (Separatists) left England because Queen Elizabeth, King James I, and later, Charles I, did not permit freedom of religion. In May of 1559, Elizabeth issued a law called the "Act of Uniformity." This law required everyone to attend divine services in the Church of England, with severe penalties for not attending. Missing church more than three times could lead to torture or life imprisonment.

In 1608, after much prayer and fasting, the Pilgrims decided to leave England for Holland, a country that permitted religious freedom. Their point of departure was on the east coast of England, at a secluded spot where the River Hull meets the English Channel. This crossing was to be the first of a series of miracles that would show the mighty hand of God in the lives of the Pilgrims throughout their earthly pilgrimage. Plymouth Colony's Governor, William Bradford, recorded the many instances of how the hand of God protected His people. Here is one.

"Next spring there was another attempt made(the first was foiled by deception) by some of the same people, i.e., Pilgrims, with others, to get over from a different place. They heard of a Dutchman at Hull who had a ship of his own belonging to Zealand, (Holland) and they made an agreement with him, and acquainted him with their plight, hoping to find him more reliable than the English captain had been; and he bade them have no fear. He was to take them aboard between Grimsby and Hull, where there was a large common a good way from any town. The women and children, with all their effects, were sent to the place at the time arranged in a small bark which they had hired; and the men were to meet them by land. But it so happened that they all arrived a day before the ship came, and the sea being rough, and the women very sick, the sailors put into a creek hard by, where they grounded at low tide. The next morning the ship came, but they were stuck fast and could not stir till about noon. In the meantime, the captain of the ship, seeing how things were, sent his boat to get the men aboard whom he saw were ready, walking about the shore. But after the first boat-full was got aboard and she was ready to go for more, the captain espied a large body of horse and foot, armed with bills and guns and other weapons, for the country side had turned out to capture them. The Dutchman, seeing this, swore his country's oath, "sacramente," and having a fair wind, weighed anchor, hoist sail, and away! The poor men already aboard were in great distress for their wives and children, left thus to be captured, and destitute of help—and for themselves, too, without any clothes but what they had on their backs, and scarcely a penny about them, all their possessions being aboard the bark, now seized. It drew tears from their eyes, and they would have given anything to be ashore again. But all in vain, there was no remedy; they must thus sadly part. At the time the estranged Pilgrims did not know when, if ever, they would be reunited. However they were reunited again within the same year meeting in Amsterdam.

Afterwards they endured a fearful storm at sea, and it was fourteen days or more before they reached port, in seven of which they saw neither sun, moon, nor stars, being driven near the coast of Norway. The sailors themselves often despaired, and once with shrieks and cries gave over all, as if the ship had foundered and they were sinking without hope of recovery. But when man's hope and help wholly failed, there appeared the Lord's power and mercy to save them; for the ship rose again, and gave the crew courage to manage her. If modesty permitted, I might declare with what fervent prayers the voyagers cried to the Lord in their great distress, even remaining fairly collected when the water ran into their mouths and ears; and when the sailors called out, 'We sink, we sink' they cried (if not with miraculous, yet with sublime faith): 'Yet Lord, Thou canst save; yet Lord, Thou canst save!' Upon which, the ship not only righted herself, but shortly afterwards the violence of the storm began to abate, and the Lord filled their afflicted minds with such comfort as but few can understand, and in the end brought them to their desired haven, where the people came flocking, astonished at their deliverance, the storm having been so long and violent."

People came flocking to see this ship because in fourteen days it was the only ship to have crossed the English Channel—all others having been lost at sea. Aboard the ship was the "cream" of the Pilgrim crop—the leaders who knew the source of Christian liberty, and the germination for the future of liberty to be planted in America. Had Satan destroyed them, America's Christian foundation perhaps would not have been laid.

I firmly believe that Satan threw everything he had in his "book of destruction" on these Pilgrims. He knew what they knew of God's Word, the Bible, and the principles of self-government, and he feared that if they ever founded a colony based on Biblical principles, he would lose his control over large numbers of people.

Satan fears and hates the fact that through Christ's death on the cross, people can receive forgiveness of sins and understand the dominion God has granted man—the dominion given to Adam and Eve, and which Satan stole from them. Satan often uses governments to control people, to rule over them, and oppress them, and to suppress their God-given liberty.

These Pilgrims were the first real threat to Satan's kingdom on earth. Satan must have thought, "If these people ever come to America and found a colony that teaches the principles of Christian-self government, free enterprise, the Christian work ethic, missionary motivation, Church order and discipline based on the Bible, Biblical discipline and training for children, and an educational system based on the Bible, I will lose my control over them." But that is exactly what happened. Satan tried to destroy the Pilgrims, as he did with Job of old, but he failed, because God's mighty hand prevailed. Satan failed with the Pilgrims when they left England for Holland, but his plan for their destruction would continue in a different form in Holland—as you will see in the next story.

"There was a man in the land of Uz, whose name was Job; and that man was perfect and upright, and one that feared God, and eschewed evil. And there were born unto him seven sons and three daughters. His substance also was seven thousand sheep, and three thousand camels, and five hundred yoke of oxen, and five hundred she asses, and a very great household; so that this man was the greatest of all the men of the east. And his sons went and feasted in their houses, every one his day; and sent and called for their three sisters to eat and to drink with them. And it was so, when the days of their feasting were gone about, that Job sent and sanctified them, and rose up early in the morning, and offered burnt offerings according to the number of them all: for Job said, It may be that my sons have sinned, and cursed God in their hearts. Thus did Job continually.

Now there was a day when the sons of God came to present themselves before the LORD, and Satan came also among them. And the LORD said unto Satan, Whence comest thou? Then Satan answered the LORD, and said, From going to and fro in the earth, and from walking up and down in it. And the LORD said unto Satan, Hast thou considered my servant Job, that there is none like him in the earth, a perfect and an upright man, one that feareth God, and escheweth evil? Then Satan answered the LORD, and said, Doth Job fear God for nought? Hast not thou made an hedge about him, and about his house, and about all that he hath on every side? thou hast blessed the work of his hands, and his substance is increased in the land. But put forth thine hand now, and touch all that he hath, and he will curse thee to thy face. And the LORD said unto Satan, Behold, all that he hath is in thy power; only upon himself put not forth thine hand. So Satan went forth from the presence of the LORD" (Job 1:1-2).

PILGRIMS PART 2 1620 A.D.

In the previous story you saw how Satan tried to destroy the leaders of the future Plymouth Colony by sinking them into the depths of the sea. With that plan thwarted, he proceeded to unfold another of his tried and trusted wiles. Often the adversary will use less obvious means to accomplish his goals.

As you may recall from the sacred Scriptures, Balak, who represented Satan in trying to destroy God's people, was the son of Zippor and King of the Moabites. He sent messengers to Balaam, the son of Beor, saying, "Behold, there is a people come out of Egypt [Israel], which covereth the face of the earth: Come now, curse me them; peradventure I shall be able to overcome them, and drive them out." And God said unto Balaam, *"Thou shalt not go with them; thou shalt not curse the people: for they are blessed"* (Numbers 22:12). Satan tried to use the false prophet Balaam to curse Israel, thus causing their defeat on the battlefield.

God's mighty hand prevailed, keeping Balaam from cursing Israel, and Israel was not attacked. There is every indication that Balaam, in his wicked desire to get rich, concocted another plan—one that would get the nation of Israel to destroy herself. Finis Dakes in his Bible commentary believes-and I concur with his observation-that Balaam probably approached Balak and suggested that he make peace with Israel, allowing the people to dwell there in the land so that in due time, letting their guard down, they would begin to adopt the ways of the Moabites. Israel would intermarry and take Moab's false gods as her gods, bringing the judgment of God and helping Satan to achieve his ultimate goal. The final results would take longer, but the end would be the same: Israel's downfall and Balak's dominion over her. Thus the scheme worked perfectly: Israel was in time destroyed through her own negligence of God's ways and by adopting the ways of the heathen.

This is precisely the same ploy Satan used with the Pilgrims while they were in Holland. Seeing that a direct assault was fruitless, he used his secret weapon of "a little leaven that leavens

-82-

the whole lump." After the Pilgrims settled in Holland, establishing their congregation of worship, and finding employment, they struggled to make a living.

For twelve difficult years, they had to work night and day to survive. In the midst of "living," they had to contend with the threat of war with Spain, the toil of work with little reward, and a serious problem with their children, as Governor Bradford later recorded: "But still more lamentable, and of all sorrows most heavy to be borne, was that many of the children, influenced by these conditions, and the great licentiousness of the young people of the country, and the many temptations of the city, were led by evil example into dangerous courses, getting the reins off their necks and leaving their parents. Some became soldiers, others embarked upon voyages by sea, and others upon worse courses, tending to dissoluteness and the danger of their souls, to the great grief of the parents and the dishonour of God. So they saw their posterity would be in danger to degenerate and become corrupt."

As with Israel of old in the land of Moab, the children of these Godly Pilgrims were becoming corrupted with the ways of the godless Dutch children. Satan saw that in time he could assimilate the Pilgrims into the Dutch culture and that they would lose their Christian distinction and the seeds of Christian self-government.

Thank the Lord that there were parents who began to see these seeds of destruction, and faced with no alternative, decided to undertake a perilous journey across the Atlantic Ocean. Governor Bradford made one last comment in regard to their going to America. The quote is almost prophetic in nature, and rest assured that Satan saw the Pilgrims' noble, Godly vision for their purpose here in America. Again, he would try to do all in his power to keep the Pilgrims from ever arriving in America.

"Last and not least, they cherished a great hope and inward zeal of laying good foundations, or at least of making some way towards it, for the propagation and advance of the Gospel of the Kingdom of Christ in the remote parts of the world, even though they should be but stepping stones to others in the performance of so great a work."

In May 1620, after prayer and Bible reading, the first band of Separatists said their farewells amid tears, knowing full well for some it would be their last sight of each other until they met again in the Kingdom of their dear Lord. The Pilgrims endured various delays but eventually began their voyage across the Atlantic.

It was now time for Satan once again to try to destroy the band of Pilgrims bound for the New World. Not long out of port, a storm arose that drove them to the four winds of the tempest-tossed ocean. Forced to stay below deck, the band of one-hundred-and-two huddled together, sharing the fears that their lives were soon to come to an end. All were seasick and were forced to eat wormy biscuits, and all were humbled to use a common toilet, a chamber pot in the presence of all. Children cried, waves slammed into the sides of the Mayflower, and the hull of the ship wrenched and creaked as if it would burst into a thousand pieces. In the midst of this the Pilgrims gathered to pray and praise the Lord in song, committing themselves to God's mighty hand of protection.

A dangerous situation soon arose: The ship's main beam began to crack. Master Jones, the ship's Captain, was sent for. After surveying the situation, he declared that without the beam being laminated together, it would surely split, sinking the ship. Much prayer ensued, and the Pilgrims suggested that Master Jones use a jack they had brought with them. The jack saved the beam and spared the ship. Satan once again failed in his attempt to destroy these Godly people.

Another incident occurred, now somewhat humorous in the telling. A Pilgrim passenger named John Howland decided to disobey the order to stay below deck and ventured up to get a breath of fresh air. Suddenly a wave slammed into the side of the Mayflower, and John Howland found himself flying over the side of the ship like the man on the flying trapeze. He hit the water with such force that he sank several feet below the surface, with the Mayflower bouncing away—a toothpick on the vast ocean.

Like Jonah of old, Howland regretted that he had disobeyed orders. I am confident that he also remembered Jonah's prayer, in

Jonah 2:1–7: *"Then Jonah prayed unto the LORD his God out of the fish's belly, And said, I cried by reason of mine affliction unto the LORD, and he heard me; out of the belly of hell cried I, and thou heardest my voice. For thou hadst cast me into the deep, in the midst of the seas; and the floods compassed me about: all thy billows and thy waves passed over me. Then I said, I am cast out of thy sight; yet I will look again toward thy holy temple. The waters compassed me about, even to the soul: the depth closed me round about, the weeds were wrapped about my head. I went down to the bottoms of the mountains; the earth with her bars was about me for ever: yet hast thou brought up my life from corruption, O LORD my God. When my soul fainted within me I remembered the LORD: and my prayer came in unto thee, into thine holy temple."*

The Lord by His mighty hand rescued John Howland. A rope "happened" to be trailing along the side of the ship. John, while underwater, felt the rope and grabbed it, and found himself being pulled up out of the water. He began calling out as a sailor on deck "happened" to notice the trailing rope and pulled it up. As the sailor pulled, to his amazement, there was the frantic, half-drowned John Howland holding onto it and bobbing like a cork in the water. After being hauled up to the ship's deck, John Howland became the most obedient Pilgrim on the Mayflower. He lived to a ripe old age, never forgetting the time the mighty hand of God delivered him from a watery grave.

Providentially, the Mayflower was driven far north of the Pilgrims' King-granted land charter. This disappointment was God's appointment. The band of Pilgrims landed on Cape Cod and deemed it necessary to accept their circumstances and entrust themselves to the Lord. After several weeks of bitter cold weather, the Pilgrims were providentially spared from death in an Indian attack and were led to Indian corn, which was to save them from starvation that winter. They finally found a good place to settle and began to build their homes.

The Pilgrims changed history by drawing up the Mayflower Compact, the first legal document based on God's Law, the Bible.

This kind of law was later to become the basis of all American law.

The Pilgrims' shelters were built as quickly as the bitter winter allowed. By the spring of 1621, half their numbers had died. In desperation, they continued to call out to the Lord, and the Lord sent them a "special instrument of God," as Governor Bradford later recorded.

In March 1621, an Indian named Samoset paid the Pilgrims a visit. He stayed two days, but not knowing how to speak English well, he left, promising to return with someone who could. Samoset, Massasoit, and Squanto showed up a week later and approached the Colony. Squanto, in an educated English manner, spoke to the Pilgrims, saying, "Greetings, English. I trust that you are faring well, and that the Lord Whom you serve has kept you through the past winter."

You can well imagine the shock the Pilgrims must have felt. Here in America was an Indian who could speak English, with proper diction and intonation! Some thought that Squanto must have been an angel in disguise. Squanto reassured them, however, that he was indeed an Indian, and he then began to tell his story.

With tears of gratefulness, the Pilgrims blessed the Lord for directing Squanto and them to each other. Had the Pawtuxets not been wiped out, the Pilgrims would have been attacked and killed. Had they not been blown off course, they would have landed in another place, where the Indians most likely would have been hostile and would have attacked. But as it was, the Indians in the Cape Cod area were afraid of the Pilgrims. Unknowingly, the Pilgrims had established their colony on the very spot where the Pawtuxets had lived, and other Indians would not venture near for fear of the "magic death" that killed that whole tribe.

Squanto now began to put the pieces of the puzzle together, and he saw how God had directed his steps. Had he not been kidnapped, he would have died, and had his village not been wiped out, the Pilgrims would likely have been wiped out. He had been educated for nine years in England; what better training could he have? And what better purpose could he have than to help these God-fearing English people and show them how to plant, trade, fish, hunt, trap, and make peace with the Indians far and wide? Thus God's mighty hand preserved the Pilgrims and gave them and our great land the seeds of liberty and self-government based on His Word, the Bible.

"O that men would praise the LORD for his goodness, and for his wonderful works to the children of men! And let them sacrifice the sacrifices of thanksgiving, and declare his works with rejoicing. They that go down to the sea in ships, that do business in great waters; These see the works of the LORD, and his wonders in the deep. For he commandeth, and raiseth the stormy wind, which lifteth up the waves thereof. They mount up to the heaven, they go down again to the depths: their soul is melted because of trouble. They reel to and fro, and stagger like a drunken man, and are at their wit's end. Then they cry unto the LORD in their trouble, and he bringeth them out of their distresses. He maketh the storm a calm, so that the waves thereof are still. Then are they glad because they be quiet; so he bringeth them unto their desired haven. O that men would praise the LORD for his goodness, and for his wonderful works to the children of men!" (Psalm 107:21-31).

O beautiful for Pilgrim feet,
Whose stern impassioned stress
A thoroughfare for freedom beat
Across the wilderness!
Katherine Lee Bates (1859–1929)

GOD'S MIGHTY HAND

OUT OF THE CLEAR BLUE 1673 A.D.

In the Provinces, during the late 1600s, Puritan leader Increase Mather wrote *Remarkable Provinces*. This rare and precious book contains amazing accounts of the mighty hand of God intervening in people's lives. In the following account, God's mercy is extended toward a sinner just prior to his impending death (the time of which only God ever knows). The story shows that God always reaches out to the sinner before his appointed day of reckoning.

"On the Lord's day, 18th of May 1673, the afternoon sermon being ended, several of the Christians went to Mr. Newman's house for fellowship. Whilst they were in discourse there about the word and works of God, a thunderstorm arose. After awhile, a loud clap of thunder broke upon the house, and especially into the room where they were sitting and discoursing together. It was so loud it deafened them all, filling the room with smoke, and a strong smell as of brimstone. With the thunder-clap came in a ball of fire as big as the bullet of a great gun, which suddenly went up the chimney, as also the smoke did. This ball of fire was seen at the feet of Richard Goldsmith, who sat on a leather chair next to the chimney, at which instant he fell off the chair on the ground.

"As soon as the smoke was gone, some in the room endeavored to hold him up, but found him dead; also the dog that lay under the chair was found stone dead, but not the least hurt done to the chair. All that could be perceived by the man was that the hair of his head, near one of his ears, was a little singed. There were seven or eight in that room, and more in the next; yet (through the merciful providence of God) none else had the least harm.

"Richard Goldsmith, who was thus slain, was a shoemaker by trade, being reputed a good man in general, but had blemished his Christian profession by being a man who kept not his word (he,

-88-

quick to promise, but slow to fulfill). However, it must be said that half a year before his death, God gave him a deep sense of his evils, so that he made it his business not only that his peace might be made with God, but with men also (unto whom he had given just offense). He went up and down bewailing his great sin in promise breaking and became a very conscientious and Godly Christian, promoting holy and edifying lifestyles. At that very time when he was struck dead, he was speaking of some passages in the sermon he had newly heard, and his last words were, 'Blessed be the Lord.'"

"If we confess our sins, he is faithful and just to forgive us our sins, and to cleanse us from all unrighteousness" (I John 1:9).

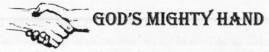

NEVER ALONE 1676 A.D.

The providence of God was favorable toward Mr. Ephraim Howe, of New Haven, Connecticut, who was for nearly a year given up by his family and friends as a dead man. But God preserved him alive on a desolate island, where he had been shipwrecked, and then returned him home to his family

On the 25th of August, in the year 1676, Skipper Howe, with his two eldest sons, set sail from New Haven for Boston, Massachusetts in a small ship. After completing their business, they set sail to return home again on September 10, but contrary winds forced them back to Boston, where Ephraim was taken ill with a violent sickness. This was a sickness which took its toll in the area, and many people died. In due course, the merciful providence of God having spared his life and restored him to health, he again with his sons set sail from Boston, this time on October 10.

By a fair wind they went forward toward Cape Cod; but suddenly the weather became very stormy, so that they could not reach the Cape, but were forced out to sea, where they were endangered by the size of their small ship. The storm was so strong and so long that the oldest son fell sick and died after eleven days at sea. Shortly after, the other son fell sick and died, also. This was a bitter cup to Ephraim.

It is noted in I Chronicles 7:22 that when the sons of Ephraim were dead, Ephraim mourned many days, and his brethren came to comfort him. Ephraim Howe had no one to comfort him, for his friends and relatives did not know what had happened. But what his friends and relatives could not do, the Lord Himself could and did, for the sons had died in such a sweet and gracious manner that their father professed he had joy in parting with them. But now his outward distress and danger were increasing, since his two sons were his only help in running the ship.

Not long after, another passenger, Caleb Jones, also fell sick and died. Thus, half of the people on the ship had died, and all that remained were Ephraim, another passenger, a Mr. Augur, and a boy who was in a very weak state, yet was willing to stand at the helm twenty-four hours at a time: In the meantime, the stormy sea buffeted the ship so much that anyone who did not hold on tightly would certainly have been washed overboard.

Ephraim did not know whether they should continue trying to return to the New England shore or sail away from America for the southern islands. He asked Mr. Augur what he thought, and they resolved that they would first seek God in prayer and then cast lots. The lot fell on New England. By this time, they had been at sea a month. The rudder of their vessel had broken off, so that now they had nothing but God alone upon which to rely.

They drifted for the next two weeks. Their entire time at sea they were wet and cold and had to ration food and water. At the end of six weeks, the ship was driven onto a reef. God's Providence allowed them to see breakers as a warning, and in the distance they were able to see a rocky island. Without the breakers as a warning, they would have been dashed to pieces on the reef. They immediately dropped anchor and got out the survival boat, and at that very moment God calmed the sea. In their haste to get out of the ship before it broke up and sank, however, they had to leave many supplies behind. When the bedraggled group came ashore, they found themselves on a rocky, desolate island near what is now Cape Sables, Florida. Because they left their food supplies on the ship, they were in danger of starving to death. Another storm finished off the anchored ship, and Providentially, a barrel of gun powder floated ashore without sustaining any damage, also half a barrel of molasses, and many things useful for building a shelter.

In spite of these blessings, there were few birds seen, and Ephraim was able to shoot only one at a time for food. Once the group went five days without food. Mercifully, the Lord took away their appetites when there was nothing to eat. After they had been on the island for about twelve weeks, Mr. Augur died. A short time later, the boy died also, so Ephraim was left alone upon the island. He lived there for another three months.

During this lonely time he saw several fishing vessels sailing by, and some came near the island, but though he used whatever he could to try to signal them, none came to close to him, fearing that he was a hostile Indian. Ephraim fasted and prayed, confessing and bewailing his sins, and begging God for deliverance.

He also realized that he should praise God for the great mercies and preservation which he had experienced up to that point. Accordingly, he set apart an entire day for that purpose, spending the time in giving thanks to God for all the mercies of his life, as many as he could remember, and especially, for those Divine favors which had been mingled with his afflictions. He humbly blessed God for His wonderful goodness in preserving him alive by a miracle of mercy. Immediately after this, a ship on its way to New England Providentially passed by the island and sent a small boat ashore—rescuing Ephraim Howe, who arrived home to be united with his family on July 18, 1677, after being gone eleven months.

"My soul shall make her boast in the LORD: the humble shall hear thereof, and be glad. O magnify the LORD with me, and let us exalt his name together. I sought the LORD, and he heard me, and delivered me from all my fears. They looked unto him, and were lightened: and their faces were not ashamed. This poor man cried, and the LORD heard him, and saved him out of all his troubles" (Psalm 34:2–6).

Jesus, Savior, pilot me Over life's tempestuous sea; Unknown waves before me roll, Hiding rock and treacherous shoal; Chart and compass came from Thee: Jesus, Savior, pilot me.

As a mother stills her child, Thou canst hush the ocean wild; Boisterous waves obey Thy will When Thou say'st to them "Be still!" Wondrous Sov'reign of the sea, Jesus, Savior, pilot me.

When at last I near the shore,   And the fearful breakers roar 'Twixt me and the peaceful Rest,   Then while leaning on Thy breast, May I hear Thee say to me, "Fear not, I will pilot thee."

Edward Hopper (1816–1888)

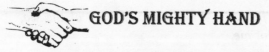

ANOTHER PRODIGAL SON 1709 A.D.

This wonderful providential account was written by Woods Rogers, a sailor who was in the rescue party that found Alexander Selkirk. Alexander Selkirk was a Scottish shoemaker's son who, in his rebellious youth, made a mistake and ran away to sea, thereby joining a band of buccaneers for a life of adventure. His adventure as a buccanear came to an abrupt end, for in September of 1704, he was put ashore by the captain due to his mutinous nature, a nature which was to be broken as he was forced to live on the uninhabited Mas a Tierra Island in the Juan Fernandez cluster, four-hundred miles west of Valparaiso, Chile. He was dubbed the real Robinson Crusoe of his time. The beauty of this story is that when a person finds himself alone, destitute, and forgotten, the Lord can be ever present to help those who call upon His name in humility and repentance. *"The LORD is nigh unto all them that call upon him, to all that call upon him in truth"* (Psalm 145:18).

"Our pinnace return'd from the shore, and brought an abundance of craw-fish with a man cloth'd in goat skins, who look'd wilder than the first owners of them. He had been on the island four years and four months, being left there by Captain Stradling in the Cinque Ports. His name was Alexander Selkirk, a Scotchman, who had been Master of the Cinque Ports, the ship that came here last with Captain Dampier, who told me he was the best man in her. Therefore, I immediately agreed with him to be a mate on board our ship.

"Twas he that made the fire last night when he saw our ships, which he judg'd to be English. During his stay here he saw several ships pass by, but only two came in to anchor. When he went to view them, he found them to be Spanish and retired from 'em, at which time they shot at him. Had they been French, he would have submitted, but chose to risk dying alone on the land, rather than fall into the hands of the Spaniards in these parts, because he apprehended they would murder him or make him a slave in the mines; for he fear'd they would spare no stranger that might be capable of discovering the South Sea. The Spaniards had landed before he knew who they were, and they came so near to him that he had much ado to escape: for they not only shot at him, but pursued him into the woods, where he climbed to the top of a tree at the foot of which they boiled water and killed several goats. In due time they left the island without discovering him. He told us he was born in Largo, in the county of Fife, Scotland, and was bred a sailor from his youth. The reason he was left here was a difference betwixt him and his captain.

"He had with him his clothes and bedding, a matchlock, musket, some powder, bullets, a hatchet, a knife, a kettle, a Bible, some practical pieces, and his mathematical instruments and books. He provided for himself as well as he could, but for the first eight months had grown melancholy because of the terror of being left alone in such a desolate place. He built two huts with pimento trees, covered them with long grass, and lined them with the skins of goats, which he killed with his gun as needed, so long as his gunpowder lasted. Poor soul had but one pound of powder and when that was near spent, he made fires by rubbing two sticks of pimento wood together upon his knee. In the lesser hut, at some distance from the other, he dressed his victuals, and in the larger he slept, and employed himself in reading, singing Psalms, and praying, so that he said he was a better Christian while in this solitude, than ever he was before, or than he was afraid he should ever be again.

"At first he never ate anything until hunger constrained him, partly for grief, and partly for want of bread and salt; nor did he go to bed till he could see no longer. The pimento wood, which burnt very clear, served him both for fire and light, and refreshed him with its fragrant smell. He might have had enough fish, but could not eat 'em for want of salt, because they occasioned a looseness; except crawfish, which were very good and as large as lobsters on this island. These he sometimes boiled and at other times broiled as he did his goats' flesh, of which he made very good broth. They are not so rank as ours: He kept an account of five-hundred goats that he killed while there and caught as many more, which he marked on the ear and let go. When his powder ceased he caught them by running them down. His way of living enabled him to become extremely fit and strong so that he ran with wonderful swiftness through the woods, and up the rocks and hills. We personally witnessed this when we employed him to catch goats for us. We had a bull dog which we sent with several of our nimblest runners to help him in catching goats; but he out-distanced and tired both the dog and the men, caught the goats and brought 'em to us on his back. He told us that his agility in pursuing a goat had once like to have cost him his life: He once pursued a goat with so much eagerness that he caught hold of it on the brink of a precipice of which he was not aware. The brush having hid it from him so that he fell with the goat down a precipice a great height. He was so stunned and bruised with the fall that he narrowly escaped with his life, and when he came to his senses, he found the goat dead under him. He lay there about twenty-four hours and was scarcely able to crawl to his hut which was about a mile distant, or to stir abroad again for ten days.

"He came at last to relish his meat well enough without salt or bread. In summer season, he had plenty of good turnips which had been sowed there by Captain Dampier's men and had now overspread some acres of ground. He had enough of good cabbage from the cabbage trees and seasoned his meat with the fruit of the pimento trees. This is the same as the Jamaica pepper and smells delicious. He also found a black pepper called Maragita, which was very good to use as a wind break. He soon wore out all his shoes and clothes by running through the woods: and at last, being forced to shift without them, his feet became so hard that he ran everywhere without annoyance. It was some time before he could wear shoes after we found him. For not being used to any so long, his feet swelled when he came first to wear them again. After he had conquered his melancholy, he sometimes diverted himself by cutting his name on the trees and keeping track of the days of his stay by making marks.

"He was at first much pestered with cats and rats that had bred in great numbers from some of each species which had made it ashore from ships that put in to collect wood and water. The rats gnawed his feet and clothes while he slept, which obliged him to cherish the cats. Many of the cats became so tame that they would lie around him by the hundreds, and soon delivered him from the rats.

"He likewise tamed some kids, and to divert himself would now and then sing and dance with them and his cats so that by the care of Providence, and vigor of his youth, (being now about thirty years old,) he came at last to conquer all the inconveniences of his solitude and became satisfied and contented. When his clothes wore out he made himself a coat and cap of goat skins, which he stitched together with little straps. He made the leather straps by cutting strips of goat skins with his knife. He had no other needle but a nail, and when his knife was worn too thin to use, he made others as well as he could of some iron hoops that were left ashore. He beat the hoops thin and ground the edge upon stones. Having some linen cloth with him, he sewed himself shirts with a nail and stitched them with the worsted of his old stockings, which he unraveled on purpose. He had his last shirt on when we found him on the island.

"At his first coming on board with us, he had forgotten his native language for want of use, that we could scarcely understand him. He seemed to speak his words by halves. We offered him a dram, but he would not touch it, having drunk nothing but water since his being there. Twas some time before he could relish our victuals. He could give us an account of no other product of the island than what we have mentioned except small black plums. They were very good, but hard to come by since the trees which bare them grow high among the mountains and cliffs.

"As for Mr. Selkirk, we took him back to the native place of his birth. It was there that this deliverance account was written in full. Mr. Selkirk spent the rest of his days sharing of his faith and how the Saviour Christ rescued him. He never passed an opportunity to press home the need for sinful men to trust Christ for their salvation and rescue from their sinful conditions."

"The LORD rewarded me according to my righteousness; according to the cleanness of my hands hath he recompensed me. For I have kept the ways of the LORD, and have not wickedly departed from my God. For all his judgments were before me, and I did not put away his statutes from me. I was also upright before him, and I kept myself from mine iniquity. Therefore hath the LORD recompensed me according to my righteousness, according to the cleanness of my hands in his eyesight.

"With the merciful thou wilt shew thyself merciful; with an upright man thou wilt shew thyself upright; With the pure thou wilt shew thyself pure; and with the froward thou wilt shew thyself froward. For thou wilt save the afflicted people; but wilt bring down high looks. For thou wilt light my candle: the LORD my God will enlighten my darkness. For by thee I have run through a troop; and by my God have I leaped over a wall. As for God, his way is perfect: the word of the LORD is tried: he is a buckler to all those that trust in him.

"For who is God save the LORD? Or who is a rock save our God? It is God that girdeth me with strength, and maketh my way perfect. He maketh my feet like hinds' feet, and setteth me upon my high places. He teacheth my hands to war, so that a bow of steel is broken by mine arms. Thou hast also given me the shield of thy salvation: and thy right hand hath holden me up, and thy gentleness hath made me great" (Psalm 18:20-35).

CHARMED LIFE, OR TRUST IN THE LORD 1718 A.D.

Very few Americans know of Israel Putman, born in Danvers, Massachusetts, in 1718, yet his life was as adventurous as that of Daniel Boone and Davy Crockett. Those who did know him said he lived a "charmed life," but they came to know that his strength and providential protection came from his trust in the Lord. There are many remarkable accounts of God's mighty hand superintending protection over Israel's life.

At twenty-two years of age, Putnam bought a farm in Pomfret, Connecticut, at that time a wild frontier. His new farm was in the midst of deep, dark forests, sugar maples, and rivers that were frequented by wild beasts and warring Indians. It happened that there was an old she-wolf living nearby who had attacked settlers, killed their livestock, and caused a general alarm for all who ventured into the woods to hunt or to travel from one farm to another. Most of the settlers had all but given up trying to kill the elusive wolf.

Seeing this as a great challenge, Israel set about to rid the area of this dreaded canine. One day while hunting, Israel caught sight of the wolf and was able to follow her to her den. The den was a cave with a perilously small opening. Only one person could enter it at a time, and only by crawling on his belly. Such a position would not be very advantageous in approaching a vicious wolf.

Israel was very bold—but he was also smart, so he asked the help of a couple of friends and returned with them to wait for the wolf. Israel decided to go in the den and look around. The other men tied a rope around his feet in case the wolf overpowered him and he needed to be pulled out.

Crawling into the small cave opening with a lighted torch, he discovered a fairly large cavern. Slowly he stood looking around, waiting, knowing that at any moment he could be pounced upon by the wolf. He had his musket ready for action. He did not see the wolf, so he lifted the torch and proceeded through the darkness to the back of the cave. Peering into the darkness he saw two eyes glaring at him. Before the wolf could spring, Israel fired a shot, and his foe lay dead on the ground. Israel became the hero of the territory.

Being a young man of courage and faith, Israel did not hesitate to join the army, in defense of his country during the French and Indian War. In 1755, as captain of a regiment of 1,000 men, he was sent by the state of Connecticut to repel a threatened French invasion of New York, and was present at the battle of Lake George. Israel's personal courage and patriotic spirit animated his troops and earned him the reputation needed to command men. The French and Indian War gave Israel and other leaders the experience they would later need to defeat the British in their battle for independence.

In 1758, Israel was captured by Indians while fighting the French. His life seemed to be doomed by these fierce and bloodthirsty warriors. After consulting with one another, his captors decided to burn him at the stake. Putnam pleaded with them, but to no avail. He was tied to an old tree in a clearing, and the wood was placed beneath his feet. While he watched the Indians prepare to set fire to what would be his funeral pyre, Israel appealed to God and committed his life to Christ, trusting that God's will would be done. After performing a feverish war dance, the Indians lifted their torches and placed them at Israel's feet. The flames leaped up and were nearly touching him when God's hand intervened. An officer from the enemy army—the French—rushed forward and kicked the fire brands in all directions and then freed Israel. Israel now knew the truth found in Proverbs 16:7: *"When a man's ways please the LORD, he maketh even his enemies to be at peace with him."*

In 1759, after the French and Indian War, Israel was given command of the Connecticut militia. In 1764, he helped to relieve the city of Detroit, then besieged by Pontiac, the Indian chief. Within eleven years he was given a commission as a Major General and proved himself worthy at the Battle of Bunker Hill, at the Battle of Long Island, in the defense of the Hudson River, and throughout the American Revolution. One last example of God's protection on this man's life bears repeating.

In 1778, Israel Putnam made his famous escape from British Governor William Tryon's dragoons in western Connecticut by riding down the steep embankment at a place called Horseneck, and was almost captured. To escape, he decided to charge his horse down the steep, rocky, forested crag at full gallop. When the British arrived at the edge of the steep incline they halted their horses, for they knew that going over the hill in pursuit would certainly bring death or serious injury. They watched Israel, expecting to see him ride to his death by smashing into a tree or tumbling headlong over a small cliff. To their consternation and disbelief, they witnessed him escape, unharmed, riding out to safety beyond their reach. Later Israel commented that in such a desperate situation he could only commend himself to the hand of God. Israel lived to tell of all his adventures to friends and family until his death on May 19, 1790, at the age of seventy-two.

" The LORD is my light and my salvation; whom shall I fear? the LORD is the strength of my life; of whom shall I be afraid? When the wicked, even mine enemies and my foes, came upon me to eat up my flesh, they stumbled and fell. Though an host should encamp against me, my heart shall not fear: though war should rise against me, in this will I be confident. One thing have I desired of the LORD, that will I seek after; that I may dwell in the house of the LORD all the days of my life, to behold the beauty of the LORD, and to inquire in his temple. For in the time of trouble he shall hide me in his pavilion: in the secret of his tabernacle shall he hide me; he shall set me up upon a rock. And now shall mine head be lifted up above mine enemies round about me: therefore will I offer in his tabernacle sacrifices of joy; I will sing, yea, I will sing praises unto the LORD. Hear, O LORD, when I cry with my voice: have mercy also upon me, and answer me" (Psalm 27:1-7).

God is love; His mercy brightens All the path in which we rove; Bliss he wakes and woe He lightens; God is wisdom, God is love.

Chance and change are busy ever;   Man decays, and ages move;But His mercy waneth never; God is wisdom, God is love.

E'en the hour that darkest seemeth, Will His changeless goodness prove; From the gloom His brightness streameth; God is wisdom, God is love.   John Browring (1792-1872)

HARDENED HEART CONVERTED 1725 A.D.

Apart from the Incarnation of Christ, the most dramatic evidence of the mighty hand of God may be witnessed in the conversion of a sinner. The life of John Newton is a testimony to this truth.

The Apostle Paul once said that he was the "chief of sinners." John Newton might well be called the "assistant chief."

John Newton was born in London in 1725. Before his conversion he was one of the most ungodly, foul-mouthed, crude, blasphemous, evil, hateful reprobates this world has ever known. But the real tragedy of the early part of his life was this: He had been raised by a Godly mother to be a God-fearing, well-behaved boy.

Though no excuse can be made in defense of John's wickedness, the point at which he turned from his childhood faith in Christ can be clearly seen.

By the age of four, John showed signs of having a brilliant mind. He could read and communicate well. When John was six, his mother began to teach him Latin. His studies included much memorization, and he could recite whole passages from the Latin Bible. Along with his Bible study John also learned the tenets of the Christian faith known as the Catechism. He later wrote that he would often awaken at night hearing the sound of a voice and would find his mother in earnest prayer over his soul, asking the Lord to make her son a Godly and useful Christian. Unfortunately, she didn't live to see the answer to her prayers.

John's father was a ship captain, and when he was at sea, John's mother often placed John in the care of friends while she went to visit relatives. The day before John turned seven he received the sorrowful news that his beloved mother had died. The family with whom he was staying tried to console him, but to no avail. From that day, John's life went downhill. Rather than draw closer to the Lord as his "refuge and strength," he chose to turn away from God and blame Him for taking his mother.

John's father, longing for a companion, remarried quickly. He and his new bride tried to cheer John, but because Captain Newton would often be at sea for great lengths of time, there was little to encourage John. Seeking affection and acceptance elsewhere, John made the mistake of choosing wrong companions. His friends were mostly uneducated, godless, profane, mischievous youths bent on destructive habits. John's father tried taking his son on several voyages to separate him from his godless friends, but without success. John's heart was with his friends.

At times during his teen years, John tried to rid himself of his bad habits and bad friends and even tried to do some religious good works. However, he found that it was impossible to develop Christian virtues on his own, and the religion of good works left him frustrated. He didn't understand that a man must be "born again" from above and that the work of salvation is a free gift of Christ to any sinner who will simply call upon the Lord.

Because of his failed attempts at virtue, John found it easy to fall into the bad habits and sinful pleasures of wicked sailors. Thus he slid into a rebellious, hard-hearted life. However, the further John sank into sin, the more God's mighty hand of grace was extended to bring him back to the faith his mother had tried to instill in him. The foundation of prayer that his mother laid before her death was more critical than she had ever dreamed.

The following examples from John Newton's life show how God works to answer the prayers of His faithful children and to bring sinners to Himself.

Once, when John was nearly twelve, he was thrown by a horse. Picking himself up, he was alarmed to see a sharp branch only inches from his head. He realized he could have been killed instantly.

One fair Sunday afternoon, John and some friends decided to go aboard a man-of-war ship that was anchored in the harbor.

John was late in meeting his friends and found that they had left the dock without him and were rowing out in a small boat. With his fist raised in anger, he watched as an unexpected swell raised the small boat and capsized it. The boys helplessly drowned. John lowered his fist and counted himself lucky, refusing to admit that it was God who had saved him.

In 1742, at the age of seventeen, John visited the Catletts, distant relatives who lived in Chatham, England. While there, he met his future wife, Mary. This saintly girl of fourteen gave John hope, and he dreamed that someday he would be worthy to have her as his wife. Although poor and socially unsuited for her, he set a goal to better himself, more for the sake of Mary than for the Lord. His love for her sustained him through many difficult times and even through a time of depression when he considered taking his own life.

John became a sailor and a slave trader, and after sailing for several years on various ships and daily growing more reprobate, his speech had become so foul that even the other sailors were shocked by it. John would often take well-known hymns and compose sacrilegious rhymes to the tunes. During one of these voyages he contracted jungle fever and was placed under the care of a trader named Clow. Mr. Clow's servant was given charge over John to nurse him back to health. This black lady had, understandably, no fondness for John Newton, and she would mock him in his sickness. She would neglect to feed him for hours, then give him garbage not fit for dogs. During this ill treatment at the hand of a slave, he came to understand how the slaves must have felt when they were treated worse than dogs.

The Lord used this humbling experience to change John's life profoundly. When he was finally converted, he did not immediately end his involvement with slave trading, but he did begin to treat the slaves on his ships with compassion, and he seldom lost a slave due to neglect.

John made many enemies over the years—enemies who would have killed him, given the opportunity. Once John anchored his ship in the Mater Harbor off the beautiful shores of

Ireland. He lowered a skiff and tried to row to the dock, but the current was so strong he could make no progress. Exhausted, he returned to the ship, pulled anchor, and left the harbor. Several months later he learned that on that day, a band of men had waited for him on shore, planning to ambush and kill him.

In 1747, John's father sent a man named Captain Stanwick to find and bring home his wayward son. John had not left word of his whereabouts for more than a year, and only God could have orchestrated the necessary events that helped Captain Stanwick to find him. After days of fruitless searching, Captain Stanwick was heading south along the African coast when his crew spotted a smoke signal from the beach. This was the usual sign that someone wanted to sell slaves. The Captain hesitated to stop, deploring the thought of further delays, but he felt compelled to take a look. When he arrived on shore, much to his amazement, he found "the prodigal son"—John Newton. The captain convinced John to return with him to England, and that journey was the turning point in John's life.

One calm, moonlit night during the long journey home, the ship was anchored off the Gabon Estuary in West Africa. John was usually a "light" drinker, but out of boredom he challenged the other sailors to a drinking match. He got so drunk he could hardly walk. As he tried to make his way back to his cabin, his hat blew overboard. Lunging after it, he found himself going overboard along with the hat. At that very moment, a couple of sailors walking by quickly grabbed his feet and pulled him up. John, unable to swim and being very drunk, would certainly have perished. He continued to see God's hand on his life, yet he still ran from the reality that God was calling him to surrender his stubborn will to Christ.

On the ship was a copy of the book *The Imitation of Christ*, by Thomas`a Kempis, along with a Bible. With nothing better to do, he began to read these books and became aware of his utterly depraved and sinful condition. Although he was still rebellious and not ready to surrender to Christ, John knew that the Lord was pursuing him. He did not like the thought of being hounded by the

Lord.

During this time of conviction, a storm hit the ship, the *Greyhound*. It was so severe that "all hands" were needed to help keep the ship afloat. John worked the bilge pump for hours, but the ship's seams were so loose that water came in faster than he could pump it out. John, who feared neither Heaven nor hell, was suddenly struck with the awareness that the ship was sinking and that he was headed for a Christ-less eternity.

He panicked, and for the first time in his life, he cried out to God: "Lord have mercy on us all! I don't want to die!" The ship was being beaten by the wind, its sails torn and its rigging ripped apart by the waves, and it was impossible to control. In the midst of all this, John's still-sharp mind recalled a Bible verse he had learned at his mother's knee:

"Because I have called, and ye refused; I have stretched out my hand, and no man regarded, But ye have set at nought all my counsel, and would have none of my reproof, I also will laugh at your calamity; I will mock when your fear cometh; When your fear cometh as desolation, and your destruction cometh as a whirlwind; when distress and anguish come upon you. Then shall they call upon me, but I will not answer; they shall seek me early, but they shall not find me; For that they hated knowledge, and did not choose the fear of the LORD. They would have none of my counsel: they despised all my reproof. Therefore shall they eat of the fruit of their own way, and be filled with their own devices. For the turning away of the simple shall slay them, and the prosperity of fools shall destroy them. But whoso hearkeneth unto me shall dwell safely, and shall be quiet from fear of evil" *(Proverbs 1:24-33).*

John was like Jonah of old, below deck and trying to run from God, yet finding no peace. His duties required him to return to the deck. As he proceeded to climb up the ladder, the captain called out to him and told him to get his knife. Because of his rebellious nature he was normally unresponsive to commands, but this time he obeyed quickly. As he stepped on the ladder the second time, another sailor pushing him aside, squeezed by, and climbed up to the deck. Perturbed at being pushed aside, John looked up to see who the sailor was. Just then, the ship lurched, and the man was thrown overboard, never to be seen again. John realized that had it not been for his obedience to the captain's order, he could easily have been in that spot on the deck, and he found himself thanking God for sparing his life.

The storm continued through the night, abating for only a short time. In the morning it hit again with full fury, this time flooding the food supplies and fresh water. With little food and barely enough water to last a day, the superstitious captain and crew blamed the mishaps on John, the "Jonah" on board. It became apparent that in a matter of hours John would probably be murdered, as the hungry sailors began to discuss the possibility of cannibalism as they looked at him. Once again, God's hand mercifully rescued John. Just as the last bit of food and water was consumed, the cry of "land ahoy" was heard. John knew the Lord had intervened to save his wretched life. John finally broke into tears, thus beginning his return to the faith once delivered to him by his mother.

In February of 1750, John and Mary—the girl who had given him hope of reforming his godless life—were married. For the next forty years, with her by his side as they studied the Bible and prayed together, John continued to grow in the grace and knowledge of Jesus Christ. As he began to mature in Christ, he came to hate the evils of slavery, left the slave trade, and vowed to help end the practice. The fulfillment of that vow came to fruition when John met William Wilberforce, the man who was instrumental in ending England's involvement with the slave trade. John became a beloved pastor and wrote a number of hymns, many of which are still sung today. (See the index of authors in the back of any hymnal.) However, John Newton is best remembered for the hymn "Amazing Grace," which was the testimony of his own conversion by the grace of God through Christ Jesus.

Much more could be said of John Newton, but it is best to conclude with what he said of himself. He requested that these words be inscribed on his tombstone:

JOHN NEWTON,
Clerk,
Once an infidel and libertine
A servant of slaves in Africa,
was by the Rich Mercy of our Lord and Savour,
Jesus Christ
Preserved, Restored, Pardoned,
And appointed to Preach the Faith
He had Long Labored to Destroy.

Amazing grace,
how sweet the sound that
saved a wretch like me!
I once was lost but now am found,
Was blind but now I see.
John Newton (1725–1807)

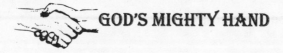

THEY STOOD STILL TO SEE THE SALVATION OF THE LORD 1746 A.D.

Wherever the French settled, they allowed only the Roman Catholic religion to be practiced. New Englanders greatly feared and resented this forced religious practice. During the mid 1700s, the Stuart monarchs in England were sympathetic to France's Catholic monarchs. But when the Protestant king, William of Orange, ascended the English throne, the French began to attack the English colonists in America with great savagery. New England forces, with the aid of the British, captured Louisbourg in Nova Scotia. During the battle, God used the weather to the advantage of the New Englanders. The French residents, viewing the events of war, later wrote, "The English appear to have enlisted Heaven in their interest, so long as the expedition lasted they had the most beautiful weather in the world: no storms, no unfavorable winds, and no fog; which was most surprising for the area."

After the capture of Louisbourg, the French retaliated. They sent half of their navy, under the command of the Duc d'Anville, to lay waste to the whole sea coast from Nova Scotia to Georgia. God miraculously protected the colonies. This was acknowledged in a sermon of thanksgiving, preached by the Rev. Thomas Prince, pastor of the South Church in Boston. He referred to God's protective hand when New England was "a long while wholly ignorant of their designs against us."

Even when rumors of French aggression reached New England, the colonists were not greatly worried about the French attacking. Admiral Martin's English squadron, posted off the French coastline, had been guarding America from a French naval attack. However, the French had eluded Admiral Martin's squadron and had slipped out to sea.

Rev. Prince observed, "While we knew nothing of danger, God beheld it and was working salvation for us. And when we had none to help in America, He even prevented our friends in Europe from coming to succor us; that we might see our salvation was His work alone, and that the glory belongs entirely to Him."

God delights in the display of His mighty hand, lest men boast of their own might. God often arranges the course of events so He receives all praise in His deeds. Having eluded the British, the proud French fleet of about seventy, set sail on June 20, 1746. As the vessels crossed the Atlantic, heading for Halifax, God's intervention took several forms. First, they were delayed in a prolonged calm. Then they encountered storms in which several ships were disabled by lightning. Next, pestilence broke out among them, and then the entire fleet was scattered to the four winds by tremendous storms. They were so dispersed in the midst of the ocean, that by August 26 they had but twelve ships left out of the seventy that had set sail on June 20. As they were nearing the dangerous shoals off the Isle of Sables, they encountered another violent storm and lost several more vessels. When the Duc d'Anville's ship finally reached Halifax, a lonely, isolated area, he fully expected to rendezvous with other French ships, sent from the West Indies to meet him. The West Indies squadron had indeed been there, but discouraged by the long delay of Duc d' Anville's fleet, had given up and left, returning to their homes.

Rev. Jonathan French, another New England pastor, wrote that as soon as the French vessels were sighted off the east coast of Massachusetts, the people were "filled with consternation." The streets filled with men marching for the defense of the seaports; and the distresses of women and children, trembling for the event, made deep impressions upon the minds of those who remember these scenes. But never did the religion, for which the country was settled, appear more important, nor prayer more prevalent, than on this occasion. God, who hears prayers, stretched forth His providential hand and destroyed that mighty armament in a manner almost as extraordinary as the drowning of Pharaoh and his host in the Red Sea.

Shortly after his arrival at Halifax, the Duc d' Anville was appalled at the loss of the major part of his fleet and, finding his few ships so shattered, so many of his men dead, many sickly, and no more of his fleet coming in, he sank into depression. On September 15, he died. It is generally accepted that he poisoned himself. He was buried in disgrace without military ceremony. More ships finally limped into port, but many of the sailors on board were ill and their food supplies were fast running out. The new commander, who took Duc d' Anville's command, committed suicide only days after their arrival, by falling on his own sword. The third in command ordered the men ashore to recruit additional French and Indians so that an attack on Annapolis could proceed. But before they could leave Halifax, almost three-thousand sailors died of a new pestilence.

Finally, still determined to teach the Americans a lesson, the fleet's new commander, La Jonquiere, set sail on October 13, 1746. Intending to attack Annapolis, he was likely unaware of the fact that on October 6 the New England churches had set October 16 as a day of fasting and prayer for their deliverance. Rev. French describes the events that followed:

"On this great emergency, and day of darkness and doubtful expectation, the 16th of October was observed as a day of FASTING AND PRAYER throughout the Province. And, wonderful to relate, that very night God sent upon them a more dreadful storm than either of the former, and completed their destruction. Some ships overturned, some floundered, and only a remnant of this miserable fleet returned to France to carry the news of defeat and of the mighty deeds of God in protection over the American colonies."

The French had been like Egypt of old, bent on the destruction of God's chosen people. God showed His mighty hand of deliverance. Throughout the history of America's early beginnings, it is obvious that without the aid of God, Americans would have been consumed many times over by Indians, France, Britain, or natural disasters through plagues or weather. God has called and preserved this nation for His divine purpose. The Sabbath after the Duc d' Anville's fleet was destroyed, the colonists turned to a passage in Exodus and gave thanks to the Lord for so great a deliverance. They took to heart their responsibility to teach their children to remember the Lord and what He had done for their preservation, and to keep His covenant.

"Is not this the word that we did tell thee in Egypt, saying, Let us alone, that we may serve the Egyptians? For it had been better for us to serve the Egyptians, than that we should die in the wilderness. And Moses said unto the people, Fear ye not, stand still, and see the salvation of the LORD, which he will shew to you today:...The LORD shall fight for you, and ye shall hold your peace" (*Exodus 14:12-14*).

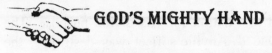

A FIGHT TO THE FINISH 1746 A.D.

Prince Charles Edward Stuart III, also known as "Bonnie Prince Charlie," was born in Rome on December 31, 1720, the eldest son of exiled King James VIII. He was an intelligent child, able to speak English, French, and Italian. Rather than pursue higher learning, he preferred military engagements in Europe. "Bonnie Prince Charlie" became the center of hopes of an ongoing Stuart restoration, which was an attempt to bring England back into the "fold" of the Roman Catholic Church. Therefore, Prince Charles was seen by the French government as an important pawn in their constantly shifting power game with Britain.

The Catholic French attempted to take power in England in 1744, but the promised invasion never came about because of God's providential power. As French ships prepared to set sail for England, bad weather moved in, and ships from the Royal Navy "happened" to be patrolling the English Channel on the day of the attempted invasion.

Despite these setbacks, Charles was determined that the time had come for him to make his move, and he set sail for Scotland in the summer of 1745, landing in the Hebrides with seven men. He was welcomed by several of the Catholic Highland chiefs, but they had little enthusiasm for a revolt without the aid of France. However, the prince had charm and courage, and when the chiefs told him that he should go home, he replied, "I am come home!"

His determination inspired many, and by the time he raised his standard at Glenfinnanon on August 19, six-hundred men had joined him. The ever-growing army marched south through Perth, where they were joined by Charles' great general, Lord George Murray, before going on to Edinburgh. The capital surrendered on September 17, with only the castle holding out. Charles held court at Holyrood Palace.

The Jacobites were a military faction helping to establish the Stuart Monarchy in England by force. Their crushing victory at the Battle of Prestonpans, on September 21, alarmed the government in London, and, for the first time, troops were hastily recalled from Europe. On November 1, Charles' army marched out of the capital—headed for London. Carlisle fell on November 8, and under Murray's guidance the Jacobite forces outmaneuvered two government armies, under Wade and Cumberland, while waiting for French troops to arrive at Derby,by December 1.

By now, however, the chiefs were increasingly nervous at their own isolation. Their men were far from their homelands and began to desert. The promised back-up of French troops had not arrived, and the English Jacobites had not joined them. The Highland chiefs, though, were unaware of the panic which was spreading through London, where George II, fearing the loss of his throne, hurriedly prepared to return to Hanover.

In this light, it is irresistible to speculate about what might have happened if Charles' plan of making a dash for London had prevailed. God had other plans for England, as will shortly be seen.

Despite Charles' arguments and pleas, the will of the chiefs prevailed, and the Jacobite army marched north on December 6, skillfully outmaneuvering the government forces again and then defeating them at Falkirk on January 17. But the army of the Duke of Cumberland caught up with them at Culloden Moor in April of 1746, where Charles, despite desertion and fatigue among his men and against Murray's advice, chose to fight. Because of stubborn pride the Jacobites were decimated.

The Battle of Culloden Moor marked the end of the Stuart monarchy and the claim of the Roman Church in Britain. Charles spent the next few months a fugitive in the Highlands and islands with a 30,000-pound sterling bounty on his head. He escaped on a French ship in September 1746, having been helped by many, including Flora MacDonald, an intriguing character. Flora MacDonald helped Prince Charles escape to the Isle of Skye, dressed as a woman named 'Betty Burke.' Although she succeeded in getting the prince to safety, she was later apprehended and imprisoned for a year. The Highlands were frightfully punished for aiding the prince in trying to overthrow the British Government. Consequently, the British Government set out to dismantle the social and cultural fabric of Scottish Gaeldom.

After Prince Charles devoted several years of his life to restoring Catholicism in England, he experienced a shattering defeat, which was almost an unbearable blow. Charles' personality crumbled under the dreadful weight of the failure. He spent the rest of his life in France and Italy, sinking into alcoholism and mistreating his wife, Princess Louise of Stolberg.

He continued to hope for a Stuart restoration and made secret trips to London in the 1750s to try to revive flagging Jacobite hopes. However, disintegration from dashing youth into shambling middle age meant that when he became the head of the Jacobite cause upon his father's death in 1766, his restoration as King of Scotland, England, and Ireland became more impossible than ever. Charles was always racked with guilt over the tragedy which had befallen his men in 1745 and the vicious punishments subsequently meted out in the Highlands by the British Government. When he died in Rome on January 31, 1788, a lone piper played the lament "Lochaber."

Having married a Scottish woman and in visiting Britain several times, unlike most Americans, I have had the opportunity to study some British history. How God has blessed that land and showered His divine favor on it! It is obvious that England has been used by God in marvelous ways to advance His Kingdom and to spread Christianity throughout the world.

The struggle between the Roman Catholic Church and the Protestant Reformation was fierce, causing death on both sides. One has to trust that because the power of the Roman Catholic Church in England was broken, a beachhead was established for the Protestant Reformation, which has affected the world in a multitude of ways, producing amazing results.

England has birthed some of this world's greatest Christian hymn writers, musicians, theologians, authors, statesmen, inventors, church leaders, and missionaries. The foundations of our nation's government can be found in the writings of Blackstone and Locke. The Battle of Culloden was a major event in history—affecting the world in untold ways and showing how God's mighty hand will prevail and carry out His will.

"There is no king saved by the multitude of an host: a mighty man is not delivered by much strength. An horse is a vain thing for safety: neither shall he deliver any by his great strength. Behold, the eye of the LORD is upon them that fear him, upon them that hope in his mercy; To deliver their soul from death, and to keep them alive in famine. Our soul waiteth for the LORD: he is our help and our shield. For our heart shall rejoice in him, because we have trusted in his holy name. Let thy mercy, O LORD, be upon us, according as we hope in thee" (*Psalm 33:16–22*).

"You'd Think Someone Was Trying to Kill You" 1755 A.D.

Between 1754 and 1763, England and France began to fight over land that had been claimed in the New World. This conflict became known as the "French and Indian War." The Bible declares, *"God that made the world and all things therein, seeing that he is Lord of heaven and earth, dwelleth not in temples made with hands; Neither is worshipped with men's hands, as though he needed anything, seeing he giveth to all life, and breath, and all things; And hath made of one blood all nations of men for to dwell on all the face of the earth, and hath determined the times before appointed, and the bounds of their habitation"* (Acts 17:24–26).

Keep in mind as you read this book that war does not take God by surprise. God directs and determines the outcome of wars which come from disputes over land, and indeed, all wars, for *"The earth is the Lord's and the fullness thereof"* (Psalm 24:1). Men may think that they plan and win or lose wars, but God gives the outcome as He wills.

The French and Indian War not only served in God's providential planning to determine land disputes, but it also brought to light a new leader: George Washington. The events of the French and Indian War were tools in God's mighty hand for shaping America's future—a future which included George Washington as a great general in the Revolutionary War and as the nation's first President. Washington's life would also become an example to future world leaders and to many others who would choose a life of sober-minded, diligent service.

It has been said by many that as Israel had Moses to bring deliverance from bondage to another nation, America had George Washington. Washington has been described as, "First in war, first in peace, and first in the hearts of his countrymen." He was a leader who stood for justice and the human rights of "life, liberty, and property" for every man. He exposed the tyranny of wicked rulers and became an example of a true leader—one who serves. He was a leader who admitted unashamedly that without God, he could do nothing and would be nothing.

During the French and Indian War, Washington was a young, energetic twenty-two-year-old colonel appointed from the Virginia militia. After being involved in service to Lieutenant Governor Dinwiddie of Virginia, he was placed under the command of English General Braddock, as an aide-de-camp. His first duty to General Braddock was to try to convince him of the folly of thinking he could march his trained British Regulars to Fort Duquesne (pronounced "due-KANE") in the wilderness of the Ohio Valley (now western Pennsylvania), fight a battle, whip the French, take the fort, and go home.

General Braddock, a proud and conceited veteran soldier, must have turned red in anger over this young officer's trying to tell him how to wage war on American soil. He reportedly said, "The Indians may frighten Continental troops, but they can make no impression on the King's Regulars!" Though the General's statement was bold, his troops proved they were not when they finally faced the warrior Indians. It was the Continental soldiers, under George Washington's leadership, who kept the French and Indian forces from completely annihilating the English.

The Battle of Monongahela (muh-non-guh-HEEL-uh), as it became known, was one of the most humiliating English defeats of the French and Indian War. Washington had suspected that the French and Indians would try to ambush the English. On July 9, 1755, it happened.

Several accounts reveal how Washington was preserved and protected from what should have been certain death at Monongahela. In the opening moments of battle, almost every mounted field officer had fallen—either killed or wounded—except Washington. Of the 86 officers who had gone into the fight, 26 were killed and 37 were wounded, leaving only 23 unharmed. Of the non-officer soldiers, 714 were killed or disabled. In every instance where the wounded could not drag themselves away from the battlefield, they were tomahawked and scalped by the savages. No prisoners were taken. Colonel Washington, one of the very few unhurt, wrote the following to his brother shortly after the battle:

> *"By the all-powerful dispensation of Providence, I have been protected beyond all human probability or expectation; for I had four bullets through my coat, and two horses shot under me, and escaped unhurt, although death was leveling my companions on every side of me."*

Fifteen years after the battle, Washington and his family physician, Dr. Craik, were traveling near the junction of the Kanawha and Ohio Rivers. They were approached by a party of Indians headed by a venerable chief, who, through an interpreter, addressed Washington and said,

> *"I great Chief; I Chief from here to the waters of the Great Lakes and to the far blue mountains beyond lakes. I have traveled a long and weary path, that I might see the young warrior of the great battle. It was on the day when white man's blood mixed with the streams of our forest that I first beheld this chief. I called to my young men and said, 'Mark tall and daring warrior. He is not of the red coat tribe. He hath an Indian's wisdom, and his warriors fight as we do. See him alone—exposed. Quick, let your aim be certain so he dies.' Our rifles were leveled, rifles which, but for him, knew not how to miss.*
>
> *"Twas all in vain. A Power, mightier far than we, gave him protection from bullets. He cannot die in battle. I am old and soon shall be gathered to the Great Council Fire of my fathers in the Land of Shades, but ere I go, there is something bids me speak in voice of Indian Great Spirit. Listen! The Great Spirit protects this warrior Washington and will guide his path. He will become the chief of great*

*nations and of many people, yet unborn. People will say of
him, he like me, Chief of a mighty nation!"*

Dr. Craik, after witnessing the encounter, recorded the
experience in detail and circulated it throughout the Colonies. The
Rev. Samuel Davies, a Presbyterian minister in Hanover,
Virginia, in a written sermon, said of Washington in 1759, "I
cannot but hope Providence has hitherto preserved him in so
singular a manner for some important service to his country."
Little did Rev. Davies imagine just what service God was going
to enable George Washington to perform. Within fifteen years,
Washington became Commander-in-Chief of the American army
and walked into the pages of American history—never to be
forgotten.

One can only surmise what the outcome of America's
Colonial history might have been had George Washington been
killed along with the other officers at Monongahela on that July
day in 1755. It is a comfort to know that God protects us for His
good purposes. However, sometimes His purposes are best served
when lives are not spared, as is illustrated in the story of Patrick
Henry, as you will soon read.

*"He that dwelleth in the secret place of the most High shall
abide under the shadow of the Almighty. I will say of the LORD,
He is my refuge and my fortress: my God; in him will I trust.
Surely he shall deliver thee from the snare of the fowler, and from
the noisome pestilence. He shall cover thee with his feathers, and
under his wings shalt thou trust: his truth shall be thy shield and
buckler. Thou shalt not be afraid for the terror by night; nor for
the arrow that flieth by day; Nor for the pestilence that walketh
in darkness; nor for the destruction that wasteth at noonday. A
thousand shall fall at thy side, and ten thousand at thy right hand;
but it shall not come nigh thee. Only with thine eyes shalt thou
behold and see the reward of the wicked. Because thou hast made
the LORD, which is my refuge, even the most High, thy
habitation; There shall no evil befall thee, neither shall any*

plague come nigh thy dwelling. For he shall give his angels charge over thee, to keep thee in all thy ways" (Psalm 91:1-11).

> *Under His wings I am safely abiding;*
> *Though the night deepens and tempests are wild;*
> *Still I can trust Him—I know He will keep me*
> *He has redeemed me and I am His child.*
>
> *Under His wings, O what precious enjoyment!*
> *There will I hide till life's trials are o'er.*
> *Sheltered, protected, no evil can harm me;*
> *Resting in Jesus I'm safe evermore.*
> *William O. Cushing (1823–1902)*

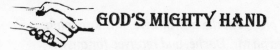

THE RIGHT PSALM AT THE RIGHT TIME 1774 A.D.

B y September of 1774, British troops were landing and taking possession of Boston and its harbor. It seemed that war with England was imminent. The leaders of various Colonies decided to hold a congress at Carpenter Hall in Philadelphia to discuss the impending war and what measures they should take. On Tuesday, September 6, Congress became alarmed over the news of British troops attacking. It was later discovered that it was a false rumor. Recognizing the seriousness of the day, they resorted to prayer, and it was resolved that the Rev. Mr. Duché be asked to open the following day with a Word from Scripture and offer a prayer of protection over the impending war with England.

John Adams wrote his wife Abigail in regard to this event as follows.

Dear Abigail,

When the Congress met, Mr. Cushing made a motion that it should be opened with prayer. It was opposed by Mr. Jay of New York, and Mr. Rutledge of South Carolina because we were so divided in religious sentiments, some Episcopalians, some Quakers, some Anabaptists, some Presbyterians, and some Congregationalists, that we could not join in the same act of worship.

Mr. Samuel Adams arose and said that he was no bigot, and could hear a prayer from any gentleman of piety and virtue, who was at the same time a friend to his country. He was a stranger in Philadelphia, but had heard that Mr. Duché deserved that character and therefore he moved that Mr. Duché, an Episcopal clergyman, might be desired to read prayers to Congress tomorrow morning. The motion was seconded, and passed in the affirmative. Mr. Randolph, was seconded, and passed in the affirmative. Mr. Randolph, our president, veiled on Mr. Duché, and received for answer, that if his health would permit, he certainly would.

Accordingly, next morning the Rev. Mr. Duché appeared with his clerk and in his pontifical and read several prayers in the established form, and read the collect for the seventh day of September, which was the thirty-fifth Psalm. You must remember, this was the next morning after we heard the horrible rumor of the cannonade of Boston.

I never saw a greater effect upon an audience. It seem as if heaven had ordained that Psalm to be read on that morning. After this, Mr. Duché, unexpectedly to everybody, struck out into an extemporary prayer, which filled the bosom of every man present. I must confess, I never heard a better prayer, or one so well pronounced.

Episcopalian as he is, Dr. Cooper himself [Adams' personal pastor] never prayed with such fervor, such ardor, such earnestness and pathos, and in language so elegant and sublime, for America, for the Congress, for the province of Massachusetts Bay, and especially the town of Boston. It has had an excellent effect upon everybody here. I must beg you to read that Psalm.

The Episcopalian service book for September 7 called for the reading of Psalm 35. This was such an inspiration to the members assembled, for it appeared that the providence of God's mighty hand was evident. Psalm 35 could not have been more appropriate to such weak and helpless colonies.

"Plead my cause, O LORD, with them that strive with me: fight against them that fight against me. Hold persecute me: say Take of shield and buckler, and Draw out also the spear, and stop the way against them that stand up for mine help. Unto my soul, I am thy salvation.

Let them be confounded and put to shame that seek after my soul: let them be turned back and brought to confusion that devise my hurt. Let them be as chaff before the wind: and let the angel of the LORD chase them. Let their way be dark and slippery: and let the angel of the LORD persecute them. For without cause have they hid for me their net in a pit, which without cause they have digged for my soul. Let destruction come upon him at unawares; and let his net that he hath hid catch himself: into that very destruction let him fall.

And my soul shall be joyful in the LORD: it shall rejoice in his salvation. All my bones shall say, LORD, who is like unto thee, which deliverest the poor from him that is too strong for him, yea, the poor and the needy from him that spoileth him?

False witnesses did rise up; they laid to my charge things that I knew not. They rewarded me evil for good to the spoiling of my soul. But as for me, when they were sick, my clothing was sackcloth: I humbled my soul with fasting; and my prayer returned into mine own bosom. I behaved myself as though he had been my friend or brother: I bowed down heavily, as one that mourneth for his mother. But in mine adversity they rejoiced, and gathered themselves together: yea, the abjects gathered themselves together against me, and I knew it not; they did tear me, and ceased not: With hypocritical mockers in feasts, they gnashed upon me with their teeth. Lord, how long wilt thou look on? Rescue my soul from their destructions, my darling from the lions.

I will give thee thanks in the great congregation: I will praise thee among much people. Let not them that are mine enemies wrongfully rejoice over me: neither let them wink with the eye that hate me without a cause. For they speak not peace: but they devise deceitful matters against them that are quiet in the land. Yea, they opened their mouth wide against me, and said, Aha, aha, our eye hath seen it. This thou hast seen, O LORD: keep not silence: O Lord, be not far from me. Stir up thyself, and awake to my judgment, even unto my cause, my God and my Lord. Judge me, O LORD my God, according to thy righteousness; and let them not rejoice over me. Let them not say in their hearts, Ah, so would we have it: let them not say, We have swallowed him up. Let them be ashamed and brought to confusion together that rejoice at mine hurt: let them be clothed with shame and dishonour that magnify themselves against me.

Let them shout for joy, and be glad, that favour my righteous cause: yea, let them say continually, Let the LORD be magnified, which hath pleasure in the prosperity of his servant. And my tongue shall speak of thy righteousness and of thy praise all the day long" (Psalm 35:1-28).

After prayers from the *Book of Common Prayers*, Rev. Duché prayed as the Spirit would lead. Closing his eyes and looking toward Heaven with pathos he prayed.

Be Thou present, O God of Wisdom, and direct the counsel of this Honorable Assembly; enable them to settle all things on the best and surest foundations; that the scene of blood may be speedily closed; that order, harmony, and peace may be effectually restored, and the truth and justice, religion and piety, prevail and flourish among the people, Amen. Preserve the health of their bodies, and the vigor of their minds, shower down on them, and the millions they here represent, such temporal blessings as Thou seest expedient for them in this world, and crown them with everlasting glory in the world to come. All this we ask in the name and through the merits of Jesus Christ, Thy Son and our Saviour, Amen.

After prayer, Rev. Duché knelt down and was soon followed by the members of Congress. Washington was kneeling there, as was God-fearing, Christ-honoring Patrick Henry, Randolph, Rutledge, Lee, and Jay, and by their side there stood, bowed in reverence, the Puritan Patriots of New England, who at that moment had reason to believe that an armed soldiery was wasting their humble households.

They prayed fervently "for America, for Congress, for the Province of Massachusetts Bay, and especially for the town of Boston," and who can realize the emotion with which they turned imploringly to Heaven for Divine interposition. "It was enough," says Mr. Adams, "to melt a heart of stone. I saw the tears gush into the eyes of the old, grave, pacific Quakers of Philadelphia."

Americans were in constant fear that England would be the victor in any struggles that would occur between England and themselves. (Quakers are pacifists; that is, they are opposed to war or violence. From the Latin work pas, "peace.") In reality, it was like David and Goliath. Without the favor of God on this nation there was little hope of victory against the most powerful nation in the world at that time. Just as David destroyed Goliath, so too God used the soldiers of the American army to set America free from the tyranny of King George III.

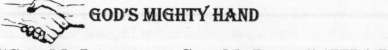

"GIVE ME LIBERTY OR GIVE ME DEATH" 1775 A.D.

W ho in the world would choose death over liberty? Were those immortal words, "Give me liberty or give me death!" spoken by Patrick Henry on March 23, 1775, just some platitude he coined to impress the House of Burgesses? What motivated our early Founding Fathers to pledge their "lives, fortunes, and sacred honor" to the preservation of liberty? These are important questions. Youth of the 1960s were quoted as saying, "Better red (Communist), than dead." Our forefathers, however, saw liberty as a divine gift and ransomed all they had to preserve it for future generations. Their experience is a testimony to the mighty hand of God, weaving His will and good purpose for mankind throughout all ages.

Keep in mind that when the triune God created Adam and Eve, He made it clear they were to take dominion over His creation. They experienced true liberty to enjoy the Lord and all His blessings. Satan, jealous of man's God given-life and liberty, succeeded in his desire to steal Adam and Eve's heritage.

I have come to see the real clash of the ages, involving wars and various historical circumstances, as being a clash of Satan's versus God's plan for man to learn to experience true liberty, by first receiving forgiveness of sins through the work of Christ on the cross, and then walking in the "newness of life."

Life really is quite simple. Satan tries to corrupt and destroy the joy God desires for His children. Satan has used ignorance to keep people from experiencing God's love and plan of salvation. People have groped in darkness, being led to forfeit their God-given rights of liberty in Christ Jesus. Satan has used various governments of the world to suppress people by taxing them to death, and keeping them ignorant by means of their godless government schools. He has used anything he can to keep people from understanding that they can learn how to govern themselves from God's great law book, the Bible. Our Founding Fathers deliberately used the Bible as their guide. They tried to ensure that schools would, likewise ,use the Bible to teach Christian self-government, the true source of liberty. These Scriptural principles were so instilled in the minds of our forefathers that they would fight and die for liberty. This divine fight, however, is not easily won. Our arch foe is ruthless in enslaving mankind.

During the middle 1700s in America, many of the colonists were waxing cold and indifferent toward religion. They continued to go to church as a tradition, more than out of a love for Christ and a desire to know and serve Him. There existed in America a religious apathy. God, in His sovereign foreknowledge, saw this danger and prepared the colonists to receive a "Great Awakening." God knew how critically they would need this revival before the coming storm of the American War for Independence.

The two men God used to stir the pot of religious stupor were Jonathan Edwards (1703-1758) and George Whitefield (1714-1770). Whitefield, known as the "lightning rod of revival," so stirred the colonists that even unbelievers were moved to either conversion or respect for God and His Word, the Bible. These colonists came to a new appreciation for the Christian heritage of America. This revival was of the most significant importance to the preservation of our nation's future. Most people today only see the fact that we won our independence from British tyranny by winning the American War for Independence. They fail to see that, behind the scenes, spiritual events were taking place which gave the Americans the will to fight and die for liberty.

Following the "Great Awakening" in our land, Americans understood that King George had usurped God-given authority to rule them. American colonists began to taste the sweet taste of liberty that can be ours in Christian self-government. Many ministers of the Anabaptists, Baptists, Methodists, Congregationalists, Dissenters, and Separatists began teaching that there was "no King, but King Jesus."

Of course, this rebellious talk did not set well with the crown in England, and soon the long arm of English law reached toward the American Colonies. Clergymen were forced to seek license for the right to preach, and then they were allowed only Anglican Church doctrine, which conveniently excluded all talk of liberty and righteous Christian dominion. All those who engaged in discourse on liberty, independence, self-government, or other such teaching were severely punished.

In November of 1769, Pastor James Ireland was warned by British magistrates in Culpeper County, Virginia, that he must obtain a license to preach or be arrested. Pastor Ireland wrote in his diary, "I sat down and counted the cost. Freedom or prison? It admitted of no dispute. Having ventured all upon Christ, I determined to suffer all for Him." He preached the next day and was arrested. While being taken to jail, he was attacked by a Tory mob, but his captors safely transported him to the jail. Pastor Ireland was confined there for six months. During his imprisonment, he would preach to listeners through the iron grating in his cell window. Opponents tossed burning pepper and sulfur into his cell, threatening to blow him up while in jail. Like the threats Nehemiah received in days of old, these too came to naught.

Many records exist that tell similar stories of preachers, stirred by the "Great Awakening," who likewise suffered for their faith and were used by God to change the course of American history. Pastor James Ireland died as an "unsung hero" for the cause of liberty, eternal liberty. *"Precious in the sight of the LORD is the death of his saints" (Psalm 116:15).*

History records that Patrick Henry, riding into Culpeper, recounted this event:

"There, in the middle of the town square, was a minister tied to a whipping post, his back laid bare and bloody with the bones of his ribs showing. When they stopped beating him, I could see the bones of his rib cage. I turned to someone and asked what the man had done to deserve such a beating as this. The reply was that the man being scourged was a minister who refused to take a license. The minister, in pain and bleeding, was jailed again.

Days later, he was given an opportunity to change his ways and apply for a license to preach."

This was a mockery, since the English government would issue only one license per county and Culpeper County had already its one licensed Anglican clergymen. A few days later, Pastor Ireland was whipped to death for continuing to refuse a license to preach. Little did the faithful, determined, non-compromising minister realize what significance his death was to play in the life of Patrick Henry.

Patrick Henry was shocked, revolted, dismayed, and angry at American suffering under the ever-growing power of the English government in the Colonies. As a deeply committed Christian, he knew God's call upon this nation. Patrick Henry began to comprehend, like so many other patriots, the extent of the ruthless tyranny England was placing upon the colonists daily. He could not shake from his mind the memory of that bleeding minister, dying for the right to preach the Gospel. Patrick, a man of keen mind, could perceive the godless outcome of England's diabolical tyranny. Unless they were stopped, British despotism would only increase in greater measure in the future. He brooded over this many a day, not knowing what he could do or say until the mighty hand of God divinely orchestrated for Patrick Henry a glorious opportunity to help determine the course of American history.

It was March 23, 1775, and Patrick Henry sat listening to the soothing tones of the American delegates gathered in the House of Burgess. These men, it seemed, wanted to continue to concede freedoms, afraid to displease the British crown. Patrick was revolted by such a weak, sickly, compromising display of English loyalty. Although he did not want to appear disrespectful of their opinions, he spoke boldly, saying: "Should I keep back my opinions at such a time, through fear of giving offense, I should consider myself as guilty of treason towards my country, and of an act of disloyalty towards the majesty of Heaven, which I revere above all earthly kings." A witness, present at the now-famous meeting, gave the following report.

"Patrick Henry, disorderly in dress, slouching in manner,

rose to his feet and, possessed of the divine, spoke in dramatic fashion so as to hold the delegates spellbound. When he said, 'Is life so dear or peace so sweet as to be purchased at the price of chains and slavery?' he stood in the attitude of a condemned galley slave, loaded with fetters, awaiting his doom. His form was bowed; his wrists were crossed; his manacles were almost visible as he stood like an embodiment of helplessness and agony. After a solemn pause, he raised his eyes and with invisible chained hands towards heaven, prayed, in words and tones which thrilled every heart, 'Forbid it, Almighty God!'

"He then turned towards the timid Loyalists of the House, who were quaking with terror at the idea of the consequences of participating in proceedings which would be visited with the penalties of treason by the British crown. He slowly bent his form yet nearer to the earth, and said, 'I know not what course others may take,' and he accompanied the words with his hands still crossed while he seemed to be weighed down with additional chains. The man appeared transformed into an oppressed, heartbroken, and hopeless felon. After remaining in this posture of humiliation long enough to impress upon the imagination the condition of the colony under the iron heel of military despotism, he arose proudly, and exclaimed, 'but as for me'—and the words hissed through his clenched teeth, while his body was thrown back, and every muscle and tendon was strained against the fetters which bound him, his countenance distorted by agony and rage. Then the loud, clear, triumphant notes, 'Give me liberty!' electrified the assembly; and as each syllable of the word 'liberty' echoed through the building, his fetters were cast off, his arms were hurled apart, and the links of his chains were scattered to the winds. He spoke the word 'liberty' with an emphasis never given it before, his hands were open, and his arms elevated and extended. His countenance was radiant! After a momentary pause, only long enough to permit the echo of *the word 'liberty' to cease, he let his left hand fall powerless to his side and clenched his right hand firmly, as if holding a dagger with the point aimed at his breast. He closed the grand appeal with the solemn words, 'Or give me death!' which sounded with the awful cadence of a hero's dirge, fearless of death, and victorious in death. He suited the action to the word by a blow upon the left breast with the right hand, which seemed to drive the dagger to the patriot's heart."*

Patrick Henry's dramatic and courageous words have lived in the hearts of bold patriots over these many years, and perhaps will continue on into eternity. What is little considered is that Patrick Henry was motivated by the vivid picture of a minister dying for liberty. That humble, faithful man of God was used by the hand of the Almighty to deeply move the heart and mind of Patrick Henry. In turn, Patrick's anointed speech persuaded the House of Burgess to join with other colonies and break ties with England, suing for "liberty or death." Had the wealthy aristocrats from Virginia, the most powerful colony, not been so inspired by Patrick Henry, Virginia would more than likely have remained tied to England. The other colonies would have followed suit and America's history would have been written differently. It is very possible that the American War for Independence would not have been fought and won.

"Stand fast therefore in the liberty wherewith Christ hath made us free, and be not entangled again with the yoke of bondage" (Galations 5:1).

"The Spirit of the Lord is upon me, because he hath anointed me to preach the gospel to the poor; he hath sent me to heal the brokenhearted, to preach deliverance to the captives, and recovering of sight to the blind, to set at liberty them that are bruised, to preach the acceptable year of the Lord" (Luke 4:18-19).

"BROTHER JONATHAN" 1775 A.D.

Jonathan Trumbull was an American statesman, born in 1710, in Connecticut, and educated at Harvard College. In 1733, he was elected to the Connecticut Assembly. He became Deputy Governor and Chief Justice of the Superior Court in 1766. From 1769 to 1784, he was Governor of Connecticut.

During the American Revolution, he was instrumental in supplying the army of General George Washington with necessary items. This invaluable service endeared him to General Washington and earned him his famous nickname, "Brother Jonathan." As a devout Christian and fiery patriot, he was constantly calling his state to prayer and fasting.

On April 19, 1775, Governor Trumbull proclaimed a day of fasting and prayer, asking that God would "graciously pour out His Holy Spirit on us to bring us to a thorough Repentance and effectual Reformation that our iniquities may not be our ruin; that He would restore, preserve and secure the Liberties of this and all the other British American Colonies, and make the Land a mountain of Holiness, and Habitation of Righteousness forever." Little did he realize that on this very day, over one hundred miles away, British troops had invaded our country and the "shot heard around the world" was fired at Lexington, Massachusetts.

Throughout the American War for Independence, days of prayer and fasting were proclaimed on numerous occasions throughout the Colonies. Christians recognized that without the aid of God's mighty hand, our victories would be short lived. Governor Trumbull recognized this dependence upon God and wrote General Washington reminding him that Congress proclaimed July 13, 1775, as another day of prayer and fasting. He told General Washington, "Congress had appointed you to your high position and to be strong and of good courage, and that the God of the armies of Israel shower down the blessings of His

Divine Providence on you, give you wisdom and fortitude, cover your head in the day of battle and danger, add success, convince our enemies of their mistaken measures, and that all their attempts to deprive these Colonies of their inestimable constitutional rights and liberties are injurious and vain."

"The LORD is on my side; I will not fear: what can man do unto me? The LORD taketh my part with them that help me: therefore shall I see my desire upon them that hate me. It is better to trust in the LORD than to put confidence in man. It is better to trust in the LORD than to put confidence in princes. All nations compassed me about: but in the name of the LORD will I destroy them" (Psalm 118:6-10).

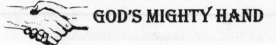

GOD'S MIGHTY HAND

MIRACLE ON LONG ISLAND 1776 A.D.

For the Americans to have won the War for Independence against the English empire without the mighty hand of God would have been impossible. Seven years before his death, George Washington reflected back over the events that transpired and wrote, "I am sure that never was there a people who had more reason to acknowledge a Divine interposition in their affairs, than those of the United States; and I should be pained to believe that they have forgotten that agency, which was so often failed, and to consider the omnipotence of that God who is alone able to protect them."

After the Declaration of Independence was signed, hopes ran high that Americans would do well against the British army on any field of battle. They were not cocky, but they felt assured that the Lord would bring a swift victory. During the early part of August, General Washington gave a speech to rally his men. He said:

> "The time is now at hand which must probably determine whether Americans are to be free men or slaves; whether they are to have any property they can call their own; whether their houses and farms are to be pillaged and destroyed, and themselves consigned to a state of wretchedness from which no human efforts will deliver them.
>
> "The fate of unborn millions will now depend, under God, on the courage and conduct of this army. Our cruel and unrelenting enemy leaves us only the choice of a brave resistance or the most abject submission. We have, therefore, to resolve to conquer or die.
>
> "Our own, and our country's honor call upon us for a vigorous and manly exertion; and if we now shamefully fail,

we shall become infamous to the whole world. Let us then rely on the goodness of our cause and the aid of the Supreme Being, in whose hands victory is; to animate and encourage us to great and noble actions. The eyes of all our countrymen are now upon us; and we shall have their blessings and praises, if happily we are the instruments of saving them from the tyranny meditated against them. Let us, therefore, animate and encourage each other, and show the whole world that a freeman contending for liberty on his own ground is superior to any slavish mercenary on earth.

"Liberty, property, life, and honor are all at stake. Upon your courage and conduct rest the hopes of our bleeding and insulted country. Our wives and children expect safety from us only; and they have every reason to believe that Heaven will crown with success so just a cause. The enemy will endeavor to intimidate by show and appearance, but remember they have been repulsed on various occasions by a few brave Americans. Their cause is bad, their men are conscious of it; and, if opposed with firmness and coolness on their first onset, with our advantage of and knowledge of the ground, the victory is most assuredly ours. Every good soldier will be silent and attentive, wait for orders, and reserve his fire until he is sure of doing execution."

Within a few days of this speech, General Washington would be faced with the first major battle of the Revolutionary War. Washington knew that the British were heading for New York; it was a strategic position they hoped to capture, for this would cut off supplies to the Colonies and bring a quick resolve to the war. Washington split his soldiers into two companies, half in New York and the other half on Long Island.

On August 27, General Howe landed troops on the southwest shore of Long Island. Immediately, he engaged Generals Green, Putnam, and Sullivan with about 8,000 American soldiers under the command of General Washington. Although the Americans were confident and inspired by the General's speech, their zeal was quickly squashed, and their brave resistance gave way under the overwhelming force of General Howe's British and hired German soldiers. The patriots fought like mother bears robbed of their cubs, but it was all in vain. About 1,000 Americans were captured, and theirs was a fate worse than death. Their lot was to suffer in the loathsome, rotted, rat-and-disease infested hulks of British prison ships in Wallabout Bay. During the course of the war, 11,000 Americans prisoners died in these hell-holes. Washington, seeing his men captured and knowing their fate, exclaimed in agony "Good God! What brave fellows I must this day lose!"

General Howe licked his chops over so easy a victory and forced Washington and his men to the very edge of Long Island, where Howe hoped to "capture the old fox himself." He was to see first hand that victory is not in the might of an army but in the hands of Almighty God. History records that General Howe made a serious mistake in not pressing for complete victory and taking Brooklyn Heights immediately. Instead, General Howe delayed his assault, waiting for his brother, Lord Admiral Howe, to arrive with more soldiers. Why this wait when complete victory was so near at hand? Battles are decided in the heavens, as this one was, and General Howe's prideful attitude cost England the end to what they thought would be a quick and speedy conclusion to the war.

For two days the patriots lay helplessly trapped, awaiting the massive British assault. During this wait many Americans went to the Lord in prayer seeking deliverance from their defenseless position. Before them lay nearly 15,000 British Regulars and 5,000 hired German Hessian soldiers. Behind them lay the East River, one mile wide and one mile from New York and the rest of the Washington's soldiers. In this predicament, General Washington was inspired to do what seemed impossible, to evacuate by the cover of night over 5,000 soldiers. In answer to prayer, the Mighty Hand of God demonstrated His control over their disastrous and perilous condition.

It was on the second night after the initial battle, and the wind was whipping up the East River, allowing both an advantage and disadvantage for the evacuation. The disadvantage was that the windy chop upon the water was too dangerously high to attempt rowing. Providentially, however, Colonel John Glover and his skilled Marblehead Massachusetts oarsmen were among the troops. These men learned to row boats practically before they learned to walk! In every disadvantage there is an advantage. The wind afforded the advantage of covering the noise of the oars which would otherwise carry into the British encampment just a few rods away.

Another major problem facing the American troops was that the light of a full moon threatened to expose the entire evacuation operation, and their location on the East River was at least partially in view of the British encampment. To help prevent the British troops from seeing the escape of his men, Washington assigned General Edward Hand, General Mifflin, and General Scammell and their soldiers to stand at attention and serve as a sort of human picket fence. About two in the morning, when the evacuation was well under way but not completed, General Mifflin mistakenly thought he received word to quit his post and leave for New York. He and his men were very anxious to leave and were milling around the shore waiting for the boats to return when General Washington, to his horror, saw the potential disaster before them. A large portion of the human fence was gone, and the evacuation in process was exposed to the British view. Washington exclaimed, "Good God! General Mifflin, I am afraid you have ruined us." God must have blinded the enemy, however, and the British sentries never noticed. General Mifflin's regiment was quickly returned to duty.

Washington realized that more boats were needed for the evacuation, so he sent scouts along the East River to confiscate boats from citizens living on Long Island. One woman, peering out her window, spied the Americans escaping and, being loyal to the crown, sent her servant to warn the British. The servant managed to elude the Americans by the color of his skin and the semi-darkness of the moon-lit night. Arriving at his destination, he proceeded to tell the soldiers, "Dat the ol' fox 'tis camping rights nows 'neath your very eyes." To his chagrin he had managed to sneak into a German encampment, and not a British one. The Germans did not understand a word of English and decided to keep him captive in their camp. The woman's plan was providentially foiled.

With more boats available, the good news was that more men could be accommodated, but the bad news was that as the wind died down, the rowing now could be heard. Only the skill of the expert oarsmen that the Lord had among them prevented the ruin of the evacuation. Rowing back and forth all night long, however, was not enough; and with dawn on the horizon, Washington still needed an additional five hours to finish ferrying his troops across the river.

Once again, the Lord showed His wonder-working power. Just as the light was getting bright enough for General Howe to resume his attack, a very dense fog (so thick that a man could scarcely see his hand in front of his face) came up the East River. Colonel Ben Tallmadge later wrote of this occurrence in his journal and stated, "It was one of the most anxious, busy nights that I ever recollect, and being the third in which hardly any of us had closed our eyes in sleep, we were all greatly fatigued. As the dawn of the next day approached, those of us who remained in the trenches became very anxious for our own safety, and when the dawn appeared there were several regiments still on duty. At this time a very dense fog began to rise, and it seemed to settle in a peculiar manner over both encampments. I recollect this peculiar providential occurrence perfectly well; and so very dense was the atmosphere that I could scarcely discern a man at six yards' distance."

At first, the rising fog caused a panic among the troops because they could not see their enemy, but that also meant that the British could not see them, either. If the fog had covered the river, it would have impeded the progress of the crossing boats, but it did not; it only rested on the two troop encampments. The sun arose, but the fog persisted. Only after the last of

Washington's soldiers had been safely ferried across the river did the miraculous fog lift, allowing the frustrated British troops to see the deserted American camp.

The British boasted of their ability in war and encouraged themselves in war counsels that the Americans were a bunch of "Yankee doodles" who would buckle under the power of the mighty British Empire. What the British did not take into account was that the Americans relied not on their own strength, but on the mighty hand of the Lord. Britain had King George III, but we had "no King but King Jesus."

"As For God, his way is perfect; the word of the Lord is tried; he is a shield to all those who trust in him" (Psalm 18:30).

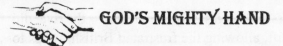

IF LOOKS COULD KILL, YOU'D BE DEAD 1777 A.D.

In the sacred Scriptures, the Gospel of John, chapter 9 records an event in which the apostle John was an eyewitness to the healing of a man who was blind from birth. The religious leaders could not accept that this man was healed by Jesus. They who could see, became blind, while he who could not see gained his sight both physically and spiritually. So it is with most historians. Because they are spiritually blinded, they reject providential occurrences in people's lives. Due to their vain philosophies, the miraculous goes untold for generations. The following is one such remarkable account in the life of George Washington that most modern textbooks of the General fail to record.

In the Revolutionary War, after unusual initial defeats, the Americans' first major victory at Trenton and Princeton inspired them to fresh courage. It appeared to all that George Washington was definitely a blessing to the American cause. His able leadership and moral fortitude kept the American army intact. As far as the British were concerned, this "rebel" was one they would give a king's ransom for if they could capture and kill him. The death of Washington, at such a critical hour, would spell the defeat of the Americans' desire for independence. The opportunity of killing Washington at the onset of the War for Independence was closer at hand than the British realized.

British Major Patrick Ferguson, inventor of the first breech-loading rifle, was known to be one of the finest sharpshooters in the British army. He was an experienced, fearless fighter and commander of a rifle corps. Preparing to move his troops toward Philadelphia to join General Howe, he set up an encampment near a creek in southeast Pennsylvania called Brandywine. On September 9, 1777, two days before what history would later record as the "Battle of Brandywine," Major Ferguson entered the following incident in his journal:

"We had just set camp when two rebel officers rode unknowing toward our army within a hundred yards of my right flank, not perceiving us. One of the two officers was dressed in dark green and blue, mounted on a bay horse, with a remarkably high cocked hat. I singled him out and ordered three of my marksmen to stand near, and fire at him; but the idea disgusting me, I recalled the order. The officers passed within a hundred yards of us; upon which I advanced from the woods towards them.

"Upon my calling, they stopped; but, after looking at us, again proceeded. I again drew their attention, and made signs for them to stop, leveling my piece at the one officer I had previously singled out; but he slowly cantered away. By quick firing I could have lodged half a dozen balls in or about him before he was out of my reach. I had only to determine; but it was not pleasant to fire at the back of an unoffending individual, who was very coolly acquitting himself of his duty, so I let it alone.

"The next day, the surgeon told me that the wounded rebel officers informed him that General Washington was all the morning with the light troops, and only attended by a French officer in the hussar dress, he himself dressed and mounted as I have before described. I am not sorry I did not know who it was at the time."

What restrained Major Ferguson? He publicly announced his hatred toward rebels to the Crown of England. He was a crack shot and loyal British soldier. The answer is the divine protection of God on the life of George Washington. The Scripture teaches that a person who pleases the Lord will find favor and protection.

"When a man's ways please the Lord, he maketh even his enemies to be at peace with him" (Proverbs 16:7).

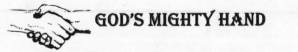

MIRACLE OF THE CONSTITUTION 1787 A.D.

After our victory over the British government at the close of the War for Independence, America was in desperate need of a body of laws that would help govern so vast a nation. England was like a vulture waiting to swoop down on a wounded animal to regain her fallen Colonies. In 1787, each Colony sent a representative to Philadelphia to form a national Constitution. The delegates nominated George Washington to be the president of the convention. On May 14, to set the stage for the convention, Washington rose to his feet and gave the delegates their charge: to work to produce a Constitution worthy of the people of the United States. Washington reminded the elected delegates that this was the work of God, and that they should not, therefore, settle for second best. He said, "If, to please the people, we offer what we ourselves disapprove, how can we afterward defend our work? Let us raise a standard to which the wise and the honest can repair; the event is in the hand of God." Washington spoke little during the proceedings, reserving his talk to after hours, during meal-times with choice delegates.

It did not take long to discover that not only did they gain an independent nation; they inherited an independent, strong-willed, opinionated people. Each delegate took part in endless rivalries and controversies, keeping things in a state of constant turmoil. Boiling hot sun outside made for boiling hot tempers inside. On several occasions, it seemed that the delegates were going to "throw in the towel" and go home, that they would simply leave America as she was with each state a separate mini-nation being sovereign over their own affairs as were the various countries in Europe.

In attempting to settle for the best, the delegates could not settle for anything. Perhaps pride was in the way. The first four or five weeks the room was filled with dissension until senior member Benjamin Franklin waved his cane and sounded a gentle convicting rebuke:

"Mr. President:

"The small progress we have made after four or five weeks of close attendance and continual reasoning with each other, our different sentiments on almost every question, several of the last producing as many noes as ayes, is, methinks, a melancholy proof of the imperfection of the Human Understanding.

"We indeed seem to feel our own want of political wisdom, since we have been running about in search of it. We have gone back to ancient history for models of government and examined the different forms of those Republics which, having been formed with the seeds of their own dissolution, now no longer exist. And we have viewed modern states all around Europe, but find none of their Constitutions suitable to our circumstances.

"In this situation of this Assembly, groping as it were in the dark to find political truth, and scarce able to distinguish it when presented to us, how has it happened, Sir, that we have not hitherto once thought of humbly applying to the Father of lights to illuminate our understanding?

"In the beginning of the Contest with Great Britain, when we were sensible of danger, we had daily prayer in this room for Divine protection. [The First Congress met in 1774.] Our prayers, Sir, were heard, and they were graciously answered. All of us who were engaged in the struggle must have observed frequent instances of a superintending Providence in our favor.

"To that kind Providence we owe this happy opportunity of consulting in peace on the means of establishing our future national felicity. And have we now forgotten that powerful Friend? or do we imagine we no longer need His assistance?

"I have lived, Sir, a long time, and the longer I live, the

more convincing proofs I see of this truth: that God governs in the affairs of men. And if a sparrow cannot fall to the ground without His notice, is it probable that an empire can rise without His aid?

"We have been assured, Sir, in the Sacred Writings, that 'Except the Lord build the house, they labor in vain that build it.' I firmly believe this; and I also believe that without His concurring aid, we shall succeed in this political building no better than the builders of Babel: We shall be divided by our partial local interests; our projects will be confounded, and we ourselves shall become a reproach and byword down to future ages.

"And what is worse, mankind may hereafter, from this unfortunate instance, despair of establishing Governments by Human wisdom and leave it to chance, war, and conquest.

"I therefore beg leave to move that henceforth prayers imploring the assistance of Heaven, and its blessing on our deliberations, be held in this Assembly every morning before we proceed to business, and that one or more of the clergy of this city be requested to officiate in that service."

Jonathan Dayton, the delegate from New Jersey, said, "As the Doctor sat down, never did I behold a countenance at once so dignified and delighted as was that of Washington at the close of the address; nor were the members of the convention generally less affected. The words of the venerable Franklin fell upon our ears with a weight and authority, even greater than we may suppose an oracle to have had in a Roman senate!"

The anointing of the Lord was so strong that within minutes, the bickering attitude of the delegates turned into constructive action. A motion for daily prayer and for pastors to be invited from time to time to preach sermons passed without delay. This was the turning point in the Convention. With God recognized and regarded in so difficult a task as forming a new national government, the mighty hand of God took control and presented the world with the greatest form of government the world has ever known or seen.

The Constitution and the Bill of Rights, written later, are regarded as brilliant documents by people who do not see the spiritual. But to the Godly who have spiritual eyes to see, they represent a divinely devised form of government. The great English Christian statesman, William Ewart Gladstone, characterized the Constitution of the United States as "the greatest piece of work ever struck off at a given time by the brain and purpose of man." Historian Melvin Evans wrote in his 1946 book, *It Works*, "The United States is undoubtedly the creation of God. We must make it worthy of this destiny."

I challenge you to find a government that has ever produced so many brilliant minds of so many men assembled at one time for so noble a purpose. You will not find it. Perhaps, as stated by Gladstone, "one or two are given by God to a nation for specific purposes. But so many at one time, all living in the same nation, with the various intellectual gifts and abilities, is nothing short of awe inspiring." There were slightly over fifty-five framers of the Constitution and the Bill of Rights at the time. Where are their intellectual types today? Has the majority of our Congress or House of Representatives had the same caliber of men since then? No! And if not, how did it occur? Apart from the mighty hand of God, it could not have occurred. When those delegates humbled themselves and sought God, God took over and blessed mankind with a form of Biblical government akin only to what Israel experienced when they were in right fellowship with God's laws and in keeping true to His word.

May the prayer of our national leaders be like Solomon of old, who, when faced with the monumental job of leading a people, cried out to God, and said:

"Thou hast shewed unto thy servant David my father great mercy, according as he walked before thee in truth, and in righteousness, and in uprightness of heart with thee; and thou hast kept for him this great kindness, that thou hast given him a son to sit on his throne, as it is this day. And now, O LORD my

God, thou hast made thy servant king instead of David my father: and I am but a little child: I know not how to go out or come in. And thy servant is in the midst of thy people which thou hast chosen, a great people, that cannot be numbered nor counted for multitude. Give therefore thy servant an understanding heart to judge thy people, that I may discern between good and bad: for who is able to judge this so great a people?" (I Kings 3:6-9).

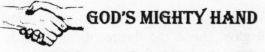

MAN OF DETERMINED WILL 1813 A.D.

David Livingstone was born on March 19, 1813, in Blantyre, Scotland. At the age of ten, because of family poverty, he went to work in a textile factory. David, along with his brothers and sisters, was raised in a Christ-honoring home. Because the family was so poor, books were not readily available, so David learned to read by using the Bible. He especially loved to hear and read of the far-off lands of the ancient world.

While his mother read, he would dream of being a missionary to foreign lands, little realizing that God's mighty hand was already at work in his heart, preparing him to be one of the greatest missionary explorers the world has ever known.

As he grew older, he worked and saved money so he could go to school in Glasgow. In a later story (Moffat—A.D. 1823), you will learn how David felt led to become a missionary as he heard of the need for the Gospel to penetrate the continent of Africa. As he was attending the University of Glasgow, he decided to study theology, and after completing the necessary studies, he began to preach. At his first meeting, a providential occurrence took place that changed the direction of his life.

His first sermon was to be delivered in Edinburgh, and excitedly, he invited his mentor, Dr. Robert Moffat, to hear him preach. As David began his sermon, he became increasingly agitated and fearful. About a fourth of the way into his message, his sharp mind went completely blank from fear, and he stopped. After what seemed an interminable silence, he said, "Friends, I have forgotten all I had prepared," and he hung his head in embarrassment and came down from the pulpit.

At that moment, Dr. Moffat kindly embraced him and advised David not to give up. He suggested that perhaps he could be a doctor instead of a preacher. That suggestion "clicked" in David's mind, for besides having a love for the Word of God, he also had hand—turning David in a direction which would ultimately bring God more glory. God gave David the desire of his heart in directing him, through Robert Moffat, to became a missionary doctor. When his years of medical studies were completed, he went to Africa and joined Dr. Moffat for a time before venturing out on his own and taking the Gospel to tribes Dr. Moffat had not yet reached—tribes that no white man had ever seen.

Livingstone began his work among the black Africans of Bechuanaland, trying to make his way northward. He encountered much hostility from the Boers, white settlers of mostly Dutch background, who occupied the same South African territory.

In one incident, God spared David's life during his extended stay in a Mabotsa tribal village. One day while he was visiting sick tribespeople, ministering Christ and medicine, a member of the village came running up to David and excitedly told him of the evil spirits sent to destroy their village through the lions that had come by day to kill their cattle. Because lions never attacked in broad daylight, this was an omen of evil to the natives. Dr. Livingstone assured the man that this was *not* an evil spirit, and that if there was any more trouble with the lions, he personally would deal with them.

The next day the lions returned, killing nine sheep. David took two rifles, rounded up as many brave natives as could be found, and said, "Come, we will seek out the lions and either destroy them or drive them away." The natives headed out to the bush, encouraged by the white man's great guns. The hunters soon traced the lions to a small clump of undergrowth where they were devouring recent kills. The natives formed a circle around the beasts, in the traditional African way of hunting, and gradually closed in to spear them. Unfortunately, the Bakatla natives lost their nerve, and when one of the lions charged, the natives broke the circle and allowed the lion to escape, to be followed a few seconds later by the flashing forms of its companions.

Livingstone, who was standing a little way down the hillside with a native schoolmaster named Mebalwe, wanted to take a shot at the escaping beasts, but he could not fire for fear of hitting the natives. He lowered his gun and sighed as he turned to his companion. "Come on, Mebalwe," he said, "let's go back to the village; they're poor, pitiful hunters with whom we can do little."

Scarcely had the two of them turned to go down the hill when the terrifying roar of a lion sounded nearby. They stopped at once, bringing their guns into the ready position. "Steady, Bwana," cautioned Mebalwe, pointing to a thick thornbush. "Simba, he behind there; he wounded; no good. He mad!" About fifteen yards ahead of them Livingstone could see the tawny shape of the lion, partly concealed by the bush, black-tipped tail lashing in fury. Slowly he raised his double-barrel shotgun, aimed it where he presumed the heart of the beast to be, then squeezed first the right and then the left trigger. For a brief moment, lion and bush were hidden from the doctor by the cloud of smoke from the gun, and at the same time he heard the tribesmen rushing down the hillside screaming, "Simba, it is dead! It is dead!"

Livingstone cautiously stepped back a little and began to reload his gun. "Don't rush in!" he shouted to the natives. "He may *not* be dead!" Then he turned again to pour more gunpowder down the muzzle. A sudden shout from the natives caused him to lift his head, and, in that moment, he saw the lion springing upon him. Down they went together, man and beast. Growling fiercely, the lion bit into Livingstone's shoulder and began to shake him as if he were nothing. The mighty hand of God was protecting David, because a lion kills its prey by the tremendous speed and weight of its body flying through the air. The prey is usually dead before it hits the ground—never knowing what happened. Miraculously, David was still alive when he hit the ground, and providentially, the lion took hold of his *arm* rather than his head and neck—the instinctive spot lions aim for in their initial attack.

Mebalwe ran to within a few feet of the beast and pulled the trigger of his gun, but it misfired, and the lion, leaving Livingstone, turned on his new foe and bit him in the leg. A second native, whose life Livingstone had saved some time earlier after he had been tossed by a buffalo, ran in with his spear, but he, too, was attacked by the lion. A third native went to the assistance of the three wounded men, and at that moment the bullets that Livingstone first shot took effect, and the lion dropped dead.

Gently, tenderly, the Bakatla natives bore their missionary doctor back to the village, and later they returned for the carcass of the lion. Livingstone records that the lion was the largest ever killed in the district, and that the Bakatla people, to break the alleged "spell" put upon them and to drive the evil spirit from the lion, burned it in a large bonfire.

For a long time, Livingstone's life hung in the balance, and he suffered terribly. The lion left him with eleven ugly gashes and a shattered arm, but the nursing of the natives and the attention he received from a fellow missionary, Edwards, saved his life, though the upper part of his arm was so badly injured that for the remainder of his life he could never raise a gun to the level of his shoulder without steadying the barrel against some support. The two natives, who were even more severely injured, both survived their ordeal, and the steadfast and loyal Mebalwe continued in Livingstone's service for many more years of missionary adventure.

When he had sufficiently recovered, Livingstone returned to Kuruman for convalescent treatment. As soon as he was fit enough to ride on horseback again, he journeyed more than 150 miles to the south to welcome Dr. Robert Moffat and his family, who had just returned from a long leave in England.

The Lord seems to have bound up the name of Moffat inextricably with that of Livingstone, as we have seen in other stories. In the first place, Moffat had encouraged Livingstone to travel to Africa and take up work there. But there was a second result. The journey Livingstone undertook to meet the Moffats ended with the Lord giving him a helpmate: Dr. Moffat gave him the hand of his daughter, Mary, in marriage.

From the time of their marriage until her death seventeen years later, Mary and her husband worked together with a devotion that has seldom been surpassed. Together they shared the toils and privations of journeys into strange lands; they experienced drought, famine, hostility from natives and Dutch settlers; and together they opened up new lands and discovered new peoples. Much more can be said of David Livingstone, but that I leave for you to discover for yourself. Suffice it to say that he survived the attack of a lion, the dangers of wild and uncharted rivers, the danger of man-killing natives, forest fires, barren deserts, ill health, and mutinous natives—all the while charting unknown territories of Africa. One of his crowning glories was exposing the horrors of African slave trading and helping to bring an end to this wicked practice in England and America. David Livingstone's life verses were Mark 16:14–20.

"Afterward he appeared unto the eleven as they sat at meat, and upbraided them with their unbelief and hardness of heart, because they believed not them which had seen him after he was risen. And he said unto them, Go ye into all the world, and preach the gospel to every creature. He that believeth and is baptized shall be saved; but he that believeth not shall be damned. And these signs shall follow them that believe; In my name shall they cast out devils; they shall speak with new tongues; They shall take up serpents; and if they drink any deadly thing, it shall not hurt them; they shall lay hands on the sick, and they shall recover. So then after the Lord had spoken unto them, he was received up into heaven, and sat on the right hand of God. And they went forth, and preached every where, the Lord working with them, and confirming the word with signs following. Amen "(Mark 16:14-20).

Far, far away, in heathen darkness dwelling,
Millions of souls forever may be lost;
Who, who will go, salvation's story telling,
Looking to Jesus, minding not the cost?
"All pow'r is given unto Me, All pow'r is given unto Me,
Go ye into all the world and preach the Gospel,
And lo, I am with you alway."
James McGranahan (1840–1907)

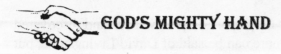

"MAN PROPOSES, BUT GOD DISPOSES" 1814 A.D.

Napoleon I, emperor of the French and, for sixteen years, master of most of Europe, was one of the greatest military geniuses of all time. To the troops he commanded in battle, Napoleon was known fondly as the "Little Corporal." To the monarchs and kings whose thrones he overthrew, he was "that Corsican ogre." Some believed him a great reformer. Others thought him a petty tyrant.

Napoleon was stationed in Paris in 1792. The French Revolution had been raging for three bloody years. It reached a climax on August 10, 1792, with the overthrow of the monarchs and the establishment of a French Republic. This was a decisive event in Napoleon's life, for it gave him the opportunity to prove himself a good soldier and leader.

Unlike our War for Independence in 1776, the French Revolution had no Biblically based moorings to establish their new form of government. Without a Christian consensus of virtuous conduct for self-government and restraint of despotism, the way was wide open for a strong leader to step in and assume control. Consequently, the strong leader became a tyrant, and the revolution that was waged to throw off tyranny became entangled in it once more, often worse than before. Without acknowledging God as its head, a nation is doomed to failure. William Penn once said, "Those who will not be governed by God will be ruled by tyrants." The French foolishly traded the overthrow of the monarch for the equally oppressive dictator. Napoleon came in on the heels of revolution. By February 1797, Napoleon had been victorious in fourteen pitched battles and seventy combats. His army had conquered rich lands. Those conquered were forced to feed and pay the French troops during the campaign. Of the millions of francs captured, much was sent back to France to relieve the financial distress of the government. This made Napoleon popular among the ruling class and gave him the support he needed in government and the military. His great love was the thrill of conquering, and conquer he did. With the support of loyal soldiers committed to him at all costs, the power given him soon went to his head. Within eight years of his involvement in the French Revolution, he then wished to be called Napoleon I rather than General Bonaparte. He held complete military and political power. Although he had partially built up a great eastern empire, he was not satisfied until he would someday restore the western empire of Charlemagne.

The Austrians had been defeated in the hard-fought Battle of Marengo in the war. The German states and England were likewise worn out by the war. They had signed a peace treaty in Amiens in 1802. For the first time since 1792, France was at peace with the whole world. Nevertheless, Napoleon continued his ambitious plans. Like Alexander the Great, Napoleon was not satisfied with peace. What he wanted were conquests. He lived for the challenge of battle.

During the fourteen months that peace lasted, he became president of the Italian Republic, reshaped Switzerland with France as "Protector," and annexed Piedmont, Parma, and the Island of Elba off the coast of France. In addition, he planned the partition of Turkey and the founding of a colonial empire which would include America and Australia.

With delusions of conquering the old kingdom of Charlemagne, he set out to conquer Russia, making his first major mistake. The Bible says, " Pride goeth before destruction, and an haughty spirit before a fall" (Proverbs 16:18). His Russian campaign was the beginning of his end and the judgment of God's mighty hand.

Fighting the Russians was difficult, for they often spent time running farther into the interior of their country. Like a "sheep led to slaughter," Napoleon followed. On September 7, 1812, the Russians finally made a stand at Borodino. The results were indecisive. On September 14th, Napoleon reached Moscow. He had expected to find shelter and provisions for his tired troops. Instead, he found the city in flames. Since it was impossible to winter in the ruined city, Napoleon began his retreat on October 19th, across the snow-covered plains. The retreat from Moscow was one of the great disasters in military history. At the crossing of the Berezina River, thousands died. Of the nearly 500,000 men who had set out in June, fewer than 20,000 ragged, freezing, and starving men staggered back across the Russian frontier in December.

"Such is war," he thought to himself. A study of military history would show the casual attitude in far too many military leaders. The majority of godless leaders are careless about the cost of others' lives. They are blinded by their power, and as long as they live in their ivory towers, they find it easy to give orders for soldiers to engage in battle at any cost.

Two years after Napoleon's Russian fiasco, the combined efforts of the European countries opposed to Napoleon were successful. He was defeated on March 13, 1814, and exiled to the Island of Elba. Less than one year after his internment, Napoleon escaped from his island prison!

Fear struck over Napoleon's escape. The governments of Europe began preparations to defeat, once and for all, this megalomanic whose armies had wreaked havoc in Europe for twenty years.

Well aware of their anxiety and animosity, Napoleon planned to strike fast before his opponents had time to organize an effective effort against him. He rapidly collected his loyal soldiers and reentered Paris on March 10, 1815. Napoleon was able not only to put down the Royalist forces there, but also to provide troops for the defense of southern France and enlarge his own army in the northeast, now 130,000 soldiers strong.

In the meantime, England had landed the Duke of Wellington in Belgium with an army which, including the hired European mercenaries, totaled 106,000 men. Blucher's army of 116,000 Prussians was only a thirty-six hours' march behind Wellington. Napoleon was also aware that Russia, Bavaria, and Austria would soon be sending armies to oppose him. He reasoned that he must strike before the forces of Wellington and Blucher could join and while his troops still outnumbered both of theirs.

Napoleon had a more capable army when he faced Wellington. He had twice as many cannons and far more artillery and cavalry. His troops were all of one nationality, seasoned in war, and full of confidence in their general. Wellington's men, on the other hand, were of five nationalities, many of them recently indentured, and none fully trained in the skill of war.

Napoleon's first attack was on Blucher's forces. He succeeded in temporarily preventing them from joining Wellington. Since they were weary from forced marches, Napoleon gloated over the fact that he was able to pin them down and keep them away from Wellington. He then made ready for his masterly attack on Wellington. Everything was proceeding according to his well-laid plans.

On June 17, Napoleon assembled his men and boasted, "We will attack at six in the morning. Blucher is too far away to reinforce Wellington before late tomorrow afternoon. My heavy artillery shall have a complete and overwhelming victory by two o'clock in the afternoon." One of the commanding officers said in reply to his boast, "But we must not forget that man proposes, but God disposes." Full of pride and confidence, Napoleon stretched his little body to full height, puffed his chest out and said, "I want you to understand, sir, that Napoleon proposes and Napoleon disposes." The major force Napoleon failed to recognize was the Lord of Hosts, the Captain of battle. Once again his pride was about to destroy him. The Bible gives the answer as to how battles are won or lost. *"Therefore the flight shall perish from the swift, and the strong shall not strengthen his force, neither shall the mighty deliver himself: Neither shall he stand that handleth the bow; and he that is swift of foot shall not deliver himself: neither shall he that rideth the horse deliver himself. And he that is courageous among the mighty shall flee away naked in that day, saith the LORD"* (Amos 2:14-16).

That very night, after his boastful speech of victory, rain and wind swept the battlefield at Waterloo, a village in central Belgium, south of Brussels. In the morning, the deluge still continued. On that momentous 18th day of June, 1815, the weather did not even clear sufficiently to see the position of the opposing troops until 9. By that time, the ground was far too soft for the cavalry and artillery to maneuver.

Napoleon had often boasted of his heavy artillery, how far superior it was to what most of Europe could use against him. His boasting came to naught. Being stuck in the mud, they were now useless. Waiting for the ground to achieve sufficient firmness for his battalions to move, Napoleon lost nine critical hours of time.

Napoleon recalled his troops from pinning down General Blucher's army. He figured Blucher's army's progress would be slowed down by the rain and mud.

Finally, the battle of Waterloo began at 11:30. To Napoleon's consternation, Blucher's force arrived in the nick of time. By 8, the French ranks broke, and the English and Prussians had the French on the run. The French were completely routed. Napoleon himself fled and was captured in a matter of weeks, once more to be exiled from France.

His dream of a world empire came to a close on the tiny island of St. Helena, to which he was exiled on July 15, 1815. The island is located in the south Atlantic Ocean well off the coast of Africa. Alone and deserted by his friends and family, Napoleon died there at the age of fifty-one, on May 5, 1821.

His exile, those six years was a blessing in disguise, for, like Nebuchadnezzar of old, who was humbled by the mighty hand of God, Napoleon, in his humbled exile, began to read and study the Bible while pondering over his life, reflecting on where he had gone wrong. He later wrote, "Alexander, Caesar, Charlemagne, and myself founded empires; but upon what foundation did we rest the creation of our genius? Upon force! But Jesus Christ founded His upon love; and at this hour millions of men would die for Him."

Napoleon humbled himself, and it appears from the following account that Napoleon may have found faith in Christ while in exile on St. Helena. Speaking with one of his former generals who had come for a short visit, Napoleon shared his faith in Jesus Christ. When the former comrade at arms did not take up the Savior's cross to which Napoleon was testifying, Napoleon said,

"The Gospel possesses a secret virtue, a mysterious efficacy, a warmth which penetrates and soothes the heart. One finds in meditating upon it that which one experiences in contemplating the heavens.

"The Gospel is not a book; it is a living being, with an action, a power, which invades everything that opposes its extension.

"Behold it upon this table, this Book surpassing all others. I never omit to read it, and every day with new pleasure.

"Nowhere is to be found such a series of beautiful ideas, and admirable moral maxims, which pass before us like the battalions of a celestial army...The soul can never go astray with this Book for its guide....

"Everything in Christ astonishes me. His spirit overawes me, and His will confounds me. Between Him and whoever else in the world, there is no possible term of comparison; He is truly a Being by Himself. His ideas and His sentiments, the truth which He announces, His manner of convincing, are not explained, either by human organization or by the nature of things.

"Truth should embrace the universe. Such is Christianity, the only religion which destroys sectional prejudices, the only one which proclaims the unity and the absolute brotherhood of the whole human family, the only one which is purely spiritual; in fine, the only one which assigns to all, without distinction, a true country, in the bosom of the Creator God in His eternal home in heaven.

"Christ proved that He was the Son of the Eternal by His disregard of time. All His doctrines signify one and the same thing: eternity. What a proof of the divinity of Christ! With

an empire so absolute, he has but one single end: the spiritual melioration of individuals, the purity of the conscience, the union to that which is true, the holiness of the soul....

"Not only is our mind absorbed, it is controlled; and the soul can never go astray with this Book for its guide. Once master of our spirit, the faithful Gospel loves us. God even is our friend, our Father, and truly our God. The mother has no greater care for the infant whom she nurses.... If you, General, do not perceive that Jesus Christ is God, very well: then I did wrong to make you a general."

After all was said and done, Napoleon came to see that the real victor of life is the one who humbles himself and submits to the only true Ruler of the eternal empire.

"Not by might, nor by power, but by my spirit, saith the LORD of hosts" (*Zechariah 4:6*).

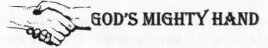

HIDDEN FROM VIEW, BUT NOT
FROM GOD 1823 A.D.

When Robert Moffat, Scottish missionary to South Africa, came back to his homeland to recruit co-laborers in the African harvest of souls, he was greeted by the fury of a cold Scottish winter. Planning to speak at an old stone church, Robert was excited at the prospect of being among his own countrymen to share his vision of the wilderness of Africa and the desperate need for missionaries to go to the "Dark Continent."

Braving the snow, wind, and bitter cold of that night, he finally arrived at his destination. He anticipated that the journey would be profitable, for by prayer, he was prepared with a Bible text he believed the Lord had impressed upon him to give to the congregation. The divinely inspired text was *"Unto you, O men, I call; and my voice is to the sons of man" (Proverbs 8:4).*

Because of the severity of the weather, Dr. Moffat was not surprised to have only a small gathering, but what did cause him to wonder if he had indeed heard from the Lord as to the text was this: There were no men assembled that night. Only ladies. How was he to appeal to a congregation of women to take the Gospel to Africa? Surely, they would not likely respond. Few women could be expected to withstand the dangers and inconveniences of the jungles of the continent where he labored. He decided, however, not to change his text. Perhaps the Lord was going to raise up some prayer warriors from among those faithful few attendants that blustery night.

After the message, the ladies graciously thanked Dr. Moffat for his inspirational sermon and promised to pray that the Lord would raise up a mighty man of God to take the hope of Christ to the Africans. Bidding him farewell, they bundled up to face the bitter cold and left the old kirk (Scottish word for "church").

Perhaps feeling a bit disappointed and perplexed at what

-161-

seemed to have been an inappropriate message to a female-only gathering, Dr. Moffat began to put away his notes. Thinking that the church had long been emptied, he was a bit startled to see a young boy approach him. The whole evening the lad had gone unnoticed by the guest speaker, because he had been in the loft, pumping the billows for the church organ.

The young boy respectfully stepped forward and relayed his newly sparked heart's passion to Robert Moffat. He explained that during the missionary's message, he felt a desire to pray about and study toward going to Africa to serve the Lord with Dr. Moffat when he grew up.

Trying not to dampen the youth's zeal, Moffat smiled, patted him on the head, and counseled him to pursue whatever God would call him to do in life. Just before leaving the chapel, the missionary asked, "What's your name, laddie?" Looking up in admiration, the boy replied, "David Livingstone, sir!"

Years later, Dr. Moffat would stand in awe at the mighty hand of God and chuckle at the irony of that wintry night in a wee Scottish kirk, where only a few ladies and one boy would have ears to hear his message. For not only did this lad grow up to become God's chosen vessel to reach the uncharted depths of Africa for Christ, but David also won the heart of Dr. Moffat's daughter, Mary, becoming not only his partner in ministry, but also his son-in-law.

Had Dr. Moffat not been obedient to the Lord in following through with the text, David Livingstone may never have heard the call to go to Africa, where he was involved in slaying the "Goliath" of the slave trade. Had Dr. Moffat abandoned his message with its descriptions of the undiscovered secrets of the "Dark Continent," young Livingstone may never have braved the depths of Central Africa on expeditions to prepare the interior for the spreading of the Gospel. And most profoundly, had Dr. Moffat wavered in his intensity of proclaiming the need for more missionaries among the Africans, David Livingstone may not have felt the compelling desire to devote thirty years of his life on the mission field to evangelize the perishing souls of the African

Continent.

"For who hath despised the day of small things?"(Zechariah 4:10).

"Let no man despise thy youth, but be thou an example of the believers, in word, in conversation, in charity, in spirit, in faith, in purity" (I Timothy 4:12).

Little children, little children who love their Redeemer, Are the jewels, precious jewels, His loved and His own. Like the stars of the morning, His bright crown adorning, They shall shine in their beauty—Bright gems for His crown.
William O. Cushing (1823–1902)

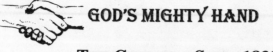

THE GIFT OF A SONG 1833 A.D.

Just as John and Charles Wesley were prominent religious leaders in 18th-century England, Providence brought forth John Henry Newman as a leader in the 19th century. Similarly, the Wesleys and Newman were educated at Oxford; each feared the growing indifference and coldness towards religion within the Church of England during this time; they had devoted their lives to striving for great revival with the purpose of reawakening religious intensity and conviction throughout England. However, there were differences between Newman and the Wesleys.

The Wesleys led a progressive and unconventional movement that went out into the countryside and crowded industrial centers preaching a religion filled with warmth and ardor. This offered a new appeal to great masses of people who, otherwise, would not have been attracted to the Gospel presented within the established Church of England.

The Oxford Movement, of which John Henry Newman played such an important role, was completely opposite in character to that of the Wesleyan movement. Newman, particularly, being extremely conservative and reactionary, felt that popular religion, as it was being spread in such an unorthodox manner, lacked dignity and reverence. Thus, he advocated an increased emphasis on form and ceremony as a way of gaining power and intensity for religion. The Oxford Movement viewed the Wesleyan Movement as too liberal and wanting after its century of introduction.

Newman had a brilliant career as an Oxford student. He was ordained and made vicar of St. Mary's Church in Oxford. Immediately, he attracted notice for preaching "like a fine strain of unearthly music" which affected his hearers deeply with its charm and religious power. His rare and magnetic personality strongly influenced his listeners. His friends thought him to be a near saint, while his opponents viewed him as "the most dangerous man in England."

In 1833, as a result of strenuous labor, Newman, age thirty-two at the time, acquired a prolonged illness which forced him to take several months off for rest. During this time, he visited the pope in Rome. Just a year before, in 1832, England had passed the Reform Bill, which was considered a great victory for the Liberals. As a result, political worries assailed Newman as he was sure England's political condition was uncertain and chaos would follow. These disturbances, along with being perplexed by religious doubts, caused him to be extremely anxious to return to England so he could fight for his own ideas.

In Sicily, he was delayed while waiting for a boat bound for England. Soon after embarking upon his earnestly awaited voyage, fog caused the vessel to halt just off the straits of Bonifacio. Still ill and perplexed by his conflicting spiritual and political doubts Newman, unable to escape the sudden still and quiet, found the peace that surpasses all understanding. Thus, inspired, he beautifully expressed this God given peace in his prayer-hymn entitled "Lead, Kindly Light." Newman was not aware that God's mighty hand had intervened to cause his present setback for a greater purpose that would demonstrate the glory of Jesus Christ to eight men who would be grasping for hope 109 years later, during World War II. While in seafaring and emotional doldrums, John Newman had no way of knowing the profound effect "Lead, Kindly Light" would have on these survivors floating adrift in the vast Pacific Ocean of a downed B-17 aircraft. But, the Alpha and Omega, Jesus Christ, knew! Once rescued, the soldiers testified that the words of a hymn, "Lead, Kindly Light" had given them divine courage and perseverance to hope for their deliverance from death. (See chapter on Eddie Rickenbacker - 1942 A.D.)

Newman had once said the words of "Lead, Kindly Light," "They are not a hymn, nor are they suitable for singing; and it is that which at once surprises and gratifies me, and makes me thankful that, in spite of their having no claim to being a hymn, they have made their way into so many collections."

> *Lead, kindly Light, amid the encircling gloom.*
> *Lead Thou me on.*
> *The night is dark, and I am far from home;*
> *Lead Thou me on.*
> *Keep Thou my feet; I do not ask to see*
> *The distant scene; one step enough for me.*

> *I was not ever thus, nor prayed that Thou*
> *Shouldst lead me on;*
> *I loved to choose and see my path,*
> *but now Lead Thou me on.*
> *I loved the garish day, and, spite of fears,*
> *Pride ruled my will; remember not past years.*

> *So long Thy pow'r hath blest me, sure it still*
> *will lead me on,*
> *O'er moor and fen, o'er crag and torrent, till*
> *The night is gone, And with the morn those angel*
> *faces smile Which I have loved long since, and lost awhile.*

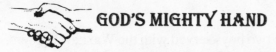
WHEN THE ODDS ARE AGAINST YOU,
IT'S GOD 1835 A.D.

In 1765, Andrew Jackson's family sailed from northern Ireland near the little coastal town of Carrickfergus (Crag of Fergus), about nine miles from Belfast. Looking for a better life in America, they landed in Charleston, South Carolina. After following a wagon train, they ended up at the Scotch-Irish settlement called Waxhaw, near the North Carolina border.

Shortly after the family arrived in Waxhaw, Mr. Jackson died, leaving his family in a log-hewn cabin on a small tract of forested land on Twelve Mile Creek. Just a few days later, on March 15, 1767, Andrew Jackson was born, destined to become the first "poor-boy" President of the United States, at the same time he became the best-loved and the most-hated President the young nation had known. He was the first President to be elected from the frontier and the first to be called "the People's President." Foes in politics and in finance accused him of being a tyrant and angrily called him "King Andrew," but the frontiersmen, the farmers, the workers, and the small businessmen loved him.

Andrew lived an early "colorful" life. Being reared in a Christian home did not seem to quell his unruly behavior, and with no father to guide and control him, he got into plenty of trouble, to the grief of his Godly mother.

When Andrew was thirteen, the American Revolution swept the Waxhaw region. In May 1780, Colonel Tarleton, a British soldier serving under Cornwallis, raided the settlement close to the Jackson farm. Andrew and his brother Robert helped their mother bind up the wounded. Their older brother, Hugh, a volunteer in a light-horse company, had died a few months earlier fighting for the cause of liberty. Following Hugh's example, Andrew and Robert took up their muskets and joined the volunteers in the battle of Hanging Rock, South Carolina, August

1, 1780.

The next year the two boys served with the Waxhaw fighters, battling the British in backwoods skirmishes. In the spring, British soldiers captured the lads but failed to break their spirits. When a red-coated officer pointed to his muddied jackboots and commanded Andrew to clean them, the boy refused. The officer slashed his saber at Andrew's head. Andrew partially blocked the blow with his arm but carried the scars of the wounds the rest of his life. Robert, too, refused the British officer's demand and was cut severely. The soldiers marched the wounded lads forty miles over wilderness roads to prison in Camden, South Carolina. Their wounds were not treated; they had no bedding, little clothing, and almost no food or water. Smallpox broke out in the filthy prison, striking both Robert and Andrew.

Their courageous mother managed to obtain their release in exchange for British prisoners at Waxhaw, and took the sick, half-starved boys home. Andrew, fighting delirium, stumbled behind the horses that carried his mother and dying brother. Mrs. Jackson's nursing care saved Andrew. As soon as he began to recover, she made her way 160 miles to Charleston to help nurse American troops held in British prison ships. Soon after, however, she died of ship fever.

Andrew eventually settled down, studied law, and became a lawyer in Tennessee, in a small village on the wooded bank of the Cumberland River, near Nashville. He lodged at the home of Mrs. John Donelson, widow of Colonel Donelson, one of the founders of Nashville. There he met their daughter: slim, black-haired Rachel Donelson Robards, also twenty-one. Rachel was living at home, having been separated from her godless husband, Lewis Robards, of Kentucky. She had made the tragic mistake of marrying Lewis when she was only sixteen, without getting to know his character. After a time, Andrew Jackson heard that Rachel's husband had obtained a divorce, and with his (Andrew's) less-than-thorough knowledge of law in other states, he got himself into a most grievous situation.

Without looking into the legality of the divorce filings, he married Rachel. In his ignorance, he did not realize that the divorce was not final. As soon as possible, this was taken care of, but years later, when Andrew was a candidate for President, his enemies accused him of "running off with another man's wife." The unfounded scandal hastened Rachel's death—which crushed Andrew. Till the end of his days he never stopped loving his wife, and he always carried a locket with her picture in it.

I cannot Biblically condone Jackson's marrying a divorced woman. For singles, waiting for God's best is the only thing to do. God's best will never be someone who has already spoken wedding vows to another living person. Even though Jackson was deeply in love with his wife and they had a happy marriage, Rachel's previous marriage caused him untold grief throughout his life.

At the same time, I cannot condemn Jackson, for every man will have to give an account of himself before the Lord. The behavioral boundaries of Scripture are God's will for you, and they ensure an abundant, joyful, and peaceful life. The Bible is clear about not remarrying after divorce, although this position is not popular in many Christian circles in America today.

Jackson practiced law in Tennessee, and in 1796, the year "the Volunteer State" was admitted to the Union, he helped forge its Constitution and was elected to its one Congressional seat for one year.

He also became a member of the Tennessee Supreme Court, but in 1804 he resigned from the Court and gave up political life in order to devote himself to paying off his debts, developing his estate, the Hermitage, and training the militia. It seemed that he would spend the rest of his days as just another well-to-do farmer.

But the Lord had other plans for Andrew. Because of the influence of his wife, he was beginning to "see the light" of the Gospel and understand the "old-time religion" in which his mother had reared him. He became so dedicated to the Lord that he built a church on his estate so all the plantation owners near him could attend divine services.

Those happy days were interrupted by the War of 1812, in which Andrew participated. During the war he proved his mettle in battle and became known as "Old Hickory," a rough-and tough-fighting soldier. Indeed, he was so capable in battle that he was commissioned a Major General in the "regular" Army. Jackson was then ordered to defend the city of New Orleans. He quickly put the city under martial law and rallied the citizens to prepare for an attack by the British.

To build up his small army, he recruited frontier riflemen from Tennessee and Kentucky and organized a force of raw volunteers from free blacks, as well as planters and pirates, the latter group headed by the colorful character Jean Lafitte. With this raw, undisciplined, rough-and-tumble fighting force, Jackson saved New Orleans.

Beyond the crude American "ramparts" of cotton bales lay 10,000 British soldiers. These were veteran troops who had fought in Europe's Napoleonic Wars. Beginning late in December 1814, they bombarded the American defenses, setting the cotton-bale ramparts on fire. Between skirmishes and shellings, Jackson's men doggedly threw up earthen breastworks alongside the cotton bales.

On January 8, 1815, with contempt for Jackson's amateur army, the British troops pridefully charged. It was a slaughter. Wave after wave of the charging redcoats fell before the grapeshot and bullets of the grim American defenders. Shattered, the British withdrew, having suffered 2,237 casualties, including three generals. Jackson's casualties numbered 71.

In the era of slow communication, the tragedy of the battle of New Orleans was that it was fought after the peace treaty between England and America had been signed, December 24, 1814, ending the War of 1812.

Jackson's victory, of course, did not affect the outcome of the war, but it did make him a national hero. With the exception of General William Henry Harrison, no other American general had achieved anything close to what General Jackson had done.

Jackson's resounding defeat of the British at New Orleans set the course for his future Presidency. His victories were not only on the battlefield, but also on the dueling field. Dueling had not been completely outlawed in all states and was considered a gentlemanly way of settling problems.

Charles Dickinson, a celebrated duelist, made the mistake of slandering Jackson's wife, which left Jackson with no course but to defend the name of his precious wife. On May 30, 1806, at 10, Jackson stepped to the dueling line, twenty-four paces from death and eternity. His wife, many miles away, prayed for God's hand of protection over her husband and sorrowed over the reality that if her husband were the victor, Charles Dickinson's wife would be a widow with child and fatherless children. To her, this was a "no-win" fight and utter foolishness.

Jackson's friend, General Overton, called out, "Gentlemen, are you ready?"

"Ready," said Dickinson quickly.

"Yes, sir," said Jackson.

"Fire!" cried Overton.

Dickinson fired almost instantly. A fleck of dust rose from Jackson's shirt. Jackson raised his left hand to hold his chest steady and thought himself dying, but, determined to shoot, he raised his pistol, affirming again the validity of his nickname, "Old Hickory."

Dickinson, horror-stricken, recoiled a step. "Have I missed him?"

General Overton raised his pistol and said at gunpoint, "Back to the mark, sir!"

Dickinson folded his arms. Jackson's weak form straightened. He aimed and fired. Dickinson fell to the ground and died that night from a gunshot wound to the stomach.

Jackson had been shot in the chest, but because of his loose coat and providential protection, the bullet was deflected by his breastbone, hit and broke two ribs, and lodged in his chest cavity. It missed his heart by an inch. Jackson's doctors, fearing that removing the bullet would kill him, left it where it was, and he carried it to his grave thirty-nine years later. Throughout those thirty-nine years, however, he lived with constant pain and coughing of blood.

One of the divine mysteries of life is how and why God protects some people. Andrew Jackson should have been killed on numerous occasions, but the mighty hand of God rested on him in order to accomplish His will for His purposes. One final account shows the protection and care of God for Andrew Jackson.

As America's seventh President, on January 30, 1835, Jackson visited the House chamber in Washington, D.C., to attend funeral services for the late Representative Warren R. Davis of South Carolina. The sermon the minister gave stirred Jackson to the depths of his heart. It had been seven years since his wife's funeral, and he still grieved. He had trusted Christ for his salvation because of his faithful, praying wife. Reflecting on death—a thought process which funerals are so apt to engender—he realized that he was prepared to die and enter the abode of the dead in Christ. The discourse finished, he filed past the casket and, with the Cabinet, descended to the rotunda of the Capitol.

A man whose face was shrouded by a thick black beard was standing a few feet away. No one noticed him draw the small pistol. He aimed it at President Jackson and pressed the trigger. The report startled and froze everyone. Calmly, the would-be assassin produced another pistol, reserved in the unlikely event that the first pistol did not fire properly. Jackson was one of the first to realize what was happening. He lunged at the man while clubbing the air with his cane. Crack went the second pistol. Old Hickory closed in on his assailant, but a young army officer reached the man first.

The President was miraculously unharmed. Only the caps of the pistols had exploded; the black powder charges in the chambers had failed to go off, even though the weapons had been properly loaded.

Later, a friend of the President recapped one of the pistols and squeezed the trigger. It fired perfectly. A small-arms expert calculated that the chance of two successive misfires was 1 in 125,000.

The important thing to remember is not that President Jackson escaped being shot, but that moments before, while attending the funeral of a dear friend, he realized that he was ready to meet his Maker because years before, he had trusted Christ as his Savior.

We will all die sooner or later. In Andrew Jackson's case, it was ten years later, at the age of seventy-eight. None of us knows how many years we have left on this earth. Are you ready to meet Christ and enter the gates of His Kingdom?

"No weapon that is formed against thee shall prosper, and every tongue that shall rise against thee in judgment thou shalt condemn. This is the heritage of the servants of the LORD, and their righteousness is of me, saith the LORD" (Isaiah 54:17).

"Praise to the Lord, Who doth prosper thy work and defend thee;
Surely His goodness and mercy here daily attend thee.
Ponder anew What the Almighty can do,
If with His love He befriend thee!"
Joachim Neander (1650–1680)

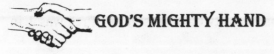

A FATEFUL NIGHT 1837 A.D.

One pitch black, pea-soup foggy English night, the London express train was suddenly shaken by the unexpected jolting of an attempted stop. The engineer had been startled to behold, in the beam of the speeding engine's headlights, a frantic figure dressed in a black cloak, standing in the middle of the tracks and waving his arms. Finally bringing the train to a stop, the engineer and one of his crew men climbed down to investigate what all the fuss was about. Their mysterious figure had disappeared, and no one was in sight. Calling out for the ghostly figure to appear, they continued to walk up the train track. Suddenly, they stopped and stared into the fog in horror! The bridge ahead of them had been washed out in the middle and had crumbled into a torrential stream! Whoever this mysterious figure was, the train men immediately recognized the fact that, without his warning, the train would have plunged into the river, and with it, their beloved Queen Victoria and the others aboard. The men were gripped with fear and awe.

Sometime later, while the bridge and the tracks were being repaired, the train crew made a more intensive search for the strange flag man, but nothing turned up and no one came forward to confess he had saved the Queen. The mystery was finally solved while the train was being inspected for another run. At the base of the engine's headlamp, the engineer discovered a huge, dead moth. He looked at it a moment, then on impulse pasted it to the glass of the lamp. Climbing back into his cab, he switched on the lamp and saw the "flag man" in the beam. He knew the answer now: the moth had flown into the beam just moments before the train was due to reach the washed-out bridge. In the fog, it appeared to be a phantom figure, waving its arms. When Queen Victoria was told of the results of the investigation, she said, "I'm sure it was no accident. It was God's way of protecting us." She recognized her life had been spared by God.

Queen Victoria, longest-reigning monarch of the United Kingdom of Great Britain, ruled England and Ireland from 1837 to 1901 and was Empress of India from 1876 to 1901. She was born Alexandrina Victoria on May 24, 1819 in London, to Victoria Mary Louisa (daughter of the Duke of Saxe-Coburg-Saalfeld) and Edward Augustus (Duke of Kent and Strathern). Young Victoria's father was the fourth son of George III and youngest brother of British Kings George IV and William IV. King William IV had no legitimate children and thus, upon his accession to the throne in 1830, his niece Victoria became heir apparent to the British crown.

When Victoria was only eleven years old, she was told that she would probably be England's next ruler. She knew something of the sad state of the monarchy under the Georges and under her immoral Uncle William, and she resolved that her reign would be different. 'I will be good,' she announced. She was only eighteen years old when William IV died and the responsibilities of the empire fell to her on June 20,1837. Throughout the sixty-three years of her reign she fufilled this childhood resolution.

Like so many other kings and queens throughout history, Queen Victoria suffered many difficult years of political turmoil. Her greatest security apart from Christ was her husband, Prince Albert, whom she married in 1840 at the age of 21. Albert, Prince of Saxe-Coburg-Gotha, was also her first cousin. In 1857, Victoria conferred the title of Prince Consort upon her husband. Their model marriage was an inspiration to the English people and produced nine children—four sons and five daughters. After 21 years of marriage, Price Albert died tragically; and the heart-broken Victoria, in virtual mourning for many years thereafter, sought to avoid most public appearances.

When Victoria came out of mourning, she began to take a renewed interest in her nation's future. Under Queen Victoria, England grew to become the largest and most powerful nation in the world. There was a time that the "sun never set on the British empire." "England's success," she felt, was as a result of believing the Bible to be the book of the English people and, without God's mighty hand of blessing, England would not have risen to such heights.

Victoria's popularity among all classes in British society reached its height in the last two decades of her reign. Her Golden Jubilee in 1887 and her Diamond Jubilee in 1897 were occasions for great public rejoicing. British subjects were enjoying an unprecedented period of prosperous complacency, and Queen Victoria's enthusiastic execution of the Boer War in South Africa increased her appeal at home and abroad.

Victoria died on January 22, 1901, at the age of 82. Her 63-year reign was the longest in the history of England. Her descendants, including 40 grandchildren, married into almost every royal family of Europe. With her personal example of Christian faith, honesty, patriotism, and devotion to family life, Victoria became a living symbol of the solidity of the British Empire. The many years of her reign, often referred to as the Victorian Age, witnessed the rise of the middle class and were marked by a deeply conservative morality and intense nationalism.

God used Queen Victoria in marvelous ways to bless the English people. Under her influence and able leadership, England grew in such proportions that the whole world took notice. The Lord blessed Queen Victoria and granted her desire for peace and goodwill towards her subjects. Not only did Victoria's England colonize the world, but they sent their greatest missionaries throughout the Empire to convert the inhabitants and to bring the Gospel of our Lord Jesus Christ to the heretofore lost heathen.

Once when a chief from one of Britain's African colonies was entertained by Queen Victoria in London, he asked her the secret of England's greatness. The queen did not take him to the Tower of London and show him the glittering crown jewels. She did not speak to him of the brilliant politicians who debated in Parliament. Instead, she presented the chief with a Bible and said, "This is the secret of England's greatness." A prince of India also recognized this truth. 'Where did the English-speaking people get all their intelligence, and energy, and cleverness, and power?' he asked. "It is their Bible that gives it to them." And now they bring it to us and say, 'This is what raised us. Take it and raise yourselves."

"Sing unto him, sing psalms unto him, talk ye of all his wondrous works. Glory ye in his holy name: let the heart of them rejoice that seek the LORD. Seek the LORD and his strength, seek his face continually. Remember his marvellous works that he hath done, his wonders, and the judgments of his mouth; O ye seed of Israel his servant, ye children of Jacob, his chosen ones. He is the LORD our God; his judgments are in all the earth. Be ye mindful always of his covenant; the word which he commanded to a thousand generations; Even of the covenant which he made with Abraham, and of his oath unto Isaac; And hath confirmed the same to Jacob for a law, and to Israel for an everlasting covenant, Saying, Unto thee will I give the land of Canaan, the lot of your inheritance; When ye were but few, even a few, and strangers in it. And when they went from nation to nation, and from one kingdom to another people; He suffered no man to do them wrong: yea, he reproved kings for their sakes, Saying, Touch not mine anointed, and do my prophets no harm. Sing unto the LORD, all the earth; shew forth from day to day his salvation. Declare his glory among the heathen; his marvellous works among all nations. For great is the LORD, and greatly to be praised: he also is to be feared above all gods. For all the gods of the people are idols: but the LORD made the heavens. Glory and honor are in his presence; strength and gladness are in his place. Give unto the LORD, ye kindreds of the people, give unto the LORD glory and strength. Give unto the LORD the glory due unto his name: bring an offering, and come before him: worship the LORD in the beauty of holiness" (I Chronicles 16:9-29).

THE HERITAGE OF A GODLY FATHER 1844 A.D.

One of the most important roles of parents is to teach their children the legacy of their heritage, the love of their nation and its defense, a love of the precious gift of God-given liberty, and, above all, a love of God and a thankful heart for salvation through Christ's sacrifice on the cross.

From time to time, God moves upon certain Gentiles to give them eyes to see and an understanding heart of love for His chosen people, the Jews. This love for the Jews, like their heritage, seems to be passed on from one generation to the next within the family. Willem ten Boom was a remarkable man and did these things for his family. The rewards were astounding, as you will learn.

In 1837, Willem purchased a little house in Haarlem, Holland, for four hundred guilders, and set up shop as a watchmaker. His good reputation soon spread far and wide and, although he was never rich, he was able to support his family and tithe to his local church. One day in 1844, his pastor Dominee Witteveen paid him a visit to share an idea with Willem. Pastor said, "Willem, you know the Scriptures tell us to pray for the Jews. In Psalm 122:6, we are told, 'Pray for the peace of Jerusalem: they shall prosper that love thee.'"

"Ah, yes, Dominee," said Willem, "I have always loved God's ancient people, the Jews. It was that race that gave us the Messiah, the Saviour of the world."

This conversation inspired them to begin a weekly Bible study and prayer fellowship, during which time they would pray for the Jews. This was a remarkable thing in those days. The Jews were practically a non-people, a sort of vagabond race with no national rooting of their own. No special attention was given to the Jews at that time, so why would Willem's home be used for a prayer place for Jews? It must have been the mighty hand of

God; only He could move in such a fashion. No record of their prayers exists, yet one would have to surmise that they asked for the Jews to return to their homeland someday, that they might again dwell in Jerusalem. No doubt, they also prayed that the Lord would come back to rule and reign on the earth from Jerusalem as the Scriptures declare.

The amazing thing is that exactly one-hundred years later, Willem's own son, four of his grandchildren, and one great-grandson would all be arrested for helping hide Jews in the very house where, one-hundred years earlier, prayer had been faithfully lifted up for them.

Willem ten Boom passed his heritage to his son and, while the eternal rewards were great, he sacrificed his life and the lives of most of his grandchildren for the Jews. Anointed with the heritage of Great-grandfather ten Boom, this courageous family "loved not their lives unto the death"(Revelation 12:11b) and would not surrender that heritage at the expense of the Jews they had grown to love.

Read Psalm 44 and 78 in light of this story to gain an understanding of what it means to pass on our heritage.

(For further reading, refer to the Corrie ten Boom story—The Price of Love 1892 A.D.)

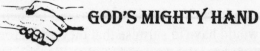

GOD KNOWS BEST 1862 A.D.

During the period of 1861-1865 America was fighting the "war between brothers," more commonly known as the Civil War, but more accurately called the "War Between the States." The horror of war can bring a beautiful rose in the midst of sorrow and darkness. When all looks lost and desperate the mighty hand of God always prevails in ways that only God can manifest.

One of these manifestations was seen in the medical treatment received for both men of the North and South. Organizations like the Sanitary and the Christian Commission were "splendid examples of organized mercy," furnished by the people of the North. They devised and provided every possible comfort for the sick and wounded, besides distributing religious reading to every soldier in the field. Ambulances, stretchers, hot coffee, postage-stamps, paper and envelopes, prayer-meetings, medicines, Christian burial, no want of body or soul was overlooked. "Homes" and "Lodges" for men on sick-leave, and for those not yet under or just out of the care of the government, or who had been left by their regiments. "Feeding Stations"for the tired and hungry; and even "Homes for the Wives, Mothers, and Children of Soldiers" who had come to visit their sick or wounded were established. On every flag-of-truce boat were placed clothing, medicines, and cordials for the prisoners who had been exchanged. With boundless mercy, they cared for all while living, and gave Christian burial and marked graves to the dead. Over seventeen million dollars, in money and supplies, were expended by these two Commissions.

In this account, Miss Mary Stafford was used by the Lord to bless dying, wounded, and sick soldiers in so many Godly ways. It was as if the Great Physician Jesus were present. One day while ministering in the hospital at Cairo, Illinois, her hometown medical unit for the Northern soldiers, she was making the rounds and wrote in her journal of a touching incident worth recording here:

As I was making the rounds of the hospital, a tall and stalwart man was brought in on a stretcher, who had been shot the night before on a gunboat. It was not a dangerous wound, apparently a little hole in the left side, that I could more than cover with the tip of my smallest finger. The grand looking man, however, was dying from the loss of blood he had already spilled before getting here. "Can we do anything for you?" One of us inquired after the surgeon had examined him, and he had been placed in bed. "Too late! too late!" was his only reply, slightly shaking his head. "Have you no friends to whom you wish me to write?" I asked.

He drew from an inside vest pocket a letter, enclosing a photograph of a most lovely woman. "You wish me to write to the person who has sent you this letter?" He nodded slightly, and feebly whispered, "My wife."

I bowed my head and offered a prayer in behalf of the dying man, bending low over him that he might hear. I remembered his wife in prayer and her bereavement. "Amen!" responded the dying man, in a distinct voice, and then we left him with the attendant to minister to others. As I left the soldier I glanced back and noticed he was lifting the photograph and gazing at it earnestly for a few moments, he pressed it to his lips and then clasped it in both hands. When I returned to his bed, some twenty minutes later he was still looking upward, his hands still clasping the photograph, and his face was irradiated with the most heavenly smile I have ever seen on any face. I spoke to him, he seemed not to hear, and there was a far-away look in the gaze, as though his vision reached beyond me to heaven. I stood still, awestruck. The ward master approached and laid his finger on the wrist. "He is dead!" he whispered. The duty of writing the widowed wife was assigned to me, and I took the letter and photograph. Ah, what a letter was that which the dying man had placed in my hands! He had evidently not replied to it, for it had been only just received, and had not the worn look of having been carried long in the pocket. It was from his wife, informing her husband of the death, on the same day, of their two children, three and five years old. It was the letter of a superior woman, who wrote nobly and tenderly, hiding her own grief, in her desire to comfort her husband. "I do not feel that we have lost our children,"thus she wrote."They are ours still, and will be ours forever. Their brief life was all sunshine and by their early departure they are spared all experience of sorrow and wrong. They can never know the keen heartache that you and I must suffer at their loss. It must be well with them. Their change of being must be an advance, a continuance of existence on a higher plane and some time, my dear Harry, we shall rejoin them. I sometimes fear, my darling, that you may meet them before I shall. Their death has taken from me all the fears of dying, which, you know, has so greatly distressed me. I can never fear to follow where my children have led. I have an interest in that other Life, whatever it may be, an attraction towards it, of which I knew nothing before. Oh, my dear Harry, do not mourn too much! I wish I were with you to share with you, not alone my hope, but the great conceptions of that other Life which have come to me." I enclosed to the wife her own letter and photograph taken from the hands of her dead husband, and told her all I knew of his death. We corresponded for three years afterwards and she resigned herself to the fact that God knew best, and that she could remain content trusting Him.

War with all its calamity can still be used by God to accomplish His will for individuals whom He calls. The mother in this story who lost her children and husband was drawn closer to seeking the Lord, and the hope of eternal life. Perhaps, had her children not died, her interest in eternal matters and the hope of salvation through Christ would not have surfaced. The Apostle Paul also learned the valuable lessons of life that can draw one towards Christ to see His mighty hand of power. Some of the greatest people who ever lived were people who lost everything but Christ.

"Not that I speak in respect of want: for I have learned, in whatsoever state I am, therewith to be content. I know both how to be abased, and I know how to abound: every where and in all things I am instructed both to be full and to be hungry, both to abound and to suffer need. I can do all things through Christ which strengtheneth me" (Phillipians 4:11-13).

GOD IS IN CONTROL 1863 A.D.

L.E. Chittenden, the Register of the Treasury during the Civil War, once asked President Lincoln how far he believed the Almighty actually directed our national affairs. Lincoln thought for some time before replying, then said:

"That the Almighty does make use of human agencies, and directly intervenes in human affairs, is one of the plainest statements of the Bible. I have had so many evidences of His direction—so many instances when I have been controlled by some other power than my own will—that I cannot doubt that this power comes from above..... I frequently see my way clear to a decision when I have no sufficient facts upon which to found it. But I cannot recall one instance in which I have followed my own judgment, founded upon such a decision, where the results were unsatisfactory; whereas, in almost every instance where I have yielded to the views of others, I have had occasion to regret it. I am satisfied that when the Almighty wants me to do or not to do a particular thing, He finds a way of letting me know it. I am confident that it is His design to restore the Union. He will do it in His own good time."

"O give thanks unto the LORD; call upon his name: make known his deeds among the people. Sing unto him, sing psalms unto him: talk ye of all his wondrous works. Glory ye in his holy name: let the heart of them rejoice that seek the LORD. Seek the LORD, and his strength: seek his face evermore. Remember his marvelous works that he hath done; his wonders, and the judgments of his mouth; O ye seed of Abraham his servant, ye children of Jacob his chosen. He is the LORD our God: his judgments are in all the earth" (Psalm 105:1-7).

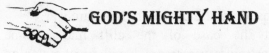

A DOUBLE PORTION 1863 A.D.

In the foolishness of war, tragically, too many young boys dream of becoming heroes at the expense of the lives of those called "the enemy." During the War Between the States, the "enemy" was other Americans in either the North or South. Of course, each side thought the other was misguided.

One of these young soldiers itching for action was a Northern, pale-faced, stripling of small stature, known as "the little adjutant." Seventeen-year-old, Arthur MacArthur soon showed himself adept at army life and won the attention of General Phil Sheridan. After seeing him in action at the Battle of Perryville, Sheridan cited him for gallantry and made him a brevet captain.

Being ranked a brevet captain, promotion with no increase in pay, mattered little to Captain MacArthur. The battle is what interested him. Soon enough he found himself in the thick of battle. At Missionary Ridge, Tennessee, Captain Edwin B. Parsons wrote to Arthur's father saying, "Arthur fought like a pack of tigers in a jungle. He has become the hero of the regiment.... He has been promoted to Major."

Author William Manchester, in his book *American Caesar* tells of the battle of Missionary Ridge overlooking the vast crescent peaks of the majestic horizon of Chattanooga, Tennessee. Manchester sets the stage, illustrating how the mighty hand of God preserves people for His greater purposes.

On Wednesday, November 25, 1863, now eighteen-years old, Captain MacArthur of the 24th Wisconsin was put into action by 4:20 . He and his men were ready. The signal guns were heard—six cannon shots fired at intervals of two seconds—and the assault began. It was still meant to be no more than a feint, drawing off some of the graycoats facing Sherman, but events swiftly acquired a momentum of their own; after the pits had been taken at bayonet point there occurred, what James M. Merrill later called, "one of the most dramatic moves in the entire war."

The situation at the base of the cliff had become impossible.The demonstrators were trapped, with fire threatening them from above, an exigency unanticipated by their commanders. Logic suggested immediate retreat; they had fulfilled their mission. Instead the troops advanced upward. According to one account, General Phil Sheridan raised his hat, a gesture interpreted by the soldiers as a command to charge. But when a staff officer rode up to find out what was happening, Sheridan said he had done nothing and was mystified. The truth is that they were witnessing an act of colossal insubordination; eighteen thousand blue-clad boys, infuriated by the musketry decimating their ranks, had sprung at the heights on their own.

General Ulysses S. Grant, watching the advancing white line of musket fire from Orchard Knob, turned in his saddle and asked angrily, "Thomas, who ordered those men up the ridge?" Major General George Henry Thomas said he didn't know; he certainly hadn't.

Then Grant wheeled on General Gordon Granger: "Did you order them up?" Granger answered, "No, they started up without orders." Fuming, Grant muttered, "Well, it will be all right if it turns out all right."

By now sixty Union battle flags were rising toward the crest, among them the banner of the 24th Wisconsin. Meanwhile the Confederate defenders on the summit were taking a murderous toll. A Union bugler, having lost his leg to a cannonball, sat on an outcrop of rock, blowing the call to charge until he collapsed. In one regiment six color-bearers fell. The 24th's first color-bearer was bayoneted; the second was decapitated by a shell.

In the heat of battle, young MacArthur grasped the flagstaff and leaped upward, crying, "On, Wisconsin!" His face blackened with smoke, his muddy uniform tattered and bloodstained, he reached the top of the precipice, and there—silhouetted against the sky, where the whole regiment could see him—he planted the standard. Other blue-clad troops gained the crest at about the same time, thus winning the battle.

Arthur MacArthur was one of the most distinguished men on the field of battle that day. He was shot in the chest, but providentially the bullet struck the wad of folded papers he had hastily shoved into his pocket early that fateful morning. Had those papers not been there , the bullet would have been lodged in his heart and killed him.

Arthur in due time rose to the rank of General, yet he felt he had never completely accomplished his desires in the military, nor gained the recognition he deserved. Very few people know Arthur MacArthur apart from serious historians, but there is hardly a person alive today who does not know of his son Douglas MacArthur. Had eighteen-year-old Arthur not placed those papers in his chest pocket that November 25, he would have been killed, and Douglas would not have been born. The mighty hand of God saved the father to produce the son, and like Elisha's mantle with the double portion falling on Elisha, so too the mantle of Arthur MacArthur fell on this son.

The son, General Douglas MacArthur, played a critical role during World War II. Douglas MacArthur was used of God to save thousands of lives and help bring the war to an end. His leadership was a blessing to mankind. It is hard to imagine how tragic history might have been had he never been born. Where the father felt a failure the son by the will of God rose in his stead.

We who are parents have a blessing in our children. May they rise to greater purposes for the work of the Lord in His eternal glory.

"Praise ye the LORD. Blessed is the man that feareth the LORD, that delighteth greatly in his commandments. His seed shall be mighty upon earth: the generation of the upright shall be blessed. Wealth and riches shall be in his house: and his righteousness endureth for ever. Unto the upright there ariseth light in the darkness: he is gracious, and full of compassion, and righteous.

"A good man sheweth favour, and lendeth: he will guide his affairs with discretion. Surely he shall not be moved for ever: the righteous shall be in everlasting remembrance. He shall not be

afraid of evil tidings: his heart is fixed, trusting in the LORD. His heart is established, he shall not be afraid, until he see his desire upon his enemies.

"He hath dispersed, he hath given to the poor; his righteousness endureth for ever; his horn shall be exalted with honour. The wicked shall see it, and be grieved; he shall gnash with his teeth, and melt away: the desire of the wicked shall perish" (Psalm 112:1-10).

GOD'S MIGHTY HAND

AM I MY BROTHER'S KEEPER? 1864 A.D.

Mary Livermore, a New England girl of nineteen, was hired as a school teacher several years before the War Between the States erupted. She was employed on a large Southern plantation to teach the three children of Master Robert Colton: Lucy, Mary, and little Robert, Jr. Unfortunately, like many children of the affluent, these three heirs had been spoiled rotten. It appeared to Mary Livermore that their parents were more attentive to their wealth than to the nurture of their children. By the Godly persistence of young Mary Livermore, however, the youngsters received a good education. She saw to it that they had daily Christian training along with their studies. The change wrought in these children by Mary's firm but loving hand and by the conviction of God's Holy Spirit was nothing short of miraculous.

One morning, while Mary was having breakfast, one of Master Colton's slave girls, "Car'line" (Caroline), a pretty and graceful mulatto, was serving in the dining room. While giving a cup of coffee to Mr. Colton, her master and owner, he accidentally knocked it from the tray on which she served it. The hot liquid spilled into his lap, instantly soaked through his light linen trousers, and scalded him. Jumping up with an oath, he raised his hand and struck the girl, who fell stunned to the floor. The angry man continued to beat her even after she fell. Bruised, bleeding, and unconscious, Car'line was carried to the cottage of her mother, known as Aunt Aggy; she had witnessed the brutal scene from an adjoining room. Mary Livermore later wrote in her journal, "I left the table and withdrew to my own apartment, shocked beyond expression at the brutal outrage of the passionate master."

Later in the day, she wrote, "Aunt Aggy came to my room on some household errand, and I expressed my indignation at the brutal treatment her daughter had received. I spoke with the frankness of a New England girl of nineteen who had been trained to be true to her convictions, and I was astonished at the change that came over the usually taciturn, dignified woman. Turning squarely about and facing me, her large, lustrous eyes blazing with excitement, she spoke in a tone and manner that would have befitted a seer uttering a prophecy:

"Thar's a day a-comin'! Thar's a day a-comin'! she said, with right hand uplifted; 'I hear de rumblin' ob de chariots! I see de flashin' ob de guns! White folks' blood is a-runnin' on de ground liked a riber, an' de dead's heaped up dat high!' she emphasized, measuring to the level of her shoulder. 'O, Lor'! Hasten de day when de blows, an' de bruises, an' de aches, an' de pains, shall come to de white folks, an' de buzzards shall eat 'em as dey's dead in de streets. O, Lor'! Roll on de chariots, an' gib de black people rest an' peace. O, Lor'! Gib me de pleasure ob livin' till dat day, when I shall see white folks shot down like de wolves when dey come hongry out o' de woods!' And without another word she walked from the room. She did not speak again of the beating given Caroline that morning.

"At the close of the war years later, I reminded Aunt Aggy of the occurrence. I found that the beating of her precious daughter had been photographed on her memory as distinctly as it had been on mine. She reflected back to that time we consoled one another over the treatment of her daughter and the misery of being a black slave.

"'I'd allers knowed it was a-comin', she said. 'I allers heerd de rumblin' o' de wheels. I allers 'spected to see white folks heaped up dead. An' de Lor', He's keept His promise, an 'venged His people, jes' as I knowed He would. I seed 'em dead on de field, Massa Linkum's sojers an' de Virginny sojers, all heaped togedder, wid de dead hosses, an' de smash-up waggins, all de fightin' done done for dis yer world foreber. Ole massa and missus both done died afore de war, an' young Massa Robert, one what you teached in de school-room, he done died in dese yer my arms. Little Mass' Batt, what liked to say his prars in yer room, he went to de war, an' was shot in ole Car'lina, an' buried wid his sojers. Miss Lucy an' little Courty before done died when de war begin, an' dey was buried in Liberty Hill. De ole place is all done broke up, an' de colored folks go jes' whar dey please no passes now. O, de Lor' He do jes' right, if you only gib Him time enough to turn Hisself.'"

As she had prayed, Aunt Aggy lived to see the mighty hand of God deal out His justice and vindication upon the South, which cruelly mistreated the Negro slaves, and upon the North, which paid a fearful price for victory. As the Bible says, "... *Your Father which is in heaven ... maketh his sun to rise on the evil and on the good, and sendeth rain on the just and on the unjust" (Matthew 5:45-46).* The young nation suffered unmercifully for four long and dark years.

As she also had prayed, Aunt Aggy lived to see God's judgment fall upon her cruel masters, as Mr. Colton's entire dynasty was wiped out by the close of the Civil War. Aunt Aggy likewise lived long enough to see the fulfillment of the Bible's promise, *"For we know him that hath said, Vengeance belongeth unto me, I will recompense, saith the Lord. And again, The Lord shall judge his people. It is a fearful thing to fall into the hands of the living God" (Hebrews 10:30-31).*

Many historians of our day spend long hours discussing the South's "States' Rights issue" and their Constitutional reasons for seceding from the Union. Both sides had sound Constitutionally based reasons for the War Between the States; however, the issue of slavery is often underplayed. It is reasoned that only 18 percent of the South had slaves, that the War Between the States was fought, not over the slavery issue but over Constitutional issues, that the slave problem would have corrected itself in due course, and even that the Bible condones slavery.

In dealing with this issue, I have consider it first of all from God's perspective, not a political perspective. I must address the subject by asking how the Lord looks at wars in general and, in this case, the Civil War. In writing a book such as this, one has to consider the questions: Does God intervene in the affairs of men, and wars? If so, all wars? Does God choose sides in wars? Does He determine the outcome?

Obviously the answer to those questions is a resounding "Yes!" God is sovereign, omnipotent, omnipresent, and omniscient. Wars and their outcomes are directly decided according to His will; God determines who will win or lose.

"We have heard with our ears, O God, our fathers have told us, what work thou didst in their days, in the times of old. How thou didst drive out the heathen with thy hand, and plantedst them; how thou didst afflict the people, and cast them out. For they got not the land in possession by their own sword, neither did their own arm save them: but thy right hand, and thine arm, and the light of thy countenance, because thou hadst a favour unto them. Thou art my King, O God: command deliverances for Jacob. Through thee will we push down our enemies: through thy name will we tread them under that rise up against us. For I will not trust in my bow, neither shall my sword save me. But thou hast saved us from our enemies, and hast put them to shame that hated us. In God we boast all the day long, and praise thy name for ever. Selah." (Psalm 44:1-8).

The War Between the States, I am sorry to say, was not primarily a Constitutional issue as many historians would have us believe. Many have swallowed that pill and thereby fallen into deception. In my opinion, the real cause of the Civil War was the moral issue surrounding the South's use and abuse of many slaves. The idea of Constitutional or States' Rights issues should not be allowed to confuse the fact that four million human slaves were used, abused, sold as cattle, often times naked before the crowds, separated from family at auctions, thought to be animals with no human emotions, and were overworked and underfed. The list of atrocities goes on and on. Some people justify this by saying, "Well, not all slaves fared so." Hogwash! If the slaves liked their lot so well, why was it necessary to have laws to keep them bound to their "good masters"? A slave is a slave no matter how well he is treated.

Abraham Lincoln is looked upon by some historians as a man who destroyed our nation. His bent on preserving the Union and freeing blacks is considered by these historians the straw the broke the camel's back. Yet when one considers Lincoln's turmoil, one cannot but help feel the pain and sorrow he carried. It is easy for us armchair historians to pass judgment. Lincoln understood all too well the dilemma of the slavery issue that was so interwoven in the South's economy. This is why he once wrote:

> *"My paramount object in this struggle is to save the Union. And is not either to save or destroy slavery. If I could save the Union without freeing any slave, I would do it; and if I could save it by freeing all the slaves, I would do it; and if I could do it by freeing some and leaving others alone, I would also do that."*

On March 4, 1865, just 45 days before he was assassinated, President Lincoln gave his second Inaugural Address. As he reflected on the devastating Civil War that continued to tear apart his long-suffering nation, he said:

> *"Neither party expected for the war the magnitude or the duration which it has already attained. Both read the same Bible and pray to the same God, and each evokes His aid against the other. It may seem strange that any men should dare ask a just God's assistance in wringing their bread from the sweat of other men's faces, but let us judge not, that we be not judged. The prayers of both could not be answered. That of neither has been answered fully. The Almighty has His own purposes. 'Woe unto the world because of offenses; for it must needs be that offenses come, but woe to that man by whom the offense cometh.'*
>
> *"If we shall suppose that American slavery is one of those offenses which, in the providence of God, must needs*

come, but which, having continued through His appointed time, He now wills to remove, and that He gives to both North and South this terrible war as the woe due to those by whom the offense came, shall we discern therein any departure from those divine attributes which the believers in a living God always ascribe to Him?

"Fondly do we hope, fervently do we pray, that this mighty scourge of war may speedily pass away. Yet, if God will that it continue until all the wealth piled by the bondsmen's two hundred and fifty years of unrequited toil shall be sunk, and until every drop of blood drawn with the lash shall be paid by another drawn with the sword; as it was said three thousand years ago, so still it must be said, 'The judgments of the Lord are true and righteous altogether.' With malice toward none, with charity for all, with firmness in the right, as God gives us to see the right, let us strive on to finish the work we are in, to bind up the nation's wounds, to care for him who shall have borne the battle, and for his widow, and his orphan, to do all which may achieve and cherish a just and lasting peace among ourselves and with all nations."

America is at the same crossroads today as it was just prior to the War Between the States. Today the slave has been morally replaced by the unborn child. The cry "States' Rights" has been replaced with "Women's Rights." Woe to this or any nation, heading on a course that will lead to the wrath of God's mighty hand in judgment! America, like Nineveh of old, must repent in total humility and surrender to God to avert judgment. This is my prayer. Remember Moses, who by prayer stayed the mighty hand of God from Israel's judgment.

SAVED BY A SONG 1875 A.D.

Ira D. Sankey was a man to whom God had given wonderful power to sing of the gospel of Jesus Christ. For years, he and D.L. Moody worked together, Moody preaching and Sankey singing.

On Christmas Eve, 1875, Mr. Sankey was traveling by steamboat up the Delaware River. It was a calm, starlit evening and there were many passengers gathered on deck. Mr. Sankey was asked to sing, and, as always, he was perfectly willing to do so.

He stood leaning on one of the outside boat rails, admiring the starry hosts of heaven, in quiet prayer contemplating which Christmas song would be appropriate. Driven almost against his will he felt the Lord instruct him to sing "Shepherd Song," written by Dorothy Thrupp and William Bradbury. He reasoned with the Lord in silent prayer that being Christmas the "Shepherd Song" would not be ideal. However, the Lord's conviction was so strong, Sankey submitted and began the song.

Savior, like a shepherd lead us, Much we need Thy tender care; in Thy pleasant pastures feed us, for our use Thy folds prepare: Blessed Jesus, Blessed Jesus, Thou hast bought us, Thine we are; Blessed Jesus, Blessed Jesus, Thou hast bought us, Thine we are.

We are Thine; do thou befriend us, be the Guardian of our way; keep Thy flock, from sin defend us, seek us when we go astray: Blessed Jesus, Blessed Jesus, Hear, O hear us when we pray; Blessed Jesus, Blessed Jesus, Hear, O hear us when we pray.

Thou hast promised to receive us, poor and sinful

though we be; Thou hast mercy to relieve us, grace to cleanse, and pow'r to free: Blessed Jesus, Blessed Jesus, early let us turn to Thee; Blessed Jesus, Blessed Jesus, early let us turn to Thee.

Early let us seek Thy favor; early let us do Thy will: Blessed Lord and only Savior, with Thy love our bosoms fill: Blessed Jesus, Blessed Jesus, Thou hast loved us, love us still; Blessed Jesus, Blessed Jesus, Thou hast loved us, love us still.

There was a deep Stillness as those who heard Mr. Sankey sing those words and melody as they came forth from the singer's soul. The peace that passes all understanding seemed to float over the deck and quiet river. Every heart was touched, and quietly left in pensive thought. After all left, and Ira turning to gaze out across the river a man with a rough, weather-beaten face came up to Mr. Sankey and said, "Did you ever serve in the Union army?"

"Yes," Mr. Sankey answered.

"Do you remember those dark and difficult days over twelve year ago?"

"Everyone like it was yesterday," Ira replied, "Why do you ask?"

The stranger then said, "Do you remember what you were doing the May of 1862, just outside of Shiloh on a bright, moonlit night much like the one tonight?"

"Why, yes I believe I do," answered Sankey surprised. "That was the month I had night duty, how could I forget those dark lonely and sometimes dreary nights?"

"I too was on picket duty," the stranger answered, "but I was in the Confederate army. I now know who you are, I saw you standing at your post across the river from me and I decided to myself that I was going to pick you off. I raised my musket and took deliberate aim. I was standing in the shadow, completely concealed, while the full light of the moon was falling upon you.

"At that instant, just as a moment ago, you raised your eyes to heaven and began to sing. Mr. Sankey, music, especially song, has always had a wonderful power over me, and I took my finger off the trigger. 'Let him sing his song to the end,' I said to myself. 'I can shoot him afterwards-he ain't going nowhere.' The song you just sang I recognized as the song you sang that night. I heard the words perfectly: 'We are thine; do Thou befriend us. Be the Guardian of our way.'

"Those words stirred up many memories. I began to think of my childhood and my God-fearing mother. She had many times sung that very song to me. But she died all too soon, otherwise much in my life would, no doubt, have been different.

"When you had finished your song along the river, it was impossible for me to take aim again. I thought, 'The Lord who is able to save that man from certain death must surely be great and mighty and my arm, of its own accord, dropped limp at my side.

"Since that time I have wandered far and wide, but when I saw you here tonight singing just as on the other occasion, my heart was stirred deeply. How I wish you could help me find a peace for my wandering and troubled soul."

Deeply moved Mr. Sankey threw his arms about the man who in the days of the war had been an enemy. On this Christmas night the two went together to the manger in Bethlehem.

There, the stranger found Him who was their common Saviour, the Good Shepherd, who seeks for the lost sheep until He finds it. And when He has found it, He lays it on His shoulders, rejoicing.

I cannot help but think when I learn of a story such as the one just recounted, how the mighty hand of God watches over us, keeping us safe from all harm. Unlike Mr. Sankey,we will probable never know the times God has kept us safe from harm. Perhaps our falling at the feet of God in the kingdom to come will involve a knowledge of how God had kept us and our loved ones in so many little ways.

"Nevertheless, I am continually with thee; thou hast held me by my right hand" (Psalm73:23).

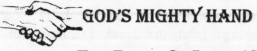

THE PRICE OF LOVE 1892 A.D.

On Good Friday in 1892, a tiny baby girl was born prematurely to the Caspar ten Boom family in Amsterdam. The infant Corrie, fourth child of Caspar and his wife Cor, clung tenaciously to her thin thread of life. With one child already passed on, the ten Booms resigned themselves to the likelihood that this sickly, pale child would be next to see the Lord, the assurance dictated by their strong faith. Mother Cor wrote in her diary: "The Lord gave us a very little, weak baby-Corrie. Oh, what a poor little thing she is. Nearly dead, she looks bluish white. Nobody thinks she will live. Uncle Hendrik has said, 'I hope the Lord will quickly take this poor little creature to His home in heaven.'"

The Lord had other plans for this new life, plans for hope and a future, plans which would take the world by surprise as the evidences of His mighty hand of power upon Corrie's life were revealed. The Bible says, *"But God hath chosen the foolish things of the world to confound the wise; and God hath chosen the weak things of the world to confound the things which are mighty." (1 Corinthians 1:27).*

For several years, little Corrie remained sickly; but by God's goodness she gradually began to gain strength. Meanwhile, her father Casper had inherited his father's watch shop and moved the family into the shop/house in Haarlem. This move was destined to play an important part in Corrie's life, for it was this very house that one-hundred years before had been the site of ongoing prayer for the Jews of the world. (See Willem ten Boom, 1844 story.)

As Corrie grew up, she and her family took active rolls in the community, often helping people with housing difficulties. Their house became a sort of train station, with people always coming and going. In the midst of all this commotion, Corrie studied the

English language; little did she know that she would someday live in America and work with Billy Graham to produce the film of her life, *The Hiding Place*. The Lord directs the steps of His children, and He knew that the knowledge of English would serve Corrie well. Betsie, Corrie's older sister, was led to study German; little did she know that she and Corrie would be sent to the Ravensbruck prison camp, where Betsie's knowledge of German would enable her to communicate the love of Christ to those Germans who had "ears to hear." Corrie's older brother, Willem, studied for the ministry, specializing in Jewish cultural studies, and he became passionately involved in the Dutch Society for Israel. Willem's studies at the Jewish Institute in Leipzig, Germany, prepared him for the large-scale persecution of Jews which would come from Hitler's Germany in a few years. How truly amazing to see God's answers to Great-grandfather ten Boom's prayers for the Jews taking root in his very home, only a generation later!

Corrie told of the 100th Anniversary of the shop (1837-1937), a landmark day in the ten Boom family: "Friends, relatives, town officials, and small children thronged the shop/house to congratulate Father and share in the hot, sweet coffee and fresh home-made cakes. Only brother Willem was missing, but he had promised to come as soon as possible. When he finally arrived with his wife, Tine, and their four children, a strange guest clung feebly to Willem's arm. The man's appearance was shocking because his face had been mutilated. 'He just arrived in Holland today from Germany,' Willem explained. 'Some German Nazi-indoctrinated youth in Munich attacked him and set fire to his beard, because he is a Jew.'

"Father rose to welcome him eagerly. Our home would always be a welcome place to any Jews who could not help themselves. Many present warned us about having anything to do with the Jews. After hearing this stranger talk of the condition of the Jewish community in Germany, a chill settled over us all. There were friends at our celebration who refused to acknowledge the reality of the Nazi regime. They tried to dismiss it to the back of their minds, refusing to admit it had any particular significance. 'It couldn't happen again,' they promised each other. 'There will never be another war in Europe in our lifetime—it's only an isolated incident of harassment.'"

All too soon, however, their half-spoken fears were to be realized. Two short years later, Britain, France, and Germany were plunged into war. Holland, although appalled by the outbreak of hostilities, was determined to remain neutral. It was only a matter of hours, however, after the Prime Minister had broadcast solemn assurances to the nation that there would be no war, that Betsie and Corrie awoke to the terrifying roar of bombs and to a sky ablaze with the red flames of burning buildings. Father slept on, but the two sisters knelt in prayer for their Queen and their beloved country. Incredibly, Betsie also prayed for the Germans.

For five long days, the brave Dutch people held off the Germans, but few doubted their valiant little nation would soon be overrun by the powerful German war machine. Corrie wept when she heard over the radio that the Queen had left. Invasion was now inevitable, and life would never be the same again.

The mighty hand of God became evident to Corrie one morning when she awoke to the sound of "dogfights" overhead between British and German planes. Unable to sleep, she went downstairs to have a cup of tea and found Betsie already there for the same reason. After the noise quieted down, Corrie returned to bed and, to her amazement, found a large piece of shrapnel lying on her pillow that undoubtedly would have killed her had she not left her bed. She and Betsie looked to the Lord with thanksgiving for His hand of deliverance.

One day, two German soldiers arrived, almost without warning, at the home of Corrie's niece, Cocky, looking for her brothers. The soldiers wanted to take them to Germany to work in the war factories. Since so many Germans had been drafted into military service, the Germans took Dutch captives to their factories to do the work. Peter and his older brother, Bob, had barely enough time to rush into the kitchen, pull up the trapdoor underneath the table, and throw themselves into a small chamber made from a shallow potato cellar for just such an emergency. Their two aunts and sister Cocky quickly threw a large cloth over the table and started setting it for a meal.

When asked where her brothers were hiding, Cocky, who couldn't bring herself to tell a lie, admitted to the soldiers that the boys were under the table. Taking her literally, the soldiers pulled aside the long cloth but saw nothing. They marched out furiously, realizing they had been made to look like fools. The joyful sister embraced her brothers, thanking God for blinding the eyes of the Germans to the truth.

The Germans were not always so easily fooled, however, and eventually Corrie and her family were betrayed for hiding Jews. For this, they were all sent to prison. The stories of Corrie's life, including her imprisonment, have been well published, and little more needs to be said except for the fact that, although most of her family died in prison or as a result of the harsh imprisonment, Corrie lived to testify to the truth that "there is no pit too deep that the Lord is not yet deeper."

Through a clerical error, Corrie was miraculously discharged from prison on December 28, 1944, at the age of fifty-two. She found out later that two weeks after her discharge, all woman of her age were put to death. The Lord's mighty hand had once again prevailed over the life of Corrie ten Boom. This "sickly" child, expected to die young, out-lived all her immediate family and died on her birthday, April 15, 1983, at the age of ninety-one. Before she went to be with her Lord, Corrie had shared the love of Christ in sixty-one countries of the world, teaching them of His power to save sinners by granting forgiveness to both Jew and Gentile, and to all people, including Nazis, who would repent and trust Christ as Savior. Corrie learned to see that all losses are gain in Christ and that, whatever difficulties lie in life's pathway, Christ is still in control and His will shall be done.

"But I rejoiced in the Lord greatly, that now at the last your care of me hath flourished again; wherein ye were also careful, but ye lacked opportunity. Not that I speak in respect of want: for

I have learned, in whatsoever state I am, therewith to be content. I know both how to be abased, and I know how to abound: every where and in all things I am instructed both to be full and to be hungry, both to abound and to suffer need. I can do all things through Christ which strengtheneth me" (Philippians 4:10-13).

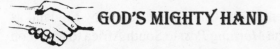 GOD'S MIGHTY HAND

THE BULL DOG OF A MAN 1874-1965 A.D.

Any student of history would have to agree that Sir Winston Leonard Spencer Churchill was one of those special gifts given by the mighty hand of God, born at the right place and at the right time. Where would Great Britain have been without Churchill during World War II? It was Churchill who warned England of the German menace of impending war, and it was Churchill who gave his people the courage and fortitude to resist Hitler.

After Churchill's censure of Prime Minister Neville Chamberlain for trying to make peace with the tyrant Hitler, many British thought him (Churchill) "excessive." Despite his unpopularity, Churchill implored England to build up its navy for the inevitable war with Germany. When war broke out, Churchill replaced Chamberlain as Prime Minister of England.

The people then no longer looked upon him with suspicion. They hung on every word he spoke, for Churchill gave the people the will to resist Hitler. In an address on October 29, 1941 at Harrow School, Churchill challenged:

> *"Never give in, never give in, never, never, never, never—in nothing, great or small, large or petty—never give in except to conventions of honor and good sense....Do not let us speak of darker days; let us rather of sterner days. These are not dark days: these are great days—the greatest days our country has ever lived; and we must all thank God that we have been allowed, each of us according to our stations, to play a part in making these days memorable in the history of our race."*

How Churchill rose to prominence is an intriguing story which could have been planned only by God.

At the age of twenty-five, Churchill was sent by England as a correspondent for the *Morning Post* to South Africa to report on the Boer War. On November 15, 1899, a Providential event took place that changed his life forever and made a relatively unknown name a household word throughout England and much of Europe.

On November 14, had you or I the opportunity to speak to Winston Churchill, he would have confessed that he was not very satisfied as a correspondent, and that he wished he had remained in military service, fighting the Boers instead of writing about them. He felt that he was "cut out of the whole exciting war with all its boundless possibilities of adventure and advancement." Little did he know that November 15, 1899, would be the beginning of a lifetime of adventure and advancement.

On that important day, Churchill was caught in an attack while riding an armored train with some British soldiers. As they were nearing the bridge at the Blue Krantz River in South Africa, the train was attacked by Boers. The Boers (Dutch farmers) were fighting for their rights over South Africa, which they had settled in 1652.

Churchill was attempting to uncouple the engine from some derailed cars. While he was running between cars and heading toward the engine, not more than 200 yards away, the Boers, riding their horses at full gallop were firing at every movement. Churchill later said that bullets were striking the metal all around him, yet he was untouched.

The train was overtaken, and as Churchill tried to make a run for the Krantz River, he was spotted by a soldier. The soldier rode up to him and leveled his rifle at him. Rather than foolishly run, Churchill froze. As he stood, however, he reached for his Mauser pistol, but then remembered he had taken it off while en route on the train. He recalled that if he had had his gun, he could have probably shot and killed his captor, but God's mighty hand was in control of Churchill's not having his gun—and of history.

Years later, that soldier became South Africa's Boer General, General Louis Botha (BOE-tuh), and later, Prime Minister of his people. Three years after the Boer War, General Botha visited

England in order to secure a loan for his country. At a luncheon he sat next to Churchill, and as the two men reminisced about the war, Churchill began to tell of his encounter with the soldier. General Botha then said, "Don't you recognize me? I was that soldier." Churchill was shocked. The soldier's wartime wild look was gone, and now that he was dressed neatly, shaven, and well possessed, Churchill admitted that he would have never guessed.

This General, whom Churchill might have killed, became one of Churchill's closest friends. General Botha, over the years, was looked upon as the father of his country and was loved by the Boers and English alike.

In 1913, General Botha was visiting Churchill, who by that time had been appointed head of the British Navy. As they talked, General Botha earnestly took Churchill by the arm and warned him not to trust the Germans—especially Kaiser Wilhelm II. He felt from his traveling throughout Prussia that the Germans were planning to take over Europe, and as a leader of his South African territory, if war broke out, he was going to drive the Germans from South Africa.

In his book *My Early Life*, Churchill shares a significant occurrence that again shows the mighty hand of God at work: "July 29, 1914, midway in the week of crisis which preceded the world explosion, I was walking away from the House of Commons after Question Time and met in Palace Yard one of the South African Ministers, Mr. De Graaf, a very able Dutchman whom I had known for a long time said, 'What does it mean? What do you think is going to happen?' I replied,'I rather think it will be war, and I think Britain will be involved. Does General Botha know how critical things are?' De Graaf slightly nodded and went away looking very grave, and I thought no more of the incident; but it had its consequences.

"That night De Graaf sent a telegram to General Botha. Telling him what Churchill had said. Botha was away from the seat of government—he was in the northern Transvaal, and General Smuts was filling in for him at Pretoria. The telegram was laid before General Smuts. He looked at it for a moment, but being busy he pushed it to one side, and continued working through his files. Then when he had finished, he noticed the telegram again. 'There must be something important to this telegram,' he thought, 'or Mr. De Graaf would not have sent it to the general.' After reading and seeing the seriousness of its contents he sent the message to the absent Prime Minister Botha in the northern Transvaal. It reached General Botha many hours later—but in time.

"That very night he was to start by train for Delagoa Bay, and the next morning he was to embark for his return journey to Cape Town on board a German ship. Had it not been for the telegram, so he afterwards told me, he would have been actually at sea on a German vessel when war was declared. The Prime Minister, the all-powerful national leader of South Africa, would have been in the hands of the enemy at the very moment when large areas of the South African nation were trembling on the verge of rebellion. One cannot measure the evils which might have come upon South Africa had such a disaster taken place. Instantly, on receiving the message, General Botha canceled all his plans and then returned by special train to Pretoria, which he reached in time, before the outbreak.

"General Botha's grand exertions in the war, the risks he ran, the steadfast courage which he showed, the great command he exercised over his people, the brilliant manner in which he overran German South-West Africa, his rugged animated counsels at the meetings of the Imperial War Cabinet in 1917, his statesmanship and noble bearing after the victory in the Peace Conference in Paris in 1919 were remarkable."

The providence of God is awesome. How He directs the steps of people never ceases to amaze me. In the grand scheme of things, the effect that young unknown soldier had upon the destiny of as-yet-unknown Churchill is glorious. As I close this account, allow me one more incident that reveals God's mighty hand upon Churchill.

When still a young soldier, Churchill was taken, along with several other British prisoners, to Pretoria, South Africa, where a prison was formed from their State Model School, a sort of university. On December 12, 1899, after twenty-eight weary, melancholy days of mundane prison life, Churchill and other key inmates decided on a daring plan of escape. There was one area in the prison—a section of the wall—which could be scaled. The escape attempt would be risky, and anyone with the wisdom of age would not try it. Yet twenty-five-year-old Churchill did not yet possess the wisdom that later years would give him. A chance of escape, with its adventure, was just what he needed to give him hope. On December 12, he, with Captain Haldane and Lieutenant Brockie, made their way to that section of the wall in hopes of escape. Here I will allow the gifted writer Churchill to tell the tale himself.

"There was no difficulty in getting into the circular office. But to climb out of it over the wall was a hazard of the sharpest character. Anyone doing so must at the moment he was on the top of the wall be plainly visible to the sentries fifteen yards away, if they were in the right place and happened to look! Whether the sentries would challenge or fire depended entirely upon their individual dispositions, and no one could tell what they would do. Nevertheless I was determined that nothing should stop my taking the plunge the next day. As the 12th wore on, my fears crystallized more and more into desperation. In the evening, after my two friends had made an attempt, but had not found the moment propitious, I strolled across the quadrangle and secreted myself in the circular office. Through an aperture in the metal casing of which it was built I watched the sentries. For some time they remained stolid and obstructive. Then all of a sudden one turned and walked up to his comrade, and they began to talk. Their backs were turned.

"Now or never! I stood on a ledge, seized the top of the wall with my hands, and drew myself up. Twice I let myself down again in sickly hesitation, and then with a third resolve scrambled up and over. My waistcoat got entangled with the ornamental metal-work on the top. I had to pause for an appreciable moment to extricate myself. In this posture I had one parting glimpse of the sentries still talking with their backs turned fifteen yards away. One of them was lighting his cigarette, and I remember the glow on the inside of his hands as a distinct impression which my mind recorded. Then I lowered myself lightly down into the adjoining garden and crouched among the shrubs. I was free!"

Now that Churchill had escaped, what was he to do? How to get out of the garden, how to pass unnoticed through the streets, how to evade the patrols that surrounded the town, and above all how to cover the 280 miles to the border, were problems which had no solutions.

He succeeded in overcoming all obstacles in his immediate vicinity and shortly found himself heading out of town toward the border and to freedom. It was easier said than done, however. Reaching a train station under cover of night, he hid in a pile of rags and soon fell asleep. Upon awakening, he decided to jump on a train in total darkness. By the mercy of God he did not break any bones in the jump. Alone, weary, and hungry, he recounts where he found the strength to move on.

"The elation and the excitement of the previous night had burnt away, and a chilling reaction followed. I was very hungry, for I had eaten only a bar of chocolate and had no dinner before starting, and chocolate, though it sustains, does not satisfy. I had scarcely slept, but my heart beat so fiercely within me and I was so nervous and perplexed about the future that I could not rest. I thought of all the chances that lay against me; I dreaded and detested more than words can express the prospect of being caught and dragged back to Pretoria. I found no comfort in any of the philosophical ideas which some men parade in their hours of ease and strength and safety. They seemed only fair-weather friends. I realized with awful force that no exercise of my own feeble wit and strength could save me from my enemies, and that without the assistance of that High Power which interferes in the eternal sequence of causes and effects more often than we are always prone to admit, I could never succeed. I prayed long and earnestly for help and guidance. My prayer, as it seems to me, was swiftly and wonderfully answered."

The mighty hand of God helped him in a most wonderful way. Providentially led by God, he found himself approaching a settlement of coal miners. It was between two and three o'clock in the morning. The danger lay in the fact that if the coal miners were Boers, he would be turned over to the authorities. What to do! After considerable time in deliberation he commended himself to God and decided to approach a small house and take a chance.

The most amazing fact is that of all the houses in the settlement, the one he approached was occupied by a British man who was managing the coal mines. The man, Mr. John Howard, was the manager of the Transvaal Collieries and was a naturalized burgher, a well-to-do member of the middle class. He said to Churchill, "Thank God you have come here! It is the only house for twenty miles where you would not have been handed over. The police were here this morning looking for you. The whole countryside is looking for you. There is a 25-pound reward for your apprehension—dead or alive. No one has ever escaped from Pretoria, and the Boers are fuming mad."

Churchill, by the providential aid of Mr. Howard, was able to hide on a train bound for the border, and he made it to freedom. Meanwhile, reports were circulated that he had been captured, and some reports even said killed.

When Churchill arrived in England, he became instantly popular. Everyone wanted to meet the hero who escaped from prison in Pretoria. Thus, Churchill's capture (and what he thought was the end of a glorious opportunity of becoming a great military leader) was turned by the mighty hand of God into a blessing.

Churchill later confided that it was his escape and the ensuing popularity that opened the doors to political advancement. Had Churchill been captured after his daring escape, he most likely would have been shot as an example. The British would have lost a great future leader, and it is not too far-fetched to say that without Churchill, Hitler may have succeeded in invading England. Moreover, had England fallen, the German war machine would have more than likely come to America. America was unprepared for war on such short notice, and thousands of lives would have been lost—in the same way that multitudes of lives were lost throughout Europe wherever the German army invaded.

God's mighty hand moves among people and nations. Churchill was a gift of God to freedom-loving people for all time. Oh, give thanks unto the Lord.

"God moves in a mysterious way His wonders to perform; He plants His footsteps in the sea, And rides upon the storm." William Cowper, 1774

"Then Mordecai commanded to answer Esther, Think not with thyself that thou shalt escape in the king's house, more than all the Jews. For if thou altogether holdest thy peace at this time, then shall there enlargement and deliverance arise to the Jews from another place; but thou and thy father's house shall be destroyed. And who knoweth whether thou art come to the kingdom for such a time as this?" (Esther 4:13-14).

"WHATSOEVER A MAN SOWETH" 1897 A.D.

The year was 1897. Dressed in the finest fashion of the day, driving an immaculate carriage with a well-trained horse, on an old muddy, bumpy, rural dirt road came the opportunity to fulfill the Biblical admonition given by Christ 1800 years earlier, *"Whatsoever a man soweth, that shall he also reap" (Galatians 6:7).*

"I say there, stranger, it appears you have gotten yourself stuck in a bad way." Sixteen-year-old Alex leaned over the stone wall viewing the perplexed face of this distinguished visitor. "Yes, lad, I am in a great hurry to arrive at Darvel where I'm scheduled to deliver a speech near the town square. I am private secretary to the Duke of Marlborough, my grandfather. My name is Lord Randolph Churchill. Can you be of any assistance?"

"Oh, yes, sir! I will hurry back with Father's team of draft horses and pull you right out, and you'll be on your way quick as a wink."

Alex, true to his word, brought the horses and the tackle necessary to accomplish the tasks at hand. As Alex was about the job, Lord Randolph was amazed how willing the lad was to get himself all muddy on his account. After the carriage was pulled out Lord Randolph offered to pay the boy for his service, when Alex said,

"Thank you, sir, but it was the least that I could do. I find it a privilege to help you. I never met a Lord like you before, and I shan't forget this meeting all my days."

"What do you plan for your life, lad, for you seem very bright," asked Lord Randolph.

"I'd like to be a doctor, but I doubt that it will happen since my family is too poor to spend for my further education."

"Then I will help you become a doctor," said Lord Randolph.

Alex stood in disbelief, gratefully smiled, and blessed his benefactor. As he bade him farewell he silently doubted his promise.

As it so happened, Lord Randolph kept his promise to the boy, and Alex was enrolled in medical school. Alex progressed quickly in his studies, specializing in the study of bacteriology at St. Mary's Hospital at the University of London.

By 1928 this boy, now forty-seven years old, was known as Doctor Alexander Fleming, the discoverer of the germ-killing power of green mold, *Penicillium notatum.* He accidently discovered this mold when he saw a bit of it growing in a culture plate in his laboratory. He observed that mold had destroyed bacteria around it. From this observation and a bit more experiments, Dr. Fleming was able to purify the substance, putting it in a usable form in which the life-saving antibiotic, penicillin, was first used.

The discovery and development of penicillin opened a new era for medicine, and World War II provided an opportune field for the drug to be used.

Nearly fifty years after the young boy Alex helped Lord Randolph out of the miry mud rut, Alex once again indirectly helped Lord Randolph, the nation of England, and perhaps the free world in a deep, profound way. Winston Churchill was lying dangerously close to death due to pneumonia. He had become ill while attending a wartime conference, at the height of the conflict against Hitler. England and the world desperately needed his leadership. Churchill—the strength of England—lay dying and helpless to get out of the miry rut of sickness. Churchill's personal physician was called in, and he immediately injected Churchill with the new wonder drug called penicillin. Needless to say Churchill recovered and lived long and well for ninety-one years—ironically outliving by ten years the younger Dr. Alexander Fleming.

Little did Winston Churchill fully realize that the Scottish farm boy, Alex Fleming, who helped pull his father, Lord Randolph Churchill, out of the mud ditch nearly a century earlier, would be the same boy who would someday save his own life.

"And I said, This is my infirmity: but I will remember the years of the right hand of the most High. I will remember the works of the

LORD: surely I will remember thy wonders of old. I will meditate also of all thy work, and talk of thy doings...Who is so great a God as our God? Thou art the God that doest wonders..." (Psalm 77:10-14).

THE BOXER REBELLION 1900 A.D.

In the summer of 1900, members of a secret society no more official than a gang of hoodlums roamed northeastern China in bands, killing Europeans and Americans and destroying buildings owned by foreigners. They called themselves "I-ho ch'uan," or "Righteous and Harmonious Fists." They practiced boxing skills that they believed made them impervious to bullets. To Westerners they became known as the Boxers, and their uprising was called the Boxer Rebellion.

Many of the Boxers were peasants or rural drifters from northern China who were provoked by the growing influence of Westerners who had systematically undermined the economy and sovereignty of China to benefit their commercial and imperialistic ambitions. Westerners were responsible for the establishment, in the early 1800's, of an opium cartel used to offset a trade imbalance that was draining their respective national coffers of silver specie.

In China's weakened and vulnerable state, as a nation alienated from God, pleas by her statesman issued to the western factions to abstain from drug trafficking were ignored.

The Christian missionary organizations, much to their detriment had closely aligned their interest with those of the opportunistic business community, living in the same compounds and demanding concessions and monetary retributions in treaty negotiations. From the Chinese perspective there was little difference between the actions and attitudes of the Christian missionaries and those of the business community.

This lack of discernment displayed on the part of the Christian organizations, placed the missionaries in the indefensible position as the objects of an indiscriminate and vehement vendetta by the Boxers, which had become organized in 1898.

In the same year the Chinese government, then ruled by the Ch'ing Dynasty, secretly allied with the Boxers to oppose such outsiders as Christian missionaries and European businessmen. The Boxers failed to completely drive foreigners out of China, but they set the stage for the successful Chinese revolutionary movement of the early 20th century.

Foreigners had entered China during an era of imperialism. In the late 1800s, Great Britain and other European nations, the United States, Russia, and Japan, scrambled for spheres of influence there. In some cases they seized Chinese territories, but usually they sought only the riches of trade and commercial enterprise. At the same time, Roman Catholic and Protestant missionaries labored to convert the Chinese to Christianity. These outsiders were resented and feared by the Chinese, who saw Western religion and business practices as a threat to their traditional ways. It did not help the true Christians, desirous of preaching the purity of the Bible, when the "pseudo" Christian missionaries came to plunder the Chinese in the guise of Christianity. The Chinese lumped all missionaries in the same category. This was Satan's way of mixing "wheat with tares."

By May of 1900, Boxers were wandering the countryside and attacking Western missionaries and Chinese converts to Christianity. In June, an expeditionary force, made up of Russian, British, German, French, American, and Japanese troops, was organized to proceed to Peking (now Beijing), put down the rebellion, and protect Western nationals.

The Chinese dowager, (a dowager was a widow of a king or royal official who takes control of the kingdom at the death of the royal offical) Empress Tz'u-hsi, the aunt of Emperor Kuang-hsu, ordered her troops to block the advance of this expedition. The foreign invasion was turned back. Meanwhile, Boxers were rampaging in Peking, burning down churches and the houses of Westerners, and killing Chinese Christians. "Death to the foreigners" was their bloodthirsty battle cry. Like many other missionaries in the field, Chauncey Goodrich, a Congregational missionary, gathered his family and fled to the missionary compound in Peking. Chinese servants of the Goodrich family who went into the compound with them said that Boxer revolutionists were afraid to attack this particular mission compound, because of a prevalent belief among them that "shen"(the Christian God) was on the protective side of the missionaries and would appear to defend them from attacks. Missionary Goodrich, during his flight to safety, was praying for the Lord to direct his steps to find a safe haven for he and his family. Little did he realize, at the time, how his steps were guided to one of the only missionary compounds in the city that was left alone by the Boxers.

From June 20 to August 14, only government soldiers and marines were allowed on the Peking wall to keep lookout for enemy movements outside the city walls. But once the missionaries were no longer seen fleeing to safety from within the walls and running to the city for safety, the guards quit their defensive positions. Now the Boxers' attacks increased. It was during an attack by a superior force that the defenders noticed how strangely the boxers were behaving. With more than adequate forces, they had fought their way to within seconds of the defense wall. Then they abruptly halted and began to point upward.

The whole attacking force, seemingly filled with consternation, suddenly turned and fled in terror. Some were captured, and when asked why they were running, replied, "We saw the walls suddenly swarming with white man's angels all dressed in white. Everyone began shouting that the 'shen' (the Christian God) had come down to fight for the foreigners and our cause was lost."

In response to the Boxer Rebellion, the allied foreign governments increased their numbers and sent some 19,000 soldiers to Peking, capturing the city on August 14, 1900. The invaders looted the city and routed the Boxers, while Empress Tz'u-hsi and her court fled to the north. By the time the rebellion ended, at least 250 foreigners, many which were missionaries had been killed. It took a year for the parties of the conflict to agree on a settlement, which was entitled the Peace of Peking. This protocol, which was signed in September 1901, was dictated by the Western powers and Japan in such a way as to humiliate

China. Heavy fines were levied against the Chinese government, and existing commercial treaties were amended in favor of the Western powers. The foreign coastal defenses were dismantled.

The history of revolutions is a bloody mess where innocent people, of all classes, needlessly lose their lives. Despite the loss of life there are always those who survive the holocaust of terrorism and escape to give glory to God in the midst of trouble. Missionary Goodrich and his family was one such family. After the city of Peking was liberated, missionary Goodrich was reminded of various passages in the Bible giving witness to the watchfulness of God's mighty hand of protection over His own, who have further work to do while here on earth for the kingdom of God.

" *The Steps of a good man are ordered of the Lord, and he delighteth in his way. Though he fall, he shall not be utterly cast down; for the Lord upholdeth him with His hand* " *(Psalm 37:23).*

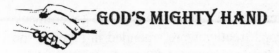

GIVE AND IT SHALL BE GIVEN UNTO YOU 1907 A.D.

My full name is Joseph Gillott Wheat, but around the old homestead my family just called me Josie. The story I am about to tell you happened many years ago but to my mind, now old and worn with years, it still seems like yesterday. I remember so well when Father, a preacher, went on a circuit riding mission just before the corn was coming to head, in the fall of 1907. It was fixing to be an early, cold winter. We were often left poor and penniless, having to trust in the Lord for our daily provisions, with Father gone.

Mother clung to Father's neck, as he was fixing to saddle up and told him about the fears she had with his leaving her and the children. Tears came slowly into his eyes and then his heart broke. He sank to his knees, struggling to trust in God to care for his children. Father said, "Let us pray," first brokenly, asking God if he should go, then triumphantly asking God with a ringing voice, "Should I go?" His answer already came. Then Father talked to God and reasoned with Him, "Now, Father, I am obeying and I am Your child; we are all Your children. You have promised to take care of Your children if they love and obey you. Now we must have better care; we will have faith and put all our trust in You and Your promises. We will expect You to keep Your word and take care of us."

Father kissed us goodbye, gave Mother all the money he had (90¢ in script), held Mother close. I heard him say, "Never fear, little woman, only trust Him." Father rose in the stirrup over his saddle bags; the mighty horse he rode settled himself to the massive load he knew so well. "God, let Father lose none of that wonderful strength." Years of sturdy frontier logging life and years of blacksmithing had given him a marvelous build of nearly 300 pounds. With his sinuous power, no backwoods bully had ever dared to rouse his anger more than once.

Father went, and Mother proudly watched him to the turn in the road. Father did not look back. As I remember him now, I believe it must have been because he could not have seen Mother, had he tried, because he was nearsighted. Father seemed to have inspired Mother with new light and courage for her face beamed. I came to her and said, "Mother, I'll soon take care of you." She placed her hand gently on my shoulder and said, "Josie, the Lord will take care of us."

Then came hard days. Mother knit and spun and sewed. Her work, at best, would earn no more than 30¢ a day and often not even that at the crossroads store, a half mile away. Sometimes we owed the storekeeper, and a few times he was cross to me. Other times he asked me if Mother was well and if we had plenty. I told him once that Mother trusted God, and I guessed God would help us. He said something about the time coming when no one else would.

When I told Mother, she looked gray and sick once more, as I had seen her other times before Father came home. I said, "Mother, will God forget us?" She clasped me in her arms and rocked me silently in her low chair and cried softly. Then I couldn't stand it any longer. I slipped down and took her head in my arms and whispered as Father did, "Never fear, little woman, only trust Him." Mother turned and kissed me and dried her tears. Then I went out into the woods and made a dead fall over a rabbit run. I began to catch some rabbits, and Mother tanned the skins and made Georgie and me warm caps and fur-lined mittens covered with old sackcloth. We gathered sticks and tied them in bundles for the winter which was coming. Days passed and sometimes we had milk and meal mush; other times only meal mush and salt. Never any butter or coffee. Some days I thought I must perish for a taste of sugar, and I did drop my wet mittens on the counter at the store where sugar had been spilt. Then I went out in the cold to save each grain and eat it. Then my heart smote me, and I went inside and dropped my sticky mitten on the sugar again. This time I saved it all and took it home to Mother and

Georgie. When I gave Mother the 23¢ which the knitting brought, she looked sadly at it, for it was less than usual. She had been almost ill that week, only able to work part of Friday and Saturday, and only 23¢ for both days. When I showed her the sugar, she refused it and made Georgie eat it. She didn't ask me how I got it, but her face looked hard, and I was afraid to tell. Years after, she told me she was afraid to ask me for fear she would learn something wrong, and she would have to refuse the sugar for Georgie, who cried for it as soon as he saw it.

That Sunday was the saddest Sabbath of our lives. God seemed to have forgotten us, and Mother talked to herself. But I couldn't hear what she said, and something in her eyes made me afraid to try to comfort her. Then came the last test for Mother, the test that Elijah put to the widow: would she share her last measure of meal and cruse of oil? Two men drove up to the side of the road in front of our house and stopped. One of them came in and knocked. Mother had been quiet for a long half hour and hadn't seen them nor heard them drive up. I had been standing by the window and watching, first Mother and then the road; Mother just seemed to be waiting for something. When the knock came, she stood and went to the door and opened it. The man spoke pleasantly and asked, "May we camp here by you tonight and secure supper for ourselves with you?" Mother turned silently to the cupboard closet and looked into the meal chest. She came out and very quietly said, "Yes, you may."

The man thanked her and turned toward the wagon, looked back, and then went to the wagon and spoke to his companion. Mother said, "Josie, take this 23¢ and go buy a quart of milk, a pint of molasses, and the rest in meal at the store." I took the money and started, but the man who came to the house saw me, and before I was across the back lot he called to me. I waited and answered. He came up and questioned me as to where I was going and what I was going to do. Then he asked me where my father was and what he was doing. When I had told him, he took me by the hand and led me wondering out to the wagon. I was a little excited, but not afraid. When we came to the wagon, the man said to his companion, "Unhitch and get ready to unload. This is the place." After a little while, we sat at supper. The men had allowed me to finish my errands while they cared for their team. In my excitement, I had not told Mother what they had said to me. She busied herself at getting supper, and I examined the wagon. It was a great, high spreading rack used in the heavy hauling trucks so common in early days in the timber country. The rack seemed just full of sacks and barrels, boxes and bundles, and apples. I could smell apples and syrup. Oh, how hungry I was for some to eat.

But as I said, we sat at supper finally, and Mother asked a silent blessing on our humble meal of corn dodgers with molasses and mush with milk. The men ate heartily and seemed to be excited over something. Sometimes they would nod at each other, and sometimes I could not understand what they meant by some of the strange remarks they made to each other. Mother looked inquiringly at them at times, but she was too gently reared in the old Pennsylvania customs to show her curiosity. When supper was finished, the man who had talked with me pushed back his chair and drew a long sigh of contentment. Then he said, "I have never had a happier hour in my life, nor eaten a better meal. And now, if you will listen, I want to tell you a story."

"A few days ago, this gentleman, Mr. Banes, who is a farmer near the town of York, came into my big general store and said to me, 'Mr. Kellogg, this has been a wonderfully prosperous year for me, and I feel very thankful. I am not a Christian, but I feel like I would willingly do something for the Lord's poor.' I thought a moment and then replied to him that it was very strange that I should have been thinking the same thing for several days. In a very short time we agreed to make up a load of goods and start out with farmer Banes' big wagon and team to find the place. The next day farmer Banes came in with his great rack wagon half-filled with turnips, cabbage, potatoes, apples, flour, meal, butter, cheese, sorghum, and other good things from the farm. Oh, I must not forget the fine fall pig that weighed 75 pounds dressed. I began to fill the space he had left us in the wagon with tea, coffee, sugar, ham, bacon, and other groceries. Then I thought of the winter, and we piled in some warm blankets and shoes and caps and mittens. My wife came in and picked out some fine warm woolen cloth, some needles, thread, buttons, and lots of other things that women need and like. My wife just runs all the buying of those things for my store. Well, we got filled up by noon, ate dinner at my house, and started. We have traveled three days and have met many people, but we felt no desire to stop or ask questions. We came to many back roads but just let the team take their heads when we didn't feel like choosing. This afternoon, farmer Banes said, 'I think we must be nearly to the place where we can find the Lord's poor.' We've come over sixty miles by now, and I cannot tell you how strangely happy it made me feel when we spoke and talked of it, but we each said it was better than being a boy once more. Then when we came to your house, the horses just looked up and neighed. I said, 'Let's stop,' and I came in. I questioned your boy before he went to the store, and we decided to take our supper with you all of what you yourself could furnish. We've made up our minds that if there are any poor that belong to the Lord, you must be the ones. And so, if you will allow us to, we will begin to unload at once so we may start home bright and early in the morning."

He rose at once, and as he turned away, I thought I saw a tear drop from his cheek. Mother had been crying silently for several minutes, but she did not speak. Her nature was very pensive and slow to speak. I came to her and clasped my arms about her neck. She seemed to shine through her tears, and she hugged me close and murmured, "God has not forgotten us, Josie, my boy." This made me cry and Mother led me to her room and left me sobbing on her iron bed. I suppose she helped the men and told them where to put things. Next morning, what a breakfast! I believe I shall never forget it, and the men started away early. I ran before their team clear beyond the turn in the road and showed them where we had seen Father last. One of the men suddenly asked me, what my name was. I said, "Joseph Gillott Wheat."

"What? Are you a Wheat? Is Elder Wheat your father?"

"Yes," I shouted, "Do you know him?"

They replied as glad as I, "Certainly no one can forget him, but we never dreamed he was not well cared for. He preached at Lancaster many weeks ago, and he prayed that those with plenty might remember the Lord's poor about them. Go home and tell your Mother, lad, and tell her we did not ask her name because it might hurt her to tell us who she was." Farmer Banes threw a dollar, a whole big dollar, at my feet and said, almost cross, "Run now, do as you are told." Then they drove away, but at the turn I looked back at them once more and they were talking earnestly and making gestures. I was sure I knew what they were talking about, but I ran home filled with joy that made my feet seem just like wings beating the air. Mother caught me in her arms and sat in her low rocker. She kissed me silently many times. At last she asked me, "Will you be like your father, Josie boy?" I think I promised her; I can't remember now, but of course I must have. Then Mother showed me what they had brought. There were many things that the storekeeper, Mr. Kellogg had not even mentioned. Then in a few days Father came; he was seldom away more than 70 or 80 days. Mother showed Father all that was in the house. He suppressed a word or choked, "Praise God," every moment. When Mother stopped, Father stepped to the middle of the floor just where he had knelt before and said, "Let us pray." I have heard prayers, but just to hear one talk with God so that you could hear the answer right along just like it was speaking back is different. I don't know what we did then, but it seems to me that Father let Georgie and me go out to bring in his saddle bags and then play with old Dobbin. I know when I came in after awhile, Father held little Mother in his great arms and was smoothing her hair away from her temples and forehead. He told me, "Josie, you have a wonderful mother." I looked at her and tears were in her eyes. I told father that Mother was God's own little girl. We never starved or were cold at home anymore. I never knew hunger after that until I went into World War I overseas.

"Trust in the Lord with all thine heart, and lean unto thine

own understanding. In all thy ways acknowledge Him, and He shall direct thy paths." (Proverbs 3:5,6).

THE GREAT WAR GOD KNEW ABOUT
1914-1918 A.D.

As an historian, I find it interesting to note that 99 percent of historical writers do an excellent job in researching the events and recording facts, but miss the most obvious. Since so many are not born-again Christians their perspective is only an earthly view and not a heavenly view.

The Bible calls the unbeliever a "natural man," and as a "natural man" he is spiritually blinded. As it says in I Corinthians 2:14, "But the natural man receiveth not the things of the Spirit of God: for they are foolishness unto him: neither can he know them, because they are spiritually discerned." These historians not only do not understand the simplicity of salvation, but neglect to see the real causes behind world events. As spiritually blinded historical writers, how can they write and record the mind of God in history?

Great cataclysmic events such as World War I and World War II, that claim the lives of millions of people, actually have eternal purposes. Yes, God is involved in war, He always has been, and He will continue to be until the final end of what we call time, the end of the age, when He will establish a new heaven and a new earth. Then war will be only a memory.

In this story and the next, I will not attempt to rewrite what has already been told and written on the "Great War," World War I, but I will reveal one of the most significant historical events in recent history. In all my hours of study on World War I, I saw no mention of this story except by Christian writers. Yet this single event set in motion the greatest fulfillment of Biblical prophecy since 70 A.D. Only the mighty hand of God could bring about circumstances in such a way to accomplish His divine will and to further fulfill prophecy.

Jesus gathered His disciples around Him on His final ascent to Jerusalem. While overlooking the city, wiping tears from His eyes, He spoke an amazing prophetic word to His disciples. He said that not one stone of the Jewish Temple would be left standing within their generation. This was too much for the disciples to believe. The Temple that Solomon and Herod the Great rebuilt with huge sums of money between 10 and 20 B.C., demolished? How could this event possibly come to pass? Yet it did in 70 A.D.

The Great Jewish Revolt against Rome in 66 A.D. and the Roman siege of Jerusalem constitute two of the most important and horrifying events in Jewish history. Unfortunately, they are sparsely recorded. Tacitus left a long account of the war, but only fragments survive. Rabbinic accounts are made up of anecdotes with no clear historical context, some of sheer legend. Virtually our only authority on the siege of Jerusalem is Josephus, 37-100 A.D., and he is not completely reliable.

Here is the story, piecing the events as best as ancient recorded history allows. After the massacre of the garrison in Jerusalem, the emperor appointed a governor in Syria. This provincial governor, named Cestius Gallus, assembled a large force in Acre, a seaport in northwestern Israel, and marched on the city of Jerusalem. When he reached the outskirts, he was dismayed by the strength of the Jewish resistance and ordered a retreat, which turned into a rout.

Rome took charge and reacted with enormous force, no fewer than four legions. The fifth, tenth, twelfth, and fifteenth legions were concentrated on Judea, and one of the Empire's most experienced generals, Titus Flavius Vespasian, was given the command. He took his time, leaving Jerusalem temporarily open until he cleared the land of Jewish zealots, who posed a threat. He then secured his communications, reduced most of the smaller Jewish fortresses, and settled his army in the countryside.

During this window of time the Christians who had "eyes to see and ears to hear" remembered the Master's words about the time the Temple would be destroyed. They hastily fled the city of

Jerusalem in time to save their lives for further service for the Lord in other parts of Israel. In 69 A.D., Vespasian was proclaimed emperor, and at the end of the year he left for Rome, leaving his eldest son, twenty-nine-year-old Titus, in charge of the final campaign, the siege and capture of Jerusalem, which lasted from April to September 70 A.D.

Titus had 60,000 men and the latest siege capabilities. He could rely on starvation and divisions among the Jews to do their work. The defenders had about 25,000 fighters, split into groups: the Zealots, under Eleazar ben Simon, held the Antonia and the Temple; the extremist Simeon ben Giora and his Sicarii ran the upper city; and there were Idumeans and other partisans under John of Giscala. The mass of the citizens and refugees were the helpless prisoners of these militants.

Josephus described the final stages of the siege in horrifying detail. The Romans had to fight all the way. They stormed the Antonia, then took the Temple, which was burned, fulfilling Jesus' prophecy to the letter: "Not one stone would be left standing." This was a remarkable feat especially considering that some of the stones were 94 feet long, 10 feet high, and 13 feet wide. The 162 solid marble columns that adorned the various porches were 52 feet high. The whole temple complex was a thirty-two-acre fortress with a temple jetting up beyond the walls that protected Jerusalem from foreign invasion.

The Temple protruded beyond the city's buildings much like the Empire State Building in New York City in the 1950s. The Temple was the highest building in Israel and stood majestically, glistening in the sun as pure gold adorned the various facades. As the Temple was being destroyed, the Romans, like a pack of wolves, headed for Herod's citadel.

Within a month the Jews were sold as slaves, or massacred, or saved to die in the arenas of Caesarea, Antioch, and Rome. Simeon ben Giora was captured alive, taken to Rome for Titus' triumphal celebration, then executed in the Forum. Titus' arch still stands there; the Temple Menorah he captured was carved on its stone. He also preserved, in his palace, the curtain which screened the Holy Ark of the Covenant, and a copy of the scriptures. If only it had survived!

The Jews for all practical purposes were nationless, a people without a home. They wandered throughout the earth, seeking a place to call home, and in time re-established themselves in various parts of the then known world.

The Jewish leaders who, by and large, rejected Christ as their Messiah and cried, "Let His blood be on us and our children," Matthew 27:25, sealed their fate and fulfilled prophecy. Jesus, on the road to Calvary, warned them of their lamentable future. The Bible states:

" And there followed him a great company of people, and of women, which also bewailed and lamented him. But Jesus turning unto them said, Daughters of Jerusalem, weep not for me, but weep for yourselves, and for your children. For, behold, the days are coming, in the which they shall say, Blessed are the barren, and the wombs that never bare, and the paps which never gave suck" (Luke 23:27-29).

"And I will make Jerusalem heaps, and a den of dragons; and I will make the cities of Judah desolate, without an inhabitant. Who is the wise man, that may understand this? and who is he to whom the mouth of the LORD hath spoken, that he may declare it, for what the land perisheth and is burned up like a wilderness, that none passeth through? And the LORD saith, Because they have forsaken my law which I set before them, and have not obeyed my voice, neither walked therein; But have walked after the imagination of their own heart, and after Baalim, which their fathers taught them: Therefore thus saith the LORD of hosts, the God of Israel; Behold, I will feed them, even this people, with wormwood, and give them water of gall to drink. I will scatter them also among the heathen, whom neither they nor their fathers have known: and I will send a sword after them, till I have consumed them" (Jeremiah 9:11-16).

PART 2

In the configuration, complications, and governmental intrigues of World War I, God's mighty hand was beginning to lead His people, the Jews, home. How this was accomplished is the beauty of the wonder and power of God.

The battle in Gallipoli, Turkey, in January 1916, was a costly failure for the British and French forces. The fiasco badly stained the reputations of Sir Winston Churchill and field marshal Herbert Horatio Kitchener. Despite its overall failure, however, the Gallipoli campaign weakened the Turks enough to facilitate the British seizure of Palestine in 1917.

Troops were withdrawn from Turkey and many were deployed to Egypt to protect the Suez Canal, which was threatened by Turkey. A part of these troops later formed a British and Arab force under General Edmund Allenby that captured Jerusalem. Thus, although the "Gallipoli Campaign" was a major loss for the British, it was a part of God's plan to arrange for His people the Jews to return home to Israel.

Now England was in control of Palestine, and the next chain of events leading to England's deeding the land of Israel back to the dispersed Jews was another wondrous providence of God.

Chaim Weizmann, a Russian Jew, was born with a passion for his Jewish people, and he did all he could to stir up Zionism among the Jews in Germany while attending school there, and throughout as much of Europe as possible. During the late nineteenth century, Zionism swept Europe affecting Jew and Gentile alike. It seemed as if the Jews were recognizing the need for their identity as a nation. However, their dilemma was "how can you have a nation without a nation?"

Along with the seeds of Zionism, the seeds of anti-Zionism were prevalent. This spirit of despising the Jews as a despicable race would come to a head in Nazi Germany in the not too distant future. Perhaps Dr. Weizmann felt an impending doom for his own people. Through many trials and tribulations he obtained an education and managed to be accepted into the Berlin Polytechnic

Institute, one of the three best science schools in Europe.

After completing his course of study, Chaim continued his education in Switzerland, where he obtained his doctorate in chemistry at Freiburg in 1899. Shortly afterward he was providentially led to teach biochemistry at Manchester University in England. England became his home, and he found many English in sympathy with Zionism. The Lord gave him key friends who, by His mighty hand, would later change the course of history, as you will see.

Just prior to the outbreak of World War I, Dr. Weizmann made friends with a man named C.P. Scott, the powerful editor of the paper *Manchester Guardian.*

He was therefore able to use the newspaper as his platform for spreading the message of Zionism, and the Lord touched the hearts of many Gentiles who had been ignorant of the conditions for Jews in Europe.

Within a matter of time the key players were in place to side with Dr. Weizmann and to help him unify the Jewish State of Israel. Those key players were Author Balfour, Sir Winston Churchill, and Lloyd George, later Prime Minister of England.

When World War I broke out, England was soon embroiled in the conflict. The might of Germany was great; the military played havoc in the air, seas, and land. They developed the U-boats, submarines that were destroying most of England's ships. Germany became bomb king, and it looked as if there was no stopping that nation in conquering the world.

By 1916, England and France were in a desperate position. The need of armaments was great. Germany had been preparing for war for years while Europe was luxuriously asleep unprepared. As the war escalated England found that one of her greatest needs was to develop greater bombs and to knock out German installations, but how? The English were ignorant of sophisticated military explosives.

The "how" was provided by none other than Dr. Chaim Weizmann, the Russian Jew who studied at Germany's Polytechnic school, a school which taught him the principles of explosives and other war material. Ironically Germany, the very nation that was destroying the world, had nurtured in her school Chaim Weizmann, the man who turned the tide of war.

At the beginning of the war, Lord Kitchener was appointed to the newly formed office Minister of War. Lord Kitchener was very cold and indifferent to the Jews; he saw no need for England to acquire the "God-forsaken land of Palestine." Providentially that all changed when Lord Kitchener was drowned at sea on a military trip to Russia.

As God's mighty hand would direct, the Christian Lloyd George, friend and sympathizer to the Jews, became the Minister of the War Department. He promoted Dr. Weizmann to be the director of the British Admiralty Laboratories (1916-1919). Aware of Dr. Weizmann's knowledge of science, he commissioned him to develop explosives of greater magnitude to use in the cause of peace, bringing an end to the war. (This was the same purpose America had in dropping the atomic bomb on Hiroshima, Japan, on August 6, 1945, to bring an end to World War II.) Dr. Weizmann developed a method for synthesizing acetone, used in explosives manufacturing.

With Dr. Weizmann's development of more powerful explosives, England was allowed for the first time to take the offensive and gain lost territory from the Germans. By 1917, England took back much of the land that had been lost in the early part of the war, to the jubilation of France. Not only was much of Europe gained, but providentially England gained control over Palestine. Dr. Weizmann went to his friend Lloyd George, the now newly appointed Prime Minister of England, and with their mutual friends A.J. Balfour, and Lord Rothschild, they drew up the Balfour Declaration on November 2, 1917.

Because God used a Jew, Dr. Weizmann, to help England in a time of need with explosives, these heads of state were now in a position to grant the request of Dr. Weizmann. The Balfour Declaration would fulfill Dr. Weizmann's desire for his people to return to their beloved land of Israel. An essential portion of the Declaration reads as follows:

"His Majesty's Government view with favour the establishment in Palestine of a national home for the Jewish people, and will use their best endeavours to facilitate the achievement of that object, it being clearly understood that nothing shall be done which may prejudice the civil and religious rights of existing non-Jewish communities in Palestine, or the rights and political status enjoyed by Jews in any other country."

The Balfour Declaration was the key piece in establishing a Jewish nation, for without it the Jewish state could never have been formed. One month after the Balfour Declaration was signed, British General Allenby walked into the Holy City of Jerusalem, the City of David. With tears streaming down his face, he realized, as did Lloyd George, that this was an historical moment of glorious import.

Thanks to Dr. Weizmann and a handful of choice players, the Jews claimed the land just in time. All over the world, nationalism was winning the day. The Allies were besieged by subject peoples demanding that the soon-coming victory and peace should guarantee them territorial rights on the basis of strict numerical head-counting, whether ethnic or racial. Although the Jews had a Biblical and historical claim to nationhood, it was a very old one, and their only appeal was that they were called of God to settle the ancient land of Palestine.

At the time the Declaration was published, there were between 85,000 and 100,000 Jews living in Palestine, out of a total population of 600,000. The general population was made up of Arabs, who were mostly Muslim. There were some Christians living in Palestine at this time. If the Arabs, as a whole, had been properly organized diplomatically during the war, there is not the slightest doubt that the Declaration would never have been issued. Even twelve months later it would have been impossible.

As it was, Dr. Weizmann pushed open the Zionists' brief window of opportunity, fated never to open again. History was changed with the stroke of a pen, a 30-06 rifle, and Dr. Weizmann's synthesizing acetone. Israel was legally back in the land for the first time in 1,875 years. God's mighty hand fulfilled a major piece of the prophetic puzzle. With Israel in the land the stage was set for the second coming of Christ.

"And it shall come to pass in that day, that the Lord shall set his hand again the second time to recover the remnant of his people, which shall be left, from Assyria, and from Egypt, and from Pathros, and from Cush, and from Elam, and from Shinar, and from Hamath, and from the islands of the sea. And he shall set up an ensign for the nations, and shall assemble the outcasts of Israel, and gather together the dispersed of Judah from the four corners of the earth" (Isaiah 11:11-12).

"Glorious things of thee are spoken, Zion, City of our God; He whose word cannot be broken formed thee for His own abode; On the Rock of Ages founded, What can shake thy sure repose? With salvation's walls surrounded, Thou mayst smile at all thy foes."
John Newton, 1725-1807

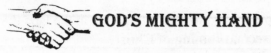

GOD'S MIGHTY HAND

MIRACLE OF THE MARNE 1914 A.D.

At the close of World War I, when an elated King Albert of Brussels made his triumphant reentry into his country, he publicly proclaimed General Foch of France "a military genius." General Foch exclaimed, "No! No! I had nothing to do with it. I have thought, planned, and reflected, but when everything was considered, and I still could not solve the war's problems, I felt myself to be the blind instrument of Providence."When General Foch was made Commander-in-Chief of the French armies on May 15, 1917, the French nation acquired the priceless leadership of a man who consciously sought and received divine guidance. But World War I was already a war of divine miracles before the promotion of General Foch. One of these was the Miracle of the Marne.

"Militarily, what happened on September 3, 1914, was simply incomprehensible," F. Herbert Stead was later to write. "[It was] too mystifying to be called anything other than a miracle."

Never up to that time had any army been better equipped with the military armaments of the day than the fast-moving army of the German Kaiser. Nor had any been more frighteningly successful as it headed toward Paris. The army's relentless progress had been so consistently victorious that the French government had moved from Paris to Bordeaux. That was on September 2. Then, strangely, on September 3 the Germans halted at the Marne. The next day the German columns began moving away in a southeasterly direction. Immediately, the French and British launched offensives which continued until September 10, driving the Kaiser's army back with heavy losses. "Someone has been praying," Lord Fisher, Admiral of the British Fleet, declared to Lord Robertson. "There is no other way of accounting for this miracle."

Sir Oliver Lodge also attributed the miracle of the Marne to supernatural causes. In his book, *The War and After*, he stated: "The Germans overran France and were close to Paris. What turned them back I do not know.... September 3 was a critical day. It was a war against principalities and powers and spiritual wickedness in high places. I must believe in assistance from on high."

Years later, in February 1952, James L. Kraft published an article in *Guideposts* magazine recounting in part how that "assistance from on high" was given. A personal friend of Brigadier General Gunn, Mr. Kraft commanded the Princess Pat Canadian Regiment on the Marne. He had the story directly from the general. Neither man was ready to speculate on what the German troops were seeing that day. That hasn't been recorded. What they do know is that both of them, and the men in the Canadian Princess Pat Regiment, saw a "man on a white horse" riding fearlessly forward through the enemy fire. General Gunn issued the order to "follow the man on the white horse," and the Princess Pat Regiment pressed valiantly forward behind him. Almost immediately, the entire invading German army began moving east. American papers carried the news that evening proclaiming that the German army was on the run, and that the Canadian Princess Pat Regiment was spearheading the pursuit.

What happened to "the man on the white horse"? No one knows. When General Gunn was questioned about it, he replied, "I don't know. He was there all right when we needed him. And then he was gone."

It was the Germans themselves who declared that the turning point of the war came at the Marne. A German monarchist, a member of the Reichstag, and a member of the imperial ruling family-each independently and at different times-made the statement that the war had been lost at the Marne. And it was pointed out that the Kaiser's armies were not defeated there. They had merely retreated.

Whatever the contributing causes of the collapse of the Kaiser's armies at the Marne, the fact remains that not only were the French and British civilians offering up heartfelt prayers that day, so were the officers in command of their armies. General Foch, who became the French commander-in-chief and later chief of all allied armies in France, is but one example of such splendid Christian military leadership. Once, while speaking with Father de Grandmaison of his daring march-to-the-sea in October 1914, Foch said, "How was I able to accomplish what I did? Because God willed it so. I do not know how. We are blind instruments of Providence."

Perhaps one of the best explanations was reported in a London news bulletin quoting Foch's request to one of his chaplains. "Father," he said, "we are to make our supreme effort in arms tomorrow. Do you make a supreme effort in prayer? All my trust is in God." Another time he stated, "It is God who guides everything." And yet again: "As far as I am concerned, when at an historic moment a clear vision is given to a man, and the event proves that this clear vision has determined movements of enormous consequence in an important war, I hold that this clear vision (such as I think I had at the Marne, at the Yscr, on the 26th of March) comes from a Providential influence in the hands of which man is an instrument, and that the triumphal decision is brought from on high by a will superior and divine."

A mysterious man observed on a white horse. Airplanes that aren't really there. Impenetrable shields of protection in times of grave danger. These strange and inexplicable events have brought dramatic changes to the lives they have touched. They are unexplainable-unless one understands the sovereign position God holds by His mighty hands throughout the pages of history. Like a majestic conductor in the symphony of world events, God uses the movements of His outstretched arm to direct each nation's fortune as only He knows best.

"So shall they fear the name of the LORD from the west, and his glory from the rising of the sun. When the enemy shall come in like a flood, the Spirit of the LORD shall lift up a standard against him" (Isaiah 59:19).

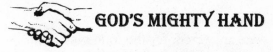 **GOD'S MIGHTY HAND**

VISCOUNT OF MEGIDDO 1917 A.D.

During World War I, the Kaiser had designs on the strategic land of Palestine, but God had other plans for His Holy Land. British General E. H. H. Allenby (1861–1936) was sent with his 60th British Division to secure Palestine. A better choice of a commander could not have been made. General Allenby was a committed Christian and a Bible scholar, often reading passages of Scripture to his soldiers and holding Sunday services. He often confided to his officers his desire to reclaim the Holy Land and see the Jews return to the Promised Land of their fathers. The Lord blessed General Allenby with the desire of his heart.

On December 9, 1917, General Allenby captured Jerusalem. Prior to his assault on the Holy City, he requested that his homeland have three days of prayer for him before he advanced upon the city. On the 9th, as his soldiers approached the city walls, the Arabs dropped their weapons, without firing a shot, and gave up the ancient City of God. With tear-filled eyes, General Allenby decided to enter the city on foot instead of in the customary way—by horse. His reason was that he wanted to reserve that honor for Christ at His Second Coming.

With Jerusalem captured, the Holy Land was taken by England, with one exception: the Turkish garrison at Michmash, Megiddo. Michmash, a small town located on a high, rocky hill overlooking the plains of Megiddo, was heavily fortified by the Turks, and without its fall, Palestine could not be taken from the Turks and Moslems.

In September 1918, General Allenby had his men in position to take the fortress of Michmash, but the Turks' high position gave them every advantage over the British. It appeared that it was going to be a costly battle. As usual, General Allenby devoted himself to private prayer, imploring the Lord to extend

His mighty hand to deliver his men from danger.

Again his prayers were answered, for the following Sunday, while giving a Bible study to his troops on the future battle of Armageddon (which would occur nearby), he researched some texts on the area and discovered that the fortifications at Michmash were once the scene of a battle between Jonathan and his armor-bearer and the Philistines.

General Allenby gathered his officers to share with them his discovery and to study the account in more detail in hopes of finding some information they could use in preparation for their impending battle. They studied the entire account in the 13th and 14th chapters of I Samuel and saw how Jonathan and his armor-bearer found a method of approaching the Philistine stronghold and taking it by surprise. The Scriptures told of a crag between two rocks, "Bozez" and "Seneh," that allowed Jonathan and his assistant to climb up on all fours under cover of night. When they reached the top and attacked, the Philistines panicked, believing that the entire Israelite army was there. In their terror and confusion, they attacked each other in the darkness, and without the ability to see clearly, killed one another. When daylight came, the Philistines were practically all dead, with the remaining ones fleeing. Jonathan and his armor-bearer became heroes among their fellow soldiers. God's mighty hand prevailed and gave Israel a great victory.

General Allenby, inspired by this passage, decided to imitate Jonathan of old and approached the Turks from the same pass. Committing himself and his men to the Lord, he began the battle. The Lord crowned them with success, and they completely routed the Turks and gained the fortress of Michmash—and shortly thereafter, the entire Holy Land. For his God-blessed service to England, General Allenby was honored with yet another title: "The Viscount of Megiddo."

One of the wonders of this story is how God's Word is so applicable over so many years. General Allenby was crowned with the same success that Jonathan had by using the same inspired strategy Jonathan had used.

Remember, God's Word is alive and will never become outdated. Study parts of Psalm 119 and see how General Allenby found the truth of the Word inspirational and useful in his battle with the Turks.

Psalm 119

v. 18: "*Open thou mine eyes, that I may behold wondrous things out of thy law.*"

v. 24: "*Thy testimonies also are my delight and my counselors.*"

v. 43: "*And take not the word of truth utterly out of my mouth; for I have hoped in thy judgments.*"

v. 49–50: "*Remember the word unto thy servant, upon which thou hast caused me to hope. This is my comfort in my affliction: for thy word hath quickened me.*"

v. 89–96: "*Forever, O LORD, thy word is settled in heaven. Thy faithfulness is unto all generations: thou hast established the earth, and it abideth. They continue this day according to thine ordinances: for all are thy servants. Unless thy law had been my delight, I should then have perished in mine affliction. I will never forget thy precepts: for with them thou hast quickened me. I am thine, save me; for I have sought thy precepts. The wicked have waited for me to destroy me: but I will consider thy testimonies. I have seen an end of all perfection: but thy commandment is exceeding broad.*" 1

v.105: "*Thy word is a lamp unto my feet, and a light unto my path.*"

v.110–112: "*The wicked have laid a snare for me: yet I erred not from thy precepts. Thy testimonies have I taken as an heritage for ever: for they are the rejoicing of my heart. I have inclined mine heart to perform thy statutes always, even unto the end.*"

v.130: "*The entrance of thy words giveth light; it giveth understanding unto the simple.*"

v.133: "*Order my steps in thy word.*"

The Bible stands like a rock undaunted 'Mid the

raging storms of time;

Its pages burn with the truth eternal, And they glow with a light sublime.

The Bible stands tho' the hills may tumble, It will firmly stand when the earth shall crumble;

I will plant my feet on its firm foundation, For the Bible stands.

Haldor Lillenas (1885–1959)

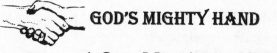 **GOD'S MIGHTY HAND**

A One–Man Army 1919 A.D.

Alvin York was born in 1887, in Pall Mall, Tennessee, a hamlet on the Cumberland Plateau in the isolated country along the Wolf River. Alvin's mother was a God-fearing woman who tried the best she could to raise her children to follow the ways of God's Son, Jesus Christ. Alvin was not interested in that "old-fashioned religion" of his mother. After the death of his father William, twenty-four-year-old Alvin went "hog wild" and began to live a Godless, wild, reckless life. He became a hard-drinking, gambling, cursing, and fighting Tennessee "redneck." Being rough in character was not unusual in those days and for those parts of the country. Life in those early days in Tennessee was hard. People lived on what they grew and hunted. Alvin soon developed a reputation as one of the best shots in all of Tennessee, winning shooting competitions for miles around.

Try as he could to run from Christ, the prayers of his Godly mother eventually hounded him to his knees. Some of his old drinking buddies said, "He was struck by lightning, which made him go crazy, 'cause he went and found religion.'" Lightning or not, Alvin York did find that "good, old-time religion." He was saved on January 1, 1915. Fortunately he had enough schooling to be able to read the Good Book, (the Bible) and very soon developed into a strong believer. The transformation was miraculous. He began to teach the Bible to children in the church and became a lay preacher and elder in the church under his beloved pastor Rosier Pile. The church was a small denomination called Church of Christ in the Christian Union.

Alvin York's peaceful existence in the hills of Tennessee was about to come to an end for a while. God had other plans for Alvin. They were plans that would change him from an obscure "nobody" to a national hero. The Bible says in I Corinthians 1:27: *"But God hath chosen the foolish things of the world to confound the wise; and God hath chosen the weak things of the world to confound the things which are mighty."*

On June 28, 1914, Archduke Francis Ferdinand of Austria-Hungary was assassinated. Many historians view this event as the beginning of World War I. However, the United States did not become involved in the war until April 6, 1917. President Woodrow Wilson instituted the draft, and it was not long before a draft notice reached the peaceful valley where Alvin was working and ministering.

As a Christian, Alvin was shocked and dismayed at the thought of going off, as he said, "to kill people with whoed I's got no feud with." In his simple way he did not understand such things as war and could not picture areas of the world such as Europe—a long way from Tennessee. His deep religious faith led him to seek exemption as a conscientious objector, but his appeals were denied.

He said of these dark days of his life, "Life's tol'ably queer. You think you've got a grip on it. Then you open your hands and you find out there's nothing in them. It doesn't go in straight lines like bees to their hives or quail from the covey. It sort of circles like foxes and goes back again to where it began."

After searching his soul and committing his ways to the Lord, he saw no choice but to report to Camp Gordon, Georgia, on November 14, 1917, where he was placed into the 82nd, the "All-American Rainbow Army Division." During basic training Alvin was given a 1903 Springfield 30-06 rifle and told to lie down on the firing line. He was amazed that the gun could shoot many times before being reloaded. He exclaimed in his Tennessee mountain drawl, "Why a feller could shoot all of a month's grub in one hunt. Why, he could shoot a bar, a deer, a couple o' coons, and a mountain lion befer them varmints knowed what hit 'em." His company Sergeant Harry Parsons looked at him with dubious eyes and told him to fire. At 200 yards Alvin hit the bull's-eye. His sergeant said it was a lucky shot and commanded him to shoot again. Alvin hit the bull's-eye again. The sergeant told him to shoot up the remaining rounds. They were all bull's-eyes.

Rubbing his eyes in disbelief, the sergeant moved York to 300, then 500 yards from the target. It made no difference to Private York whether he was firing from a standing, prone, or kneeling position; his shots were all bull's-eyes. However, when York was asked to fire at human silhouette targets, he balked. "Sir, I'd do wrong; practicing to kill people is agin' my religion." York was taken to Captain E. C. B. Danforth. The captain reasoned with him, giving him every argument he could think of to convince him that he should fight for his country, but York would not budge.

He then was brought before battalion commander Major George E. Buxton, who tried to persuade York. It was all to no avail. York felt he would rather spend time in hard labor in a detention camp for conscientious objectors. He told Major Buxton he had never killed anyone before becoming a Christian and he did not want to start killing. Major Buxton was a student of the Bible, and he continued to try to persuade York using history and the Bible. He argued the matter with the blue-eyed Tennessean for the better part of three days, pointing out the great heroes and leaders of the Old Testament and great Christian leaders, like George Washington, who fought in wars for their country. York kept saying, "But the Old Book says, 'Thou shalt not kill.'"

Finally Major Buxton sent York back to his home on the Wolf River on leave and told him to think the problem through carefully. In two weeks Alvin York was back. With a look of peace on his face, he said he was ready to fight. Through prayer and fasting for several days alone on a mountain with God and his Bible, as he told his Captain and the Major, he had "come to see that 'tis not a matter of killing folks, but a matter of keeping them from killing. If I'd be able to fight to bring this here bad war to an end sooner, then what I'd do is right in the sight of Jesus my Lord."

Thirteen months later, on October 8, 1919, Alvin York's appointment with destiny came in the Argonne Forest of France. It was the first offensive battle of the Argonne, and his battalion was one of the attacking battalions. Orders came down on the night of October 7 for them to take Hill 223 on the morning of the 8th, then drive across a narrow valley surrounded on three sides by hills fortified by German machine guns. Their mission was to destroy the machine gun nests and press on to the Decauville Railroad. The attack bogged down under the withering fire from their front and both flanks. A hurried conference concluded that the only way to continue the advance was to knock out the machine gun nests on the hill to their left. A detachment of one non-commissioned officer and sixteen men was detailed to circle around the end of the hill and attack the machine gun nests from the rear. Alvin York, then a corporal, was one of these men. Crawling through the undergrowth, they succeeded in passing around the German flank and positioning themselves behind their lines.

Now let Alvin tell the rest of the story in his own words. In his diary under the date of October 8, 1918, he wrote:

"There was 17 of us boys went around on the left flank to see if we couldn't put those guns out of action. So when we went around and fell in behind those guns, we first saw two Germans with Red Cross bands on their arms. So we asked them to stop and they did not. So one of the boys shot at them and they run back to our right. So we all run after them, and when we jumped across a little stream of water that was there, they was about 15 or 20 Germans jumped up and threw up their hands and said, 'Komrade!' So the one in charge of us boys told us not to shoot; they was going to give up anyway. (These prisoners included a major and two other officers). By this time some of the Germans from on the hill was shooting at us. Well, I was giving them the best I had, and by this time the Germans had got their machine guns turned around and fired on us. So they killed six and wounded three of us. So that just left 8, and then we got into it right by this time. So we had a hard battle for a little while, and I got hold of the German major and he told me

if I wouldn't kill any more of them he would make them quit firing. So I told him all right if he would do it now. So he blew a little whistle and they quit shooting and come down and gave up. I had killed over 20 before the German major said he would make them give up. I covered him with my automatic and told him if he didn't make them stop firing I would take his head off next. And he knew I meant it. After he blew his whistle, all but one of them came off the hill with their hands up, and just before that one got to me he threw a little hand grenade which burst in the air in front of me. I had to touch him off. The rest surrendered without any more trouble. There were nearly a 100 of them. We had about 80 or 90 Germans there disarmed, and had another line of Germans to go through to get out. So I called for my men, and one of them answered from behind a big oak tree, and the others were on my right in the brush. So I said, 'Let's get these Germans out of here.' One of my men said, 'it is impossible.' So I said, 'No; let's get them out of here.' So when my man said that, the German major said, 'How many have you got?' And I said that, 'I have got plenty,' and pointed my pistol at him all the time. In this battle I was using a rifle and a .45 Colt automatic. So I lined the Germans up in a line of twos, and I got between the ones in front, and I had the German major before me. So I marched them straight into those other machine guns and I got them. So when I got back to my major's P.C. [post of command] I had 132 prisoners."

A division inspector in the vicinity, upon hearing of this deed, personally went to investigate the story. Finding it all to be true, he called on York and asked him how he managed this incredible feat. Alvin responded with his customary drawl, "I had no time nohow to do nothing but watch them there German machine gunners and give them the best I had. Every time I seed a German, I jes teched him off.

"At first I was shootin' from a prone position, that is

lyin' down, jes like we often shoot at the targets in the shootin' matches in the mountains of Tennessee, and it was jes about the same distance. But the targets here were bigger. I jes couldn't miss a German's head or body at that distance. And I didn't. Besides, it weren't no time to miss nohow. I knowed that in order to shoot me, the Germans would have to get their heads up to see where I was. And I knowed that my only chance was to keep their heads down. And I done it. I covered their positions and let fly every time I seed anything to shoot at. Every time a head come up, I done knocked it down.

"In the middle of the fight a German officer and five men done jumped out of a trench and charged me with fixed bayonets. They had about twenty-five yards to come, and they was comin' right smart. I only had about half a clip left in my rifle; but I had my pistol ready. I done flipped it out fast and teched them off, too. I teched off the sixth man first; then the fifth; then the fourth; then the third; and so on. That's the way we shoot wild turkeys at home. You see, we don't want the front ones to know that we're gettin' the back ones, and then they keep on comin' until we get them all. Of course, I hadn't time to think of that. I guess I jes naturally did it. I knowed, too, that if the front ones wavered, or if I stopped them, the rear ones would drop down and pump a volley into me and get me.

"Then I returned to the rifle, and kept right on after those machine guns. I knowed now that if I done kept my head and didn't run out of ammunition, I had them. So I done hollered to them to come down and give up. I didn't want to kill any more'n I had to. I would tech a couple of them off and holler again. But I guess they couldn't understand my language, or else they couldn't hear me in the awful racket that was goin' on all around. I'd killed over twenty Germans by the time they gave up."

When the military leadership heard the results of York's amazing marksmanship and courage, he was promoted to sergeant by his company commander, Captain Danforth. Alvin York's daring deeds and his solo attack captured the imagination of the Allied world and made him one of the top heroes of the First World War. Ferdinand Foch, who commanded the French, British, and American armies in France, told him, "What you did was the greatest thing accomplished by any private soldier in all the armies of Europe." York humbly replied, "It was the Lord that shielded me; the men on my right and left were shot to pieces. I never got so much as a scratch or a cut on my uniform."

"The wicked flee when no man pusueth: but the righteous are bold as a lion" (Proverbs 28:1).

"But thou, O LORD, be merciful unto me, and raise me up, that I may requite them. By this I know that thou favourest me, because mine enemy doth not triumph over me. And as for me, thou upholdest me in mine integrity, and settest me before thy face for ever" (Psalm 41:1-13).

"Offer unto God thanksgiving, and pay thy vows unto the most High: And call upon me in the day of trouble: I will deliver thee, and thou shalt glorify me" (Psalm 50:14-15).

"Our Shield and Defender, the Ancient of Days; Pavilioned in splendor and girded with praise."
Robert Grant (1779–1838)

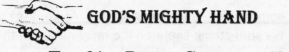

THE 91ST PSALM COLONEL 1918 A.D.

Colonel Whittlesey was a committed Christian who fought four long years for the British during World War I. As a Christian, he set out to fight with explicit faith in the fact that the God of the Bible would shield him and his men from harm in battle. When he shared his faith in the mighty hand of God's protection to other officers, many thought him a bit overconfident and presumptuous. Yet at the end of the war, his faith was no longer a laughing matter. Not a single man in his entire regiment during all those years of action died in battle. Considering the casualties of other regiments in battle, this was truly an amazing act of divine providence.

How did Whittlesey build faith in God among his men? From the beginning of the war he required every man and officer under his command to repeat the Ninety-first Psalm daily. Each officer and soldier in the regiment carried a complete copy of the Psalm and either read it or recited it from memory.

In many battles, he fought with other regiments alongside his. At times, these regiments would be completely decimated with only ten percent surviving. If they could be calculated, the chances against his entire regiment surviving four years of battle unharmed—with countless bullets flying and bombs bursting on or near them—would be astronomical! This was such an astounding phenomenon that Christian magazines on both sides of the Atlantic published the testimony of Colonel Whittlesey and his "Psalm Ninety-One Regiment."

"He that dwelleth in the secret place of the most High shall abide under the shadow of the Almighty. I will say of the LORD, He is my refuge and my fortress: my God; in him will I trust. Surely he shall deliver thee from the snare of the fowler, and from the noisome pestilence. He shall cover thee with his feathers, and under his wings shalt thou trust: his truth shall be thy shield and

buckler. *Thou shalt not be afraid for the terror by night; nor for the arrow that flieth by day; Nor for the pestilence that walketh in darkness; nor for the destruction that wasteth at noonday. A thousand shall fall at thy side, and ten thousand at thy right hand; but it shall not come nigh thee. Only with thine eyes shalt thou behold and see the reward of the wicked. Because thou hast made the LORD, which is my refuge, even the most High, thy habitation;*

There shall no evil befall thee, neither shall any plague come nigh thy dwelling. For he shall give his angels charge over thee, to keep thee in all thy ways. They shall bear thee up in their hands, lest thou dash thy foot against a stone. Thou shalt tread upon the lion and adder: the young lion and the dragon shalt thou trample under feet. Because he hath set his love upon me, therefore will I deliver him: I will set him on high, because he hath known my name. He shall call upon me, and I will answer him: I will be with him in trouble; I will deliver him, and honour him. With long life will I satisfy him, and shew him my salvation" (Psalm 91:1-16).

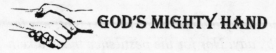

THE WHITE BATTALION 1918 A.D.

By April of 1918, World War I was coming to a swift close. The Germans were facing the inevitable, defeat. The mighty hand of God was revealed to hundreds of German soldiers in a miraculous way as they were advancing their troops near the little French town of Bethune. Perhaps this incident occurred in order to allow them an opportunity to acknowledge defeat and to turn to God who controls the destinies of men and nations.

The Bible says that it is God who raises up one and puts down another. *Psalm 75:6-7: "For promotion cometh neither from the east, nor from the west, nor from the south. But God is the judge: he putteth down one, and setteth up another."*

The account you are about to read was written by a German captain who witnessed an extraordinary event, along with hundreds of other Germans:

> *We were advancing at the head of our troops, all of whom were in excellent spirits, singing as they marched along, thinking that the British were now defeated and all that remained was to go forward without much opposition and capture Paris, where we would have a fine time—plenty of drinks and all else we desired.*
>
> *By my side was my Lieutenant Fritz, and he suddenly seized hold of my arm, saying, "Look, Herr Captain, there is a large body of mounted men approaching Bethune from the other side. See, the smoke of the burning houses is blowing away, and I can discern their uniforms. Why, they are all dressed in white and are mounted on white horses. Who can they be?"*
>
> *"I don't know," I replied. "They may be British Colonial mounted troops."*

Lieutenant Fritz replied, "I know of no British Colonial mounted troops with white uniforms and white chargers. But anyway, they will be blown to pieces now. Our heavy artillerymen are opening fire upon them."

We halted instinctively and stood watching those white-uniform-clad cavalrymen advancing quietly through the smoke, their figures clearly outlined in the shining sun against the smoke of the burning town. We saw the shells breaking amidst their ranks with shattering crashes which shook the ground. This barrage was followed by intensive machine gun fire which raked the advancing men until it seemed impossible for anyone to survive. But the White Cavalry came quietly forward at a slow trot and not a man or a horse fell!

Resistless as the incoming tide, they advanced, and in front of them rode their leader—a fine figure of a man. By his side was a great sword similar to those used by the Crusaders, and his hands lay quietly, holding the reins of his great white charger as it bore him forward. Then a terror seized me, and I found myself fleeing from that awe-inspiring body of white cavalry, frightened and terrified. All around me were the masses of my men, formerly an army, but now a rabble, broken and afraid, all fleeing from them, but more especially from that wonderful leader on his great white charger...The German army is defeated. I don't say you will not have any more fighting, for this you are bound to experience; but I do say that we have lost the war, and that it is due to the "White Cavalry."

Throughout recorded history there are various accounts of mysterious apparitions that reveal to a discerning, God-fearing believer that God has His angelic host in the midst of world conflicts. Such an account was witnessed and recorded in the days of Elisha.

"And when the servant of the man of God (Elisha) was risen early, and gone forth, behold, an host compassed the city, both

with horses and chariots. And his servant said unto him, Alas my master! What shall we do? And he answered, fear not for they who are with us are more than they who are with them. And Elisha prayed thee, open his eyes, that he may see. And the Lord opened the eyes of the young man, and he saw; and, behold the mountain was full of horses and chariots of fire around about Elisha" (II Kings 6:15-17).

The angelic army of Heaven is always present during battles. God's mighty hand is not shortened in performing His good will. It should be our desire not to look for angels to visit us and perform some mighty feat in time of trouble, but simply to lean on Him who controls our lives and who holds us in the palm of His hand.

> *Spirit of God, descend upon my heart; Wean it from earth, through all its pulses move; Stoop to my weakness, mighty as Thou art, And make me love Thee as I ought to love.*
>
> *I ask no dream, no prophet ecstasies, No sudden rending of the veil of clay, No angel visitant, no opening skies; But take the dimness of my soul away.*
>
> *Hast Thou not bid me love Thee, God and King? All, all Thine own, soul, heart, and strength and mind I see Thy cross—there teach my heart to cling. O let me seek Thee, and O let me find.*
>
> *Teach me to feel that Thou art always nigh; Teach me the struggles of the soul to bear, To check the rising doubt, the rebel sigh: Teach me the patience of unanswered prayer.*

George Croly 1780-1860

BIG BEN AT NINE 1918 A.D.

In his book *Round the World at Nine* Prominent British industrialist, W. Tudor Pole recalls a significant event in his life. While stationed at Palestine during World War I he and a soldier buddy were chatting in the mouth of a cave near Jerusalem on the eve of General Allenby's takeover of the holy city. As both chatted over the war, home, family, friends, and church a moment of silence fell. Then Pole's young friend turned to him and said,

"I shall not come through this war alive. Like thousands of others who have given their lives for Freedom, it shall be my destiny to go on now." Looking intently at me he prophetically said,"You will survive. You will live to see a greater and more vital war fought on every continent, on every ocean, and in the sky."

Pole's friend continued speaking with a plea for a spiritual response towards God from all those who would fight in that future war. He stressed to me the power of silence and urged a moment of silence each day for prayer. Then he said, "When those tragic days arrive, do not forget us, nor what we have talked about."

The next day, as had been predicted, the young man was killed in battle. Pole himself was severely wounded and was captured, but managed to escape with an overwhelming sense of God's mighty hand in the miraculous aid to shelter him in his escape.

He never forgot his friend's parting words. Years later, during that "greater, more vital war," World War II, fought on every ocean, land, and in the sky, he was amazed at the fulfillment of his friend's prediction. He also was perplexed as to how to incorporate "silent prayer" as his friend advised.

One day during the beginning of the war, while doing business in London, Big Ben chimed its time. The clock struck nine. Inspired, he came up with an idea that every day at the stroke of nine citizens should remember to have a moment of silent prayer for the progress of the War. Since Mr. Pole was an influential man in the city of London it did not take long that citizens at the stroke of nine from Big Ben would bow their heads and have silent prayer. This soon caught on and thousands, from the Prime Minister, King and Queen, Parliament, and the common labor, at the stroke of nine prayed for British victory and world peace. Only eternity will tell the results of prayer that moves the hand of God.

"Then cometh Jesus with them unto a place called Gethsemane, and saith unto the disciples, Sit ye here, while I go and pray yonder" (Matthew 26:36).

"And Jesus answering saith unto them, Have faith in God. For verily I say unto you, That whosoever shall say unto this mountain, Be thou removed, and be thou cast into the sea; and shall not doubt in his heart, but shall believe that those things which he saith shall come to pass; he shall have whatsoever he saith. Therefore I say unto you, What things soever ye desire, when ye pray, believe that ye receive them, and ye shall have them" (Mark 11:22-24).

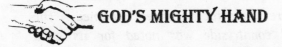

GOD'S MIGHTY HAND

PETER MARSHALL 1902-1949 A.D.

A highlight of Peter Marshall's life was his appointment as Chaplain of the U.S. Senate for two terms to a Republican, and later, a Democratic Senate. His desire was to be "all things to all men to gain them to Christ" (see I Corinthians 9:22). Most older Americans remember Chaplain Marshall, but now the younger generation knows of his wife, Catherine, because of the story called "Christy." Hollywood has produced this life story on television, bringing the Marshall name back into recognition. Catherine Marshall wrote the biography of her husband, *A Man Called Peter*, in 1951. In it she recounts his wonderful life and how God directed his steps by His mighty hand to accomplish through Peter His divine will in order to bring Himself glory.

The year 1924 was a significant year for Peter, because that year, Eric Liddell, "the Flying Scotsman," broke the world record for the 400-meter race at the Olympics in Paris. Liddell was one of Peter's heroes. He was a hero, not just because of his athletic ability, but because of his strong convictions for Christ, which were known throughout the world. Later, Peter seriously considered entering the ministry, and Liddell had a great influence over him in that area. Several other events also influenced his decisions about the ministry. Catherine Marshall writes about them in her book:

> *One summer Peter spent working in the English village of Bamburgh, sixteen miles southeast of the Scottish border. The village, which had only about four hundred inhabitants, had a charm all its own. Red-roofed nineteenth-century stone cottages, vine-covered, were set on the edge of the cold, misty North Sea. Around the village was a spacious countryside of wheat and barley fields, pasture, and*

moorland where blackfaced sheep roamed. The Northumberland countryside was noted for its good workable limestone. There were alternations of whinstone (the local name for limestone), shale, and coal, with the whin often eighty to one hundred feet thick. Craggy Ridge, Spindleston, and Belford Crags overlooked the lofty, bleak moorlands of Rayheugh and Roseborough.

Walking back from a nearby village to Bamburgh one dark, starless night, Peter struck out across the moors, thinking he would take a shortcut. He knew that there was a deep deserted limestone quarry close by the Glororum Road, but he thought he could avoid that danger spot. The night was inky black, eerie. There was only the sound of the wind through the heather-stained moorland, the noisy clamor of wild fowl as his footsteps disturbed them, the occasional far-off bleating of a sheep.

Suddenly he heard someone call, "Peter!" There was great urgency in the voice.

He stopped. "Yes, who is it? What do you want?"

For a second he listened, but there was no response, only the sound of the wind. The moor seemed completely deserted.

Thinking he must have been mistaken, he walked on a few paces. Then he heard it again, even more urgently:
"Peter!"

He stopped dead still, trying to peer into that impenetrable darkness, but suddenly stumbled and fell to his knees. Putting out his hand to catch himself, he found nothing there. As he cautiously investigated, feeling around in a semicircle, he found himself to be on the very brink of an abandoned quarry. One step more would have sent him plummeting into space to certain death.

This incident made an unforgettable impression on Peter. There was never any doubt in his mind about the Source of that Voice. He felt that God must have some great purpose for his life, to have intervened so specifically. Through subsequent years there were other close brushes with death, times when he was spared, while others around him were hurt or killed. Once an automobile killed a friend walking at his side; once fire broke out in a tiny boat ten miles out at sea; once an airplane he had just missed crashed. God's hand was very evidently on his life. This gave him a sense of destiny and purpose.

On January 24, 1949, Peter Marshall suffered a severe heart attack and died within a few hours. The loss was great. It left Catherine a widow and Peter, Jr., fatherless. The sudden shock to Catherine was overwhelming, but Psalm 23:4 gave her the promise, *"though I walk through the valley of the shadow of death, I will fear no evil: for thou art with me; thy rod and thy staff, they comfort me."* When Catherine Marshall received word that her husband had died in the hospital, she quickly saw that little Peter was cared for and traveled to the hospital to say farewell to her dead husband.

Upon entering the room, she felt the presence of the Lord, and a deep sense of peace flooded over her. Her 55-minute stay was her healing time where she received assurance that all would be well with her and her little boy—"a boy called Peter"—as he was the namesake of her dear husband. Little Peter has grown up and has received the "mantle" of both his deceased father and mother combined into one. The mantle of his father, because he has traveled throughout the United States of America proclaiming and reclaiming our Christian heritage; and the mantle of his mother, because he has become a recognized and established writer. His book, co-authored with David Manuel, *The Light and the Glory*, *From Sea to Shing Sea* and *Sounding Forth the Trumpet* has sold thousands of copies and has helped show Americans the loss of their God-given heritage. The book has affected families, Senators, Congressmen, governors, teachers, and ministries such as ours in profound ways. America is at a crossroads, and "a man and men like Peter" need to rise up and proclaim that this nation, without the Christian basis with which it was established, will not long endure. God's mighty hand moves in mysterious ways. The heritage of parents is profound, and parents' influence on their children is great. This account is testimony to that truth.

"Behold, I will send you Elijah, the prophet, before the coming of the great and dreadful day of the LORD; And he shall turn the heart of the fathers to the children, and the heart of the children to their fathers, lest I come and smite the earth with a curse" (Malachi 4:5-6).

God moves in a mysterious way
His wonders to perform;
He plants His footsteps in the sea
And rides upon the storm.
William Cowper (1731-1800)

GOD'S MIGHTY HAND

BLACK THURSDAY BECOMES "SONDAY" 1929 A.D.

What good could come from being broke? How could God's mighty hand allow well-to-do folks who do good deeds for humanity to lose all, and with the loss of all to be of little value to anyone? That is the subject of this story.

The year was 1875. Mr. and Mrs. Penny were the proud parents of a newborn son named Jim. Mr. Penny, a Baptist minister, dedicated their new son two weeks later at the church near Log Creek, Missouri. The father placed his hands upon the son and committed him to the Lord and dedicated him to "walk in the paths of righteousness for His name's sake." Jim grew up like most farm boys, with lots of good old-fashioned work, a smidgen of fishing on the side, and swimming in the river during the hot, humid summers of Missouri.

When Jim was twenty, he was apprenticed to a storekeeper in nearby Hamilton. One day Jim observed his employer using deceitful merchandising on some customers. The boss mixed some lower quality coffee with some expensive coffee and repackaged it as the expensive brand. During the evening meal Jim laughed while telling his parents of the employer's smooth tricks. The father did not laugh. He corrected Jim for thinking that cheating at another's expense was a laughing matter. He then showed what Christian character he possessed when he told Jim that he was going to have to quit working at the grocery store because he did not want his son to work for a man with very little character and principles. The father instilled in his teachable son a principle that the son was going to apply from that day forward, *"Therefore all things whatsoever ye would that men should do to you, do ye even so to them: for this is the law and the prophets"* (Matthew 7:12).

Providentially, not long after this incident, Jim's health failed, and the family was forced to move for health reasons to the dryer climate of the West. Jim ended up in the beautiful Wyoming Rockies. As a hard-working ambitious boy, he was soon able to work again and decided to try his hand in dry goods merchandising. Because he did well for his employer, he was given an opportunity to become partners in a joint store venture in Kemmerer, Wyoming. With everything looking up, Jim began to look search for a wife and soon found a lovely girl named Berta. They marred in 1901. Jim was elated. He had a new wife and a new store. What could be better! On April 14, 1902, Jim hung his sign up for his business. It was called the "Golden Rule" store. His parents were pleased with all Jim was becoming.

Jim tended that store from sunup until after the last customer left at midnight. Then he and Berta walked up the outside stairs to their home above the store.

Their room was an unfinished attic. The dining table was a dry goods box, upside down. They used shoe cases for chairs. There were no windows, and a kerosene lamp was their only light.

But the first day's receipts totaled $466.59. The Golden Rule Store was on its way.

Six years later Jim bought out his partner. Business was so good that he purchased two more stores for $30,000 in cash.

By then Jim had learned to employ other persons as he had first been employed: To allow each store manager to earn a share of the business and to divide its profits or its loss.

Jim added more links to the chain, more stores to his name, until—twelve years from that start in Kemmerer, by 1914—he was operating seventy-one stores.

On Christmas Day, 1910, his precious bride died after eight years of blissful marriage. Jim was shattered. Berta was the strength behind Jim. Without her, what could he do? To hide the pain and loss of his wife, Jim immersed himself in his business. By 1928, Jim's chain of retail stores numbered more than a thousand and grossed more than 176 million dollars a year.

Jim applied his "Golden Rule" principles outside his chain stores to all his ventures. One philanthropic venture was the establishment of a retirement home for clergymen like his father who were destitute upon retirement. With all his good works he was still empty inside. He was rich but insecure without his consort Berta. When the stock market crashed on "Black Thursday" 1929, Jim emotionally crashed. By 1931, J.C. Penny was penniless and had a seven-million-dollar debt. Jim was admitted into a sanitarium in Battle Creek, Michigan. He was frail, nervous, and physically a wreck. Burdened with debt and facing an uncertain future, he gave up the will to live. He wrote farewell letters to friends and family members and in his mid-fifties lay down to sleep hoping never to awake. The mighty hand of God could now work. God was waiting for this hard-working man to realize that the religion of "good works" will only leave one broken and an utter failure.

Instead of death, a deep sleep pervaded his body. God was doing spiritual surgery. After a long, long sleep Jim opened his eyes. It was still dark. He had no idea of what day it was, or how long he had slept. Amazingly, he was at peace. It was as if there was a "silver lining" awaiting him. He dressed himself, avoided the attending nurses seeing him, and proceeded down to the chapel to seek the Lord about his future. Providentially, there was a chapel service going on the very moment Jim walked in. The chaplain was leading in singing the song "God Will Take Care of You."

As Jim listened to the words, he was being ministered to in the inner man. He heard the words:

"All you need, He will provide. God will take care of you.

Lonely and sad, from friends apart [He reflected on the loss of his wife.]

No matter what may be the test, God will take care of you.

Be not dismayed what'er betide. God will take care of you."

The chaplain proceeded to give a message from the text, *"Come unto me all ye who are heavy laden and I will give you rest" (Matthew 11:28).* A miracle, by the mighty hand of God, occurred. Jim wept like a child as he gave all of his burden to the Lord who promised to take care of him. The warmth and love of God through Christ came into him bringing hope where there had been despair. J.C. Penny was "born anew." He went home, healed spiritually and emotionally. Things were different now. There were no more servants, no big fancy house, no large properties, just a small apartment with a small salary as he started all over again living one day at a time. He learned the secret of what Jesus taught when He said in Matthew 6:25-34:

"Therefore I say unto you, Take no thought for your life, what ye shall eat, or what ye shall drink; nor yet for your body, what ye shall put on. Is not the life more than meat, and the body than raiment? Behold the fowls of the air: for they sow not, neither do they reap, nor gather into barns; yet your heavenly Father feedeth them. Are ye not much better than they? Which of you by taking thought can add one cubit unto his stature? And why take ye thought for raiment? Consider the lilies of the field, how they grow; they toil not, neither do they spin: And yet I say unto you, That even Solomon in all his glory was not arrayed like one of these. Wherefore, if God so clothe the grass of the field, which to day is, and to morrow is cast into the oven, shall he not much more clothe you, O ye of little faith? Therefore take no thought, saying, What shall we eat? or, What shall we drink? or, Wherewithal shall we be clothed? (For after all these things do the Gentiles seek:) for your heavenly Father knoweth that ye have need of all these things. But seek ye first the kingdom of God, and his righteousness; and all these things shall be added unto you. Take therefore no thought for the morrow: for the morrow shall take thought for the things of itself. Sufficient unto the day is the evil thereof."

With faith in Christ and Christian principles, J.C. Penny started over at fifty-six years of age. It was not easy, but he was at peace. Within a few years J.C. Penny had 1,650 stores throughout America. He began an extensive traveling ministry sharing his new-found faith in Christ, the "Golden Rule" of business, and what God's mighty hand could do for lives of people who lose all to gain eternal life.

J.C. Penny, who gave up the will to live in his mid-fifties, lived to be ninety-six years old. He went to be with the Lord in 1971.

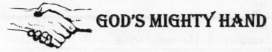# GOD'S MIGHTY HAND

SEA LION DROWNS 1940 A.D.

After the German victory at Dunkirk in June 1940, Hitler, "licking his chops," felt it was time to conquer England. In what is now known as the "Battle of Britain," Hitler planned a two-front assault to take place, starting August 25. The first front would be an air strike, amassing his Luftwaffe (German Air Force) under the leadership of his Commander-in-Chief, Hermann Goring. The second assault would be an amphibious invasion called "Operation Sea Lion."

This was a crucial moment in British history, as the odds were in the Germans' favor. The Germans were better trained for war, better equipped, stronger in air power, greater in naval strength, and confidently optimistic, having by this time defeated every major country in Europe that stood in defiance of Hitler. This was Germany's golden hour.

In August, the Germans began their air strikes on England. Deep in the underground operations room of the 11th Group Fighter Command, British Prime Minister Winston Churchill and his military advisers sat watching their electric battle charts and the lights which tracked German positions.

The British, as part of the Allied forces, had come to the aid of France in the Battle of Dunkirk, and that battle cost the British a large quantity of much-needed defense materials. The British were now dangerously short of materials with which to defend their own shores. In all of England there were only 500 eighteen-pound guns (many of them taken from museums) with which to repel, if necessary, an invading army.

Intelligence reports from the Continent indicated that an invasion of England by the enemy was being planned as early as July. Hitler ordered his Luftwaffe to begin shooting down Royal Air Force (RAF) planes to make air defense of the British Isles ineffective, if not impossible.

The Germans found their task difficult, because the Lord's mighty hand of favor was extended to the British. The RAF fought furiously and shot down 164 Nazi bombers in the month of July, with a loss of only 58 of their own aircraft. In August, despite insufficient rest, the outnumbered British downed 662 Nazi bombers, while losing only 360 of their own.

The RAF was ecstatic over their advantages in the air. But they were also realistic, because they knew that with aircraft, the German war machine was outproducing them three to one. It seemed that there was an inexhaustible supply of German aircraft. The British command, viewing the electric charts in the underground operations room, knew that the "score" could change at any time to German advantage and British loss. It was obvious to them all, that without Divine aid, it was only a matter of time before Germany would be occupying England's shores. England needed a miracle and needed it soon.

As Churchill pensively watched the electric chart, prayer warriors all over England were on their knees in prayer and supplication to the God of Israel. The British were blessed to have Dr. Wesley L. Duewel, President of the Oriental Missionary Society, living not too far from London during the war. Dr. Duewel was the head of a prayer college during the war, and he commissioned his students to pray and fast throughout the war years in England. On numerous occasions the tide of battles turned in favor of the British as the result of fervent, specific prayer. This was the case during the Battle of Britain.

In mid-September a "red alert" sounded at the British fighter command headquarters at Stanmore, England. The charts showed more than 40 Nazi aircraft approaching from the French seaport, Dieppe; more than 40 approaching from another direction; and more than 60 from still another.

As each Nazi formation neared the coast of England, British squadrons rose to meet it. Because there were only 1,000 British pilots defending southern England, all of them were soon in the air.

Tension grew in the underground shelter.

Air Vice-Marshal Keith R. Park requested reinforcements from other parts of England, but only three squadrons could be spared.

"What other resources have we?" Churchill asked.

"None, Sir," was the reply.

The room was silent.

"The odds were great; our margin small; the stakes infinite," Churchill wrote later.

Then inexplicably, the lights on the chart began to move eastward—away from England. The great Nazi air flotilla had turned back. Miraculously, in addition, the Germans did not knock out the British radar stations—a mistake that Hitler could not afford to make. With 185 of their aircraft down in flames, they were in retreat! By the mighty hand of God moving through prayer and against all logistical probability, the Royal Air Force had won the battle!

Just why Royal Air Force pilots continued to win against unbelievable odds may or may not be satisfactorily explained in the military records. But British intelligence officers later received some strange information from three different members of the Nazi armed forces.

The first bit of information was from a Nazi pilot captured after his crippled plane was downed in England. British intelligence officers asked him, "Why did your formation retreat when only a few planes were attacking you?"

"A few!" exclaimed the pilot. "There were hundreds!"

After the prisoner had been dismissed, the intelligence officers exchanged puzzled glances. They all but disregarded the strange reply until a German officer, captured later, asked them in perplexity, "Where did you get all the planes you threw into the battle over Britain?"

The interrogators managed to mask their surprise. Actually, the powerful Nazi bomber force had been met by a mere handful of outdated RAF Spitfire and Hurricane fighters. The sky was not full of Royal Air Force planes! Only a few worn-out pilots, making anywhere from their third to their seventh combat mission that day, had met Germany's mighty bombers.

Perhaps visionary planes rode the skies in formation with the Royal Air Force, and perhaps only the Nazis could see those planes that convinced them they were confronted by overwhelming numbers. It was the remarks of an imprisoned Nazi intelligence officer captured still later that came nearest to the truth of the Source of the plane-filled mirages which had confused the Luftwaffe pilots.

"With the striking of your Big Ben clock each evening at nine," the Nazi told the British intelligence officer, "you used a secret weapon which we do not understand. It is very powerful, and we could find no countermeasure against it. It is your prayers. Who can fight against God?"

This amazing testimony was corroborated by several German pilots shot down over Britain. Each one said the same thing. Like the Israelites of old, the British could sing the song Moses composed at the defeat of Pharaoh and his army.

After the war, Air Chief Marshal Lord Dowding said, "Even during the battle one realized from day to day how much external support was coming in. At the end of the battle one had the sort of feeling that there had been some special Divine intervention to alter some sequence of events which otherwise we would have occurred."

" Then sang Moses and the children of Israel this song unto the LORD, and spake, saying, I will sing unto the LORD, for he hath triumphed gloriously: the horse and his rider hath he thrown into the sea. The LORD is my strength and song, and he is become my salvation: he is my God, and I will prepare him an habitation; my father's God, and I will exalt him. The LORD is a man of war: the LORD is his name.

"Pharaoh's chariots and his host hath he cast into the sea; his chosen captains also are drowned in the Red Sea. The depths have covered them; they sank into the bottom as a stone. Thy right hand, O LORD, is become glorious in power: thy right hand, O LORD, hath dashed in pieces the enemy. And in the greatness of thine excellency thou hast overthrown them that rose

up against thee: thou sentest forth thy wrath, which consumed them as stubble. And with the blast of thy nostrils the waters were gathered together, the floods stood upright as an heap, and the depths were congealed in the heart of the sea. The enemy said, I will pursue, I will overtake, I will divide the spoil; my lust shall be satisfied upon them; I will draw my sword, my hand shall destroy them. Thou didst blow with thy wind, the sea covered them: they sank as lead in the mighty waters.

"Who is like unto thee, O LORD, among the gods? Who is like thee, glorious in holiness, fearful in praises, doing wonders? Thou stretchedst out thy right hand, the earth swallowed them. Thou in thy mercy hast led forth the people which thou hast redeemed: thou hast guided them in thy strength unto thy holy habitation. The people shall hear, and be afraid: sorrow shall take hold of the inhabitants of Palestina. Then the dukes of Edom shall be amazed; the mighty men of Moab, trembling shall take hold upon them; all the inhabitants of Canaan shall melt away. Fear and dread shall fall upon them; by the greatness of thine arm they shall be as still as a stone; till thy people pass over, O LORD, till the people pass over, which thou hast purchased. Thou shalt bring them in, and plant them in the mountain of thine inheritance, in the place, O LORD, which thou hast made for thee to dwell in, in the sanctuary, O Lord, which thy hands have established. The LORD shall reign for ever and ever" (Exodus 15).

"A mighty fortress is our God; a bulwark never failing."
Martin Luther (1453–1546)

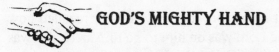

GOD'S MIGHTY HAND

WAGE WAR ON YOUR KNEES 1940 A.D.

At the outbreak of World War II Britain was soon in the thick of war. With His mighty hand, God raised key players on the side of liberty and justice. Just as during the formation of our great nation of America, key players were in position to establish our republic, so too Great Britain had leaders who were born for a "time and purpose under heaven" (see Ecclesiastes chapter 3). Some were military leaders in the Royal Air Force, Royal Navy, and Royal Army, and some were leaders of state, like Winston Churchill.

All too often the leaders of God's Royal Court in Heaven go unnoticed by the leaders of this world, but when all is said and done at the end of the age, God will reveal to humanity His eternal purpose and destiny of those He caused to be born. Those unseen and unnoticed often do the greatest work. That work is the work of prayer. Jesus said that prayer "moves mountains." Therefore we can conclude that prayer moves the mighty hand of God to direct certain events of monumental circumstances like world wars. God moved thousands of His people to pray during World War I and World War II; we will meet one of these men in this chapter.

Rees Howells was born on October 10, 1879, the sixth of a family of eleven. The little whitewashed cottage on the Llandilo Road, in the mining village of Brynamman, South Wales, was where Thomas and Margaret Howells raised their children. They were "dirt poor," but the Lord sustained them and gave them the joy of knowing Him who is above all earthly riches. Rees, from his earliest days, was conscious of the presence of God. Rees's grandparents were converted to Christ during the great Welsh Revival of 1859, and they had a profound effect on him.

By the time Rees was thirteen, he was attending church on his own and would walk miles to hear preachers speak. At the age of twenty-two Rees left home for America. He later recalled how strong the hand of the Lord was on him to go to America. It was the leading of the Spirit of God to lead him to salvation.

While in America, his cousin Evan Lewis asked him if he was "born again." Rees was dismayed and perplexed, for he had not even heard nor read of those very words spoken by Christ to Nicodemus in John chapter 3. Shortly after the challenge to be "born again" Rees was stricken with typhoid fever, always dangerous, but in those days often fatal.

While facing death, he realized he was not a saved Christian trusting in Christ by grace for his salvation. Up to then his religion was that of good works, and as he lay dying he received the revelation of his sinful condition apart from all the good he had done. He cried out to the Lord for forgiveness and saw his utter dependency on Christ. He knew he could never do anything to merit salvation. It was then that he was transformed, "born again."

Rees developed into a Godly man and found his life's vocation of serving the Lord full time, living by faith. In time he returned to Wales to reach his people with the Gospel of Christ. Rees became perhaps best known as the founder of the Bible College of Wales. He was a man peculiarly taught of God, one who learned to walk in the light of God's Word, the Bible, as the Spirit led him.

A study of his Christian life reveals great lessons in walking with the Lord. Rees faced the challenge of entire surrender to self, then learned to love the unlovely, found the key to prevailing prayer, became the channel of a mighty revival in Africa, studied the principles of divine healing, and progressed ever further in faith until world events were being affected by his prayers.

At the outbreak of World War I, Rees Howells and his wife were holding revival meetings all over South Africa and were being used of God in a mighty way. They returned to Wales six years later, where they were led by the Holy Spirit to start the Bible College of Wales. Here Mr. and Mrs. Howells began their life-long quest of training new Christians to grow in "grace and in the knowledge of Jesus Christ."

Rees had the particular gift of intercession and would spend days alone in fasting and prayer. By the outbreak of World War II Rees had become a mighty man of prayer and had dedicated his college to teaching and practicing daily prayer. When England declared war the staff and students of Wales Bible College, under the direction of Mr. Howells, dedicated themselves to daily prayer and fasting. They would all gather in the evenings and begin divine intercession. Their prayers were heard and answered in specific ways throughout the war years.

The stories in the following chapters on World War II give testimony to the mighty hand of God in answer to the prayers offered by countless God-fearing English, Scotts, and Irish. Tribute should also be paid to Wales Bible College and Rees Howells for their remarkably persistent prayers during those fearful, dark days.

After World War II was over, British General J.R.C. Fuller gave four reasons for the ultimate failure of the Nazis. Hitler's blunder number one was missing the chance to invade Great Britain. Blunder number two was his failure to attack Egypt and gain Alexandria. Blunder number three was failing to realize that everything in the Russian campaign depended on the fall of Moscow, and instead turning to other objectives. The final blunder, number four, was Hitler's attack on Stalingrad.

What is truly amazing is that Rees Howells' Wales Bible College prayed specifically for the victory in battle in the four above-mentioned battles. The Nazis' "blunders" outlined by General Fuller were accomplished by the Spirit of God against the wicked leadership of Hitler and those who followed him. Behind the scenes, demonic hosts often try to destroy God-given liberty and all that is wise and good. Through prayer, God's mighty hosts conquer these evil forces and bring victory. I would like to close this chapter by showing just how Wales Bible College practiced the call of daily prayer, giving you a glimpse into those difficult war years in Britain.

On January 20, 1940, college president Rees Howells

assembled the students and staff for prayer. He said, "I feel much more strongly today that God has shown me He wants me to pray not only for this town but for the country at large. The Lord in private prayer impressed me with the danger of these German air raids. He told me, 'If these air raids are going to be repeated, I cannot guarantee you will be safe, so come and pray them out of the country.' I said to Him, 'Lord you must protect us now!'"

Over a week was spent in prayer, and then on January 28, Rees's journal stated, "Believed for the protection of the country." This was followed by the remarkable petition: "Lord, turn the enemy down to the Mediterranean," (away from Great Britain). Just over two months later, on April 6, Hitler declared war on Yugoslavia and Greece, and this was followed by the invasion of Crete and North Africa. With these new commitments the enemy was obliged to turn its attention away from the destruction of Britain, and so the immediate crisis for that country passed. Thus, Howells' prayer was answered.

The next prayer was greater still. We suppose nothing gave the world a bigger shock through the whole course of the war than when, without a word of warning, Hitler swung around and invaded Russia. If anything was seen to be an intervention of God to help the Allies, it was this sudden change in Hitler's war plans. The secular newspapers spoke of it in the words of the pagan proverb, "Whom the gods would destroy they first make mad." From a Christian perspective it certainly was not the "gods," but God who moved Hitler to make a foolish decision. Historically, it was one of Hitler is most foolish maneuvers. It was reckoned as one of the great acts of divine intervention which spelled doom for the Nazis.

The invasion of Russia started at 4 a.m. on June 22, 1941. Seven weeks previously, on May 2, God had begun to speak to Mr. Howells about Russia, and he said that day: "Much as we long to see the war finished, it seems that God is saying, 'There is one more country I want to bring judgment on, and that is Communist Russia.' And again on the next day: "Russia comes before me. Is it right for Stalin and his followers to escape? If

God gives us the choice, would we tell Him to prolong the war, although we are losing on every point?"

He also said: "We ask the Lord to weaken Russia and Japan, even if it means prolonging the war for five years. Can't the Lord turn the enemy's drive into Russia? If God does not deal with Russia now, He will have to make another war to do so. I say He ought to bring Russia into it, no matter how long it will take, unless He has another way to get at these Communists." From that time this became the main prayer of the college: "Lord, bring Russia into the war and deal with Communism." Seven weeks later Russia was brought into the war!

After a few short weeks Russia was facing imminent collapse. Nazism was worse than Communism. As the German hordes poured into that country, the free world watched the gradual disintegration of the Russian armies and the constantly closer approach of the Nazis to Moscow. It was a race with winter. In an attempt to replicate the famous invasion of Napoleon, Hitler proclaimed that he would succeed where Napoleon had failed, before the onset of winter. Would he? Did anybody in those tense days believe he would not?

Hitler's armies were almost at the gates of the city. Mrs. Howells relates that very early on Sunday morning, October 19, 1941, Mr. Howells told her he would go down and hear the seven o'clock news to see if Moscow had fallen. When he came back he said it had not fallen, but that they were expecting bad news any time. A few minutes after that, the Lord began to speak to him: "Is there any need for Moscow to fall? Why don't you pray and believe for Me to save Moscow and give a setback to the Nazis?"

Dr. Kenneth G. Symonds, who has been a member of the college staff for twelve years, tells us of the meeting that Sunday morning. "Mr. Howells opened his message by saying that the first thing the Lord had told him that morning was, 'Pray that Moscow will not fall!' It seemed ridiculously impossible, for we had heard that its fall was inevitable; but although the prayer was so far beyond us, yet the Spirit laid it on us all, students and teaching staff alike. It seemed that He prayed in spite of us, so we travailed all day, until in the late meeting that night, He so inspired us through His servant Rees that we had the assurance that God was answering. The Lord gave us liberty to pray that the Nazis might be utterly overthrown in a Russian winter. We shall never forget the joy of victory He gave us as faith mounted up during those days."

The second day the news was that the Russians had taken fresh courage and the snow was falling heavily in some parts. Four days later in the meeting Mr. Howells said, "I say now, 'Thus saith the Lord: he (Hitler) is wintering in the Russian snows.'" We all know the end of the story; Moscow never fell, and Goering, recounting later the misfortunes of that winter, stated that thousands of the flowers of the Nazi army perished in the snow.

Victor Kravchenko in his book *I Chose Freedom* said: "The Germans could have taken Moscow those days virtually without a struggle. Why they turned back is a mystery only the Germans themselves can solve for history." As Christians we can solve that mystery. It was the mighty hand of God extended by the prayers of His children. The Bible conclusively states that God directs the outcome of wars. In II Chronicles, chapter 18, godless king Ahab is planning to go to war. He summons a prophet named Micaiah to predict the outcome of the battle. The prediction is defeat for the king, and his death in battle.

King Ahab, angered with this prophetic pronouncement of judgment on him, sends Micaiah to prison telling the prophet that he will take further action against him when he returns from battle. The prophet Micaiah says that if the king returns in peace he himself is not a prophet. In other words, *"You are not coming back."* In verses 18-22 God is pictured on His throne surrounded by angels. The Lord asks, "Who will go to earth and entice the king to battle to die?" An evil spirit comes up to the throne and says that he is right for the job, and he asks permission of God to be allowed to cause the defeat and death of the king. Permission is granted and the king is killed as predicted.

I know some people will take issue with the idea that God is involved in war, but the Bible is clear from Genesis through Revelation that God is indeed in control of battles and determines the outcomes. He gives victory or defeat to whomever He wills. I believe that Hitler's ultimate defeat was predicted in the annals of God's recorded book of His-Story in Heaven. God, in speaking of Himself to Job, tells of His power and might:

"When he (God) raiseth up himself, the mighty are afraid: by reason of breakings they purify themselves. The sword of him that layeth at him cannot hold: the spear, the dart, nor the habergeon. He esteemeth iron as straw, and brass as rotten wood. The arrow cannot make him flee: slingstones are turned with him into stubble. Darts are counted as stubble: he laugheth at the shaking of a spear. Sharp stones are under him: he spreadeth sharp pointed things upon the mire. He maketh the deep to boil like a pot: he maketh the sea like a pot of ointment. He maketh a path to shine after him; one would think the deep to be hoary. Upon earth there is not his like, who is made without fear. He beholdeth all high things: he is a king over all the children of pride.

Then Job answered the LORD, and said, I know that thou canst do every thing, and that no thought can be withholden from thee. Who is he that hideth counsel without knowledge? therefore have I uttered that I understood not; things too wonderful for me, which I knew not" (Job 41:25-34; 42-1-3).

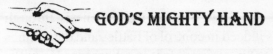

BIRD ON THE BRAIN 1942 A.D.

During World War I, Captain Eddie Rickenbacker was a household name throughout America. He had gunned down numerous German fighter planes and observation balloons which had earned his lion's share of medals. When World War II broke out, Henry Stimson, Secretary of War, asked Captain Rickenbacker to serve the American cause by inspecting Air Force bases throughout the U.S., Great Britain, and the Pacific. In accepting this position, Rickenbacker did not realize the Lord was about to show His mighty power to Americans who had "eyes to see and ears to hear."

On October 21, 1942, Captain Rickenbacker was carrying a secret message aboard a B-17-D to General Douglas MacArthur, headquartered in Port Moresby, New Guinea. Unfortunately, Captain William T. Cherry, Jr. had made a critical error in fuel calculations, and the giant aircraft came to a sudden halt over the vast Pacific Ocean. Captain Rickenbacker, Captain Cherry, First Lieutenant James C. Whittaker, First Lieutenant John J. De Angelis, Sergeant James Reynolds, Private F. Barteck, and Crew Chief Alexander T. Kaczmarczyk found themselves stranded without certainty of location and with no way to summon help. Miraculously, Captain Cherry brought the belly of the plane to rest in the ocean. Within moments, the men gathered three life rafts and scurried out the top of the plane into twelve-foot swells. It was a challenge to all, especially, to those who were injured during the crash landing. The only rations among them were eight oranges which, needless to say, did not last long. The three rafts were tied together for security and moral support. Most of the men were improperly clothed and found exposure to the sun produced horrible, life-threatening damage. Providence had prepared and equipped Captain Rickenbacker with experience to lead these men and make plans for their survival while keeping morale high. In his pocket, John Bartek had a serviceman's New Testament with Psalms which they read every morning and evening for devotions. The men discovered that Jesus was the "Living Water" that refreshed their soul and was more valuable than the natural water they so lacked. Each man took a turn reading Bible passages that meant the most to him. Their favorite passages were Psalm 23 and the following:

"Therefore take no thought, saying, What shall we eat? or, What shall we drink? or, Wherewithal shall we be clothed? (For after all these things do the Gentiles seek:) for your heavenly Father knoweth that ye have need of all these things. But seek ye first the kingdom of God, and His righteousness; and all these things shall be added unto you. Take therefore no thought for the morrow: for the morrow shall take thought for the things of itself. Sufficient unto the day is the evil thereof" (Matthew 6:31-34).

After devotions, the few songs that were remembered from bygone Sunday school days by some of the sin-hardened men were sung with sincere repentance. Their favorite songs were "Onward Christian Soldiers" and "Lead, Kindly Light." (See chapter on John Newman - 1833 A.D.) Prayers of confession were uttered to one another and to Christ Jesus, asking for forgiveness of past sins, as well as mercy to be rescued from their present danger. The God of mercy and grace heard and responded to their prayers in startling and amazing ways. After eight days, hunger pangs and thirst were met by the Lord of provision. God sent them sweet, pure rain which cleansed their salt-crusted bleeding and blistered bodies. Immediately, they set about collecting, in every device imaginable, the precious rain water God had sent. However, the rain left in the dead of that pitch black night as fast as it came. After giving thanks to the Almighty for His tender loving care, the men, being cold, soaked and exhausted, fell asleep. Later, Eddie Rickenbacker said, "It was the most refreshing water he had ever drunk."

During the night, they abruptly awoke to what they had expected and dreaded for some time. Sharks had followed them for days and were now moving in more aggressively by bumping into the rafts repeatedly. Fear gripped them, and led them all to cry out to God in prayer for His protection. The next morning, they rejoice to find that the sharks were gone. Their joy soon turned into sorrow when they realized that comrade, Alex Kaczmarczyk, was failing in health. By day fourteen, Alex knew he was on the verge of death; thus, he committed his soul to his Savior Christ Jesus and died. His comrades buried him at sea with all the honor they could bestow upon him. His final hours were spent in prayer for his mother and his fiancee's happiness.

Though thirst had been temporarily satisfied, the grim face of hunger reared its ugly head. Prayer for food now became their focus. Once again, the Lord answered in a most satisfying and unusual way. As Rickenbacker was dozing in the mid-afternoon sun, he felt something perch atop his hat. When he opened his eyes, he perceived that the Lord had sent "manna" from heaven in the form of a sea gull. Carefully and painstakingly, he slowly moved his hand toward the feet of the gull until he finally reached it. He grabbed it, wrung its neck, and divided it among the men for a most precious feast. Complete awe struck them at how Jesus had provided meat for them at such a critical time. These men had witnessed a miracle similar to the Bible stories many of them had remembered from their Sunday school days! They ate bones and every imaginable part of the gull, reserving a portion as fishing bait . They had taken equipment from their survival packs, along with the bait, and caught a couple of fish which they quickly divided amongst themselves. These Americans had "eyes to see" God's providential care, and knew they would somehow survive this ordeal. As their faith strengthened, some of the men made professions of faith, trusting their lives to the atoning blood of Jesus Christ.

On November 13, 1942, after twenty-four days, U.S. Navy planes finally spotted the crew. This was a miraculous event, in and of itself, since several American planes had previously passed over without seeing them. How does an airplane spot a little blotch in such a huge ocean? The answer is simple! No plan of God is thwarted, and He directs the ways of man through His mighty hand of deliverance. All seven men, having lost over thirty pounds each and wearing tattered clothes, were taken to field hospitals. The experiences of the rescued men brought encouragement to the war effort and had far-reaching spiritual results. Nationally publicized accounts of their survival allowed opportunity for several of the airmen to give glory to God for His direct and miraculous answers to their specific prayers. During the ordeal, grace and mercy had left a life-long impression upon the airmen. These newly converted Christians could truly give thanks to God in all things, knowing the Lord had allowed them to suffer physically because He cared more for their eternal salvation and condition. Thus, they could agree with the Psalmist that "it is good for me that I have been afflicted" (Psalm 119:71).

Columnist Ray Tucker declared, "Rickenbacker has become an evangelist without knowing it." Johnny Bartek was equally outspoken about his experiences on the raft in the Pacific Ocean. He asserted, "Then we prayed—and God answered. It was real. We needed water. We prayed for water, and we got water—all we needed. Then we asked for fish, and we got fish. And we got some meat when we prayed. Sea gulls don't go around sitting on people's heads waiting to be caught. Once again I prayed to God and said, 'If you'll send that one plane back for us, I promise I'll believe in you and tell everyone else.' That very plane came back and the others flew on. It just happened? It did not! God sent that plane back!" The entire free world was thrilled by the rescue and by Captain Rickenbacker's words: "We prayed . . . and we were spared to come back and tell Americans to pray more earnestly."

"O, give thanks unto the LORD, for He is good: for His mercy endureth for ever. Let the redeemed of the LORD say so, whom He hath redeemed from the hand of the enemy; And gathered them out of the lands, from the east, and from the west, from the north, and from the south. They wandered in the wilderness in a solitary way; they found no city to dwell in. Hungry and thirsty, their soul fainted in them. Then they cried unto the LORD in their trouble, and He delivered them out of their distresses. And He led them forth by the right way, that they might go to a city of

might go to a city of habitation. Oh that men would praise the LORD for his goodness, and for His wonderful works to the children of men! For He satisfieth the longing soul, and filleth the hungry soul with goodness " (Psalm 107:1-9).

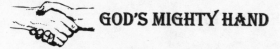

ONE NATION UNDER GOD 1942 A.D.

Following her surprise attack on Pearl Harbor on December 7, 1941, Japan did not seize her advantage by attacking California or any of the strategic cities throughout the United States mainland. Many Americans continue to wonder why. Admiral Sako, commander of the invading Japanese submarine force at Pearl Harbor, was in the best position to know, and offered an explanation some years after the war.

Speaking throughout the U.S., Admiral Sako, having become a Christian, told audiences that during repeated attempts his forces were completely unable to take the American mainland, try as they may. At the time he did not understand this powerlessness, but as a Christian he knew that God's mighty hand had intervened to protect America. He stated that Christians praying for the United States must have played an important role in this protection.

"Confess your faults one to another, and pray one for another, that ye may be healed. The effectual fervent prayer of a righteous man availeth much. Elias was a man subject to like passions as we are, and he prayed earnestly that it might not rain: and it rained not on the earth by the space of three years and six months. And he prayed again, and the heaven gave rain, and the earth brought forth her fruit." (James 5:16-18).

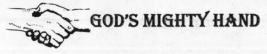

"THE DESERT FOX" 1942 A.D.

General Erwin Rommel, known as "The Desert Fox," was the high commander of the German forces attempting to conquer Africa during World War II. By 1942, the fourth year of the war, he had conquered almost all of North Africa. Opposing Rommel was British General Bernard Montgomery. El Alamein, a village in northwest Egypt, became the "Waterloo" for the indestructible Rommel.

Sir Winston Churchill so dreaded Rommel that in a war conference, hearing of the power and invincibility of Rommel, he cried out in frustration, "Rommel, Rommel, Rommel! What else matters but beating him?" It seemed that to "beat him" was impossible, but what is impossible for man is but trivial for God, as will be seen in this account. The "indestructible Rommel" was defeated, and two years later he committed suicide by drinking poison.

In the city of Alexandria, Egypt, the citizens braced themselves, fearing the inevitable bombardment and probable capture and occupation by the Germans. Along with the British forces opposing Rommel were the Greek and Egyptian armies. During World War II, Greece had been invaded first by the Italians, whom they had defeated. Then the incomparably stronger Nazi armies had forced the Greek government to yield. But the Greek soldiers, to escape capture, had embarked in boats and crossed the Mediterranean to Egypt. There they had reorganized to continue the fight alongside their British allies.

To the Christian Greeks, the village of El Alamein, west of Alexandria, had a special significance. The name of the village is an Arabic interpretation of the name "Menas," a Godly Christian man of the third century. This man's brave and noble character was evident as he served as an army officer in ancient Phrygia and later as a Christian hermit who was martyred and then buried in

El Alamein.

Greek fighting forces stationed near the church of St. Menas in El Alamein had already explored the sacred ruins of the ancient structure. With silent reverence they had studied the frescoes depicting the heroic deeds of Menas' life. One fresco showed Menas going off to war, leading camels and depicted the miraculous intervention of God in saving His people from destruction.

The proximity of this church was a comfort to the Greeks, as they worked far into the night preparing for the inevitable attack by Rommel's desert-hardened forces.

At midnight on the fateful night of October 23, 1942, certain Greek believers happened to glance at the church. They saw the figure of a man emerge, leading a procession of camels! It was exactly like the scene depicted on the fresco! They pointed excitedly, but silently, at the procession. Then they began to pray while the vision of the man trudged across the sands toward the enemy army, leading his illusory camels. The Greeks were not surprised at the confusion that ensued in the enemy camp as the camels made their noiseless way across the dunes. Shooting and shouting began and increased in intensity as the Greek and British forces returned the fire.

The silent approach of the visionary camels had filled the enemy troops with fear; pandemonium ensued, and finally, flight. They were pursued, defeated, and taken prisoner in large numbers by the Greeks, Egyptians, and British.

The victory at El Alamein marked a turning point in World War II. "Up to Alamein," Sir Winston Churchill said of that decisive battle, "we survived. After Alamein, we conquered."

Another major event during this campaign bears mention. German General Strumme of the Nazi XL Motorized Corps, commander of the Germans when they overran Greece, was also commander at El Alamein. (General Rommel was recovering from an illness in a hospital in Germany.) While patrolling the battlefield, General Strumme had a fatal heart attack and fell from the back of his moving vehicle. The driver did not even notice that the General had fallen out until he arrived at their next stop. The untimely death of General Strumme was a major setback for the German cause. General Rommel, sick as he was, had to come to take over the engagement, and he witnessed the defeat firsthand.

So dramatic was the change in Allied outcomes of war after El Alamein that when General Montgomery was decorated for his brilliant successes, which continued, he was given the title "Viscount of Alamein." Although General Montgomery received this title of honor, had the Greeks been asked where the unlikely victory for the British cause came from, they would have certainly given the answer, "From the mighty hand of God."

"Then upon Jahaziel the son of Zechariah, the son of Benaiah, the son of Jeiel, the son of Mattaniah, a Levite of the sons of Asaph, came the Spirit of the LORD in the midst of the congregation; And he said, Hearken ye, all Judah, and ye inhabitants of Jerusalem, and thou king Jehoshaphat, Thus saith the LORD unto you, Be not afraid nor dismayed by reason of this great multitude; for the battle is not yours, but God's. To morrow go ye down against them: behold, they come up by the cliff of Ziz; and ye shall find them at the end of the brook, before the wilderness of Jeruel. Ye shall not need to fight in this battle: set yourselves, stand ye still, and see the salvation of the LORD with you, O Judah and Jerusalem: fear not, nor be dismayed; to morrow go out against them: for the LORD will be with you. And Jehoshaphat bowed his head with his face to the ground: and all Judah and the inhabitants of Jerusalem fell before the LORD, worshipping the LORD. And the Levites, of the children of the Kohathites, and of the children of the Korhites, stood up to praise the LORD God of Israel with a loud voice on high" (II Chronicles 20:14–19).

Please read the entire account of this battle in II Chronicles 20 to see how God intervenes in battles. God is often referred to in the Bible as "The Captain of the Host" or the "Lord of Hosts."

The word "Sabaoth" (SAA-bay-oth) is a Greek word derived from Hebrew, which means "Lord of Hosts." (See *Strong's* Greek entry #4519 and Hebrew entry #6635.)

Did we in our own strength confide, our striving would be losing; were not the right man on our side, The Man of God's own choosing. Dost ask Who that may be? Christ Jesus, It is He. Lord Sabaoth His Name, From age to age the same. And He must win the battle.

Martin Luther (1483–1546)

THE SILVER CROSS 1942 A.D.

Clarence S. Stanford, a pilot from Auburn, New York, was fighting Japanese planes over the Pacific when he was separated from the rest of his squadron. Not knowing where he was, he flew along with nothing but water under him. When his fuel tank ran dry, he was still over the Pacific Ocean, so he put the plane into a long glide at the optimum angle, prayed, and commended himself to the mighty hand of God. He nearly made it to the land, but the plane sagged down just a bit too soon, and he had to bail out.

He landed easily in the water, but his life belt wouldn't inflate, and he was at least three miles from land. He had never swum such a distance in his life, but he disentangled himself from his parachute harness, kicked off his clothes, and swam for dear life, praying as he went.

When he finally dragged himself onto the beach he was exhausted, and he fell into a deep sleep. He awoke to feel a sharp instrument digging into his chest. Towering over him were two naked Australian aborigines.

"You Japanese?" asked the native, withdrawing his spear a moment.

"In the name of Jesus, no. I'm an American," Stanford replied. But the aborigines, not trusting him, prodded deeper with their spears, evidently intending to kill him. Then suddenly one of them noticed the only thing Stanford was wearing—a little silver cross.

Immediately they withdrew their spears and cried out reverently, "Jesus number one man!"

They helped Sanford up, gave him food, and took care of him. They led him through the jungle for twenty-five miles to an American missionary outpost. His feet were torn with the journey, and the sun baked him almost beyond recognition, for he was stark naked. Reaching the mission, he found that these two natives were the only ones who ever came to that particular beach. If they hadn't found him, he certainly would have perished.

The missionaries investigated and confirmed the natives' account in that they said they would have killed Stanford had they not noticed the cross of Christ on his chest. The cross and what it stands for had brought salvation to the aborigines. God reconciled them to Himself through the cross. Seeing the silver cross they recognized a fellow believer and knew that they were "fellow citizens" in the Kingdom of Christ.

Dear reader, God's mighty hand is most wonderfully displayed in the fact that He desires all men to come to Christ so that none should perish. I trust that you have come to the cross of Christ yourself and have committed your life to Him who died for your sins.

Consider the following story, told by one of my professors many years ago while I was in seminary. I hope it will leave as profound an impression on your mind as it did on mine about the power of the cross of Christ. The story was recorded by J. Wallace Hamilton.

An Archbishop of Paris, standing in the pulpit of Notre Dame Cathedral, said that thirty years before, three young tourists had come into the cathedral. They were rough, rude, and cynical men who thought all religion was a racket. Two of them dared the third to go into the confession box and make a pseudo confession to the priest. They bet that he didn't have the nerve, but he did. When he attempted to fool the wise, experienced, old priest, the priest, sensing haughtiness in his attitude, said, "Very well, my son. Every confession requires a penance. I ask you to go to the alter, stand before the Crucifix, look into the face of the crucified Christ, and say, 'All this You did for me, and I don't care a bit.'"

The young man swaggered out of the confessional to claim the bet, but the others insisted that before he was paid he would have to do the penance. So he went up to the alter, looked into the face of Christ and began: "All this You—" He did not finish the sentence but that moment he began the painful experience of realizing that Christ died for his sin. Falling down on his knees he made his peace with Christ, his life was forever changed. That change in his life finally led him into the priesthood. The archbishop leaned over the pulpit and said, "That young man is the same person who stands before you to preach today."

"But now in Christ Jesus ye who sometimes were far off are made nigh by the blood of Christ. For he is our peace, who hath made both one, and hath broken down the middle wall of partition between us; Having abolished in his flesh the enmity, even the law of commandments contained in ordinances; for to make in himself of twain one new man, so making peace; And that he might reconcile both unto God in one body by the cross, having slain the enmity thereby: And came and preached peace to you which were afar off, and to them that were nigh. For through him we both have access by one Spirit unto the Father. Now therefore ye are no more strangers and foreigners, but "fellow citizens" with the saints, and of the household of God; And are built upon the foundation of the apostles and prophets, Jesus Christ himself being the chief corner stone; In whom all the building fitly framed together groweth unto an holy temple in the Lord: In whom ye also are builded together for an habitation of God through the Spirit." (Ephesians 2:12-22).

BAD WATER 1942 A.D.

British Major P.W. Rainer was involved in the battle for Alexandria, Egypt, from August 31 through September 5, 1942. In his book, *Pipe Line to Battle*, he tells this story of a remarkable incident that determined who would win the battle and how it was done.

Field Marshal Erwin Rommel was the extremely capable commander of Germany's crack tank division, the dreaded Afrika Korps. He was so successful in fighting the Allies in North Africa that he earned the nickname, "Desert Fox." Between this brilliant leader with about 1,100 elite troops and the city of Alexandria stood the remnants of a British army—fifty tanks, a few score field guns, and about 5,000 soldiers.

The sides were equally matched. For, although outnumbered, the Germans had superior 88-mm. guns. And both armies were near exhaustion from heat, dust, and lack of water.

The ensuing battle was grim. In the words of Major Rainer: "The sun was almost overhead, and our men were fast reaching the end of their endurance when the Nazis surrendered. Ten minutes more and it might have been curtains for us. Slowly, sullenly, our Mark IV tanks lumbered back from their battle smoke. And then an incredible thing happened: 1,100 men of the 90th Light Panzer Division, the elite of the Afrika Korps, came stumbling across the barren sand with their hands in the air. Cracked and black with coagulated blood, their swollen tongues were protruding from their mouths. Crazily they tore water bottles from the necks of our men and poured life-giving swallows between their parched lips."

Major Rainer gives this reason for the Germans' surrender. "The Germans had been twenty-four hours without water when they overran the British defenses and found a six-inch water pipe. They shot holes in it and drank deeply. Only when they had taken great gulps, did they realize that it was sea water.

"The pipe had only just been laid. I took a water sample and found it was not yet clear to drink. I admonished my men to wait a couple of days for the salt water to be replaced with the incoming fresh water. When the Germans overran the outpost, we retreated, leaving them the water.

"The day before the Germans overran the outpost the water pipe would have been empty. Two days later it would have been full of fresh water. There was only one critical time the water was bad, and that is precisely when the Nazis overran us and drank it. The Nazis didn't detect the salt at once because their sense of taste had already been anaesthetized by the brackish water they had been used to, and by thirst."

The surrender of those 1,100 crack soldiers may have been the deciding incident in the battle for Alexandria. Such an incredible happening cannot be treated as a mere coincidence. Surely, the hand of Almighty God is evident once more, coming to the aid of righteousness and liberty—His precious gifts to humanity.

"O my God: defend me from them that rise up against me. Deliver me from the workers of iniquity, and save me from bloody men. For, lo, they lie in wait for my soul: the mighty are gathered against me; not for my transgression, nor for my sin, O LORD. They run and prepare themselves without my fault: awake to help me, and behold. Thou therefore, O LORD God of hosts, the God of Israel, awake to visit all the heathen: be not merciful to any wicked transgressors. Selah. They return at evening: they make a noise like a dog, and go round about the city. Behold, they belch out with their mouth: swords are in their lips: for who, say they, doth hear? But thou, O LORD, shalt laugh at them; thou shalt have all the heathen in derision. Because of his strength will I wait upon thee: for God is my defence. The God of my mercy shall prevent me: God shall let me see my desire upon mine enemies. Slay them not, lest my people forget: scatter them by thy power; and bring them down, O Lord our shield. For the sin of their mouth and the words of their lips let them even be taken in their pride: and for cursing and lying which they speak.

*Consume them in wrath, consume them, that they may not be: and
let them know that God ruleth in Jacob unto the ends of the earth.
Selah. And at evening let them return; and let them make a noise
like a dog, and go round about the city. Let them wander up and
down for meat, and grudge if they be not satisfied. But I will sing
of thy power; yea, I will sing aloud of thy mercy in the morning:
for thou hast been my defense and refuge in the day of my trouble.
Unto thee, O my strength, will I sing: for God is my defense, and
the God of my mercy"* (Psalm 59:1-17).

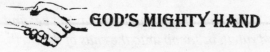

GOD'S MIGHTY HAND

THE PRAYER OF DELIVERANCE 1942 A.D.

On August 7, 1942, U.S. Marines landed on Guadalcanal in the first of the amphibious assaults against Japanese-held positions in the Pacific. The marines obtained and held Henderson Field on the island in the face of bitter ground, sea, and air attacks by the Japanese. Fighting continued in the jungles of Guadalcanal until February 9, 1943, when the U.S. Army and Marine Forces secured the island against Japanese resistance. Behind the scenes in every situation of life where God's children pray, whether in peace or in the intense danger of battle, the mighty hand of God can be seen and felt, as in the story told by Private Richard Hollinger.

Private Hollinger and six Marines were lost in a Guadalcanal jungle for five nights. There was a forty-eight-man platoon on outpost duty beyond the American positions. The Japanese swarmed around them and cut them completely off from the rest of the outfit in an attempt to recapture an airfield. Two men were killed and ten were badly wounded. The men scattered and the six were reported, "missing in action."

Those jungles were dirty, damp, dangerous places, full of swamps that a man could neither swim through nor walk across. You could take a step and sink to your thigh. Something would clutch your leg and you could not tell whether it was a reptile or a poisonous vine. Once within the depth of the jungle, all direction was lost. At times the sky was obscured in the dense jungle. At night bugs would crawl and nibble at your body. It was enough to cause a sinner to pray. Private Hollinger recalls:

"When the Japs came in around us, it was dark. There was a lot of shooting going on, and we couldn't tell what the score was. We camouflaged ourselves and lay low for the night. There were an awful lot of Japs. Well, we just prayed and kept moving. And, believe me, we did a lot of praying."

The Japs, with leaves sewn to their clothes, ran noiselessly through the shadows, looking for the boys who were lying, still as death, in plain view, praying and holding their breath. From behind them, their own outfit was firing at the Japs, and they were in the way so that one of their men was hit twice. At another time a four-man patrol of Japs spotted them, but Private Richard Hollinger managed to kill two of them. He was too modest to tell about it himself, but his pal, Pharmacist's mate Homer Berry, told it.

"Dick is the guy that shot them," he said. "He had a Springfield, and it sounded like a machine gun, he was shooting so fast." They tried to get the rice rations from the dead Japs, but there were too many live ones sniping at them to take a chance. So they had to go on being hungry for the whole five days.

God answered their prayer, for providentially they stumbled into an American patrol. All the six Marines recognized the hand of God in their deliverance. It was to Richard Hollinger that they owed their lives. He reminded them that God delivered them and to trust Him throughout their lives. They shared many personal times together during those six days. Those who had not previouly experienced personal faith and the results of faith believing prayer soon learned how to trust God and to pray themselves. Throughout the war they never forgot that God's mighty hand of deliverance was only a prayer away.

"For this shall every one that is godly pray unto thee in a time when thou mayest be found: surely in the floods of great waters they shall not come nigh unto him. Thou art my hiding place; thou shalt preserve me from trouble; thou shalt compass me about with songs of deliverance. Selah. I will instruct thee and teach thee in the way which thou shalt go: I will guide thee with mine eye. Be ye not as the horse, or as the mule, which have no understanding: whose mouth must be held in with bit and bridle, lest they come near unto thee. Many sorrows shall be to the wicked: but he that trusteth in the LORD, mercy shall compass him about. Be glad in the LORD, and rejoice, ye righteous: and shout for joy, all ye that are upright in

heart"(Psalm 32:6-11).

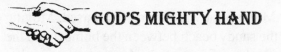

GOD'S MIGHTY HAND

NOW IS THE TIME TO PRAY 1942 A.D.

Captain Johnson was serving as chaplain on an island in the South Pacific during World War II. He had attended a bombing raid several hundred miles from the bomber's base. The raid had been a perfect success, but the return trip had scarcely begun when the plane began to lose altitude and the gasoline gauges rapidly moved toward "empty." Providentially, an island with a wide, smooth, sandy beach was spotted below. As they approached, the pilot could see a Japanese flag fluttering among the trees that shaded a Japanese military camp. It obviously was a Japanese occupied island. They had no choice. It was either this island or the surging sea. The bomber's motors misfired and sputtered as they headed for the secluded beach and miraculously touched down without sustaining any damage. Cautiously, the armed crew disembarked and inspected the area. The Japanese apparently were off the island for the moment or were hiding. After a brief survey of their situation, the staff sergeant came to Chaplain Johnson and said,

"Chaplain, you have been telling us for months about the need for praying, and believing God answers prayer in time of trouble. Now is the time to pray."

Chaplain Johnson knelt in the sand under the shade of the great bomber's wing and began fervent prayer with a firm belief in God's promises. He lay hold of the promise found in Acts 2:21, *"Whosoever shall call upon the name of the Lord shall be saved."* He prayed all afternoon. There was no means of help or rescue within hundreds of miles. As they made their landing, they had left no radio communication as to their whereabouts. Chaplain Johnson continued to pray in the darkness of night, and still no Japanese patrols had appeared. His prayer was for God to work a miracle and deliver them from the claws of the enemy so close at hand. While the chaplain prayed the crew fell asleep.

At about 2:00 AM the pilot was strangely aroused. Moving slowly, he surveyed the sandy beach between the bomber and the dark rim of trees. No shadowy figures moved in that direction, but there was a new sound to the waves. A huge, dark blob loomed at the water's edge. Stealthily, the pilot awakened his crew, one man at a time, placing a warning finger on the lips of each as he roused him. As they watched and listened, they whispered as to what and who might be there. They reasoned that the Japanese garrison hardly needed to make a long trip around by water to apprehend them when they were already within half-a-mile walking distance to their camp. Nor did they believe an attack by night would be logical on the part of the Japanese garrison. For, being so out-numbered, they could easily attack in the light of day. Some reasoned that it might be Americans.

At last, the airmen could bear the suspense no longer. They crept to the water's edge. They moved so silently that the kneeling chaplain was not disturbed. They discerned the outlines of a sizeable barge. No voices could be heard aboard, and no sounds of human footsteps were detected. A giant tow rope, dangling almost to the surface of the beach, brushed stiffly against the pilot's shoulders. Was it some kind of barge with perhaps a crew below? The gentle surf with its Pacific breeze allowed the armed airmen to make plans. It was decided that the captain must board that barge. After ordering the men to hold the rope, he boarded the barge with a knife in his teeth like a pirate. He slowly shimmied up the dangling rope and crept silently over the edge of the boat. Noiselessly, the captain sought a sentry. The deck looked abandoned. No sentry, no crew on the single-decked barge. The barge was totally deserted! The pilot discovered that the deck was covered with drums. He unscrewed the opening of a drum and perceived the unmistakable odor of the contents: Gasoline!

Sliding down the tow rope, he imparted the tremendous news to the crew. "The barge is full of gas!" The whole unbelievable answer to their prayer seemed like a dream to the stranded men, as when the angel of the Lord awoke the Apostle Peter and hastened his escape. This drifting barge had brought them the one thing in all the world that could get their bomber swiftly off this island and see them back to home base. Jubilantly, they streaked across the sand and embraced their startled chaplain.

"Your miracle's here, Chaplain!" they exulted.

In quiet haste, they counted fifty drums of high-octane gasoline. They refueled the plane, using their in-flight refueling hose, and with prayerful thanksgiving, bid farewell to the island and the Japanese, whom they never had to encounter.

A later investigation revealed that the skipper of a U.S. tanker, finding his ship in submarine infested waters, had his gasoline cargo removed to minimize the danger in case of a torpedo hit. Barrels were placed on barges and set adrift six hundred miles from where Johnson and the plane crew were forced down. Only the Creator of the high seas could navigate one of these barges through wind and current and beach it fifty feet from the stranded men. An answer beyond their wildest dreams and earnest prayer.

" Thou hast a mighty arm: strong is thy hand, and high is thy right hand. Justice and judgment are the habitation of thy throne: mercy and truth shall go before thy face. Blessed is the people that know the joyful sound: they shall walk, O LORD, in the light of thy countenance. In thy name shall they rejoice all the day: and in thy righteousness shall they be exalted. For thou art the glory of their strength: and in thy favour our horn shall be exalted. For the LORD is our defence; and the Holy One of Israel is our king. Then thou spakest in vision to thy holy one, and saidst, I have laid help upon one that is mighty; I have exalted one chosen out of the people" (Psalm 89:13-19).

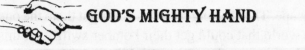

GOD'S MIGHTY HAND

IT'S ALL WE CAN DO FOR NOW 1943 A.D.

I believe you will find this an amazing story written by Mr. Elmer Bendiner, a gunner on the *Tondelayo* a B-17 bomber, during WWII.

"It was another one of those perilous days that awaited my friend and pilot Bohn, and the flight crew of which I, Elmer Bendiner, was a part of. Leaving our base the Kimbolton airfield in England, we were headed for Kassel, Germany. Kassel, located on the Fulda River about 93 miles northeast of Frankfurt was the site of a large locomotive and tank factory. It was our job to drop 4,800 pounds of explosive from our B-17 Flying Fortress we named the *Tondelayo*.

"The British Air Command thought we were nuts to fly in daylight to do our bombing raids over Europe. They much preferred the cover of darkness, but we insisted that in darkness we were not sure of what we would be hitting with our bombs, and we had specific targets assigned for us to knock out. This became a standing joke between us American pilots and the British RAF. Sometimes I sided with the British when seeing so many of my friends knocked out of the sky, flying like huge sitting ducks in our B-17's amidst German 20-mm big antiaircraft guns and fighter planes. What could a soldier do but follow orders and continue daylight bombing?

"We did, however, have a sense of confidence flying our fortress with their powerful four-engines giving us top speeds of 317 mph. Our plane which would reach altitudes of 25,000 feet would hopefully make us hard targets to hit—we hope—especially at fast speeds. The down side was our low-wing, 103-foot B-17, with the five defensive machine-gun turrets, which could shoot down Nazi aircraft that buzzed around us like flies at a Sunday picnic, was so big it made a somewhat easy target from ground guns.

"Over the war years the Germans got pretty clever developing all kinds of wicked explosives to put us out of commission. Flak explosives were annoying pesky bombs that would explode in our flight vicinity and send out shrapnel in all directions often perching our planes and playing havoc with our crew. Many times I would be hit and saved by the multitudes of layers of clothing we would have to wear to keep warm while flying at such altitudes. It got down right cold flying in our airship in 40-below zero weather.

"Worse than the flak bombs were the Nazi 20-mm anti-aircraft shells that would blow huge pieces out of our aircraft, and unless we were hit in a serious location that would instantly blow us into eternity, we could bail out and hope the Germans would treat us civil in a Nazi concentration camp.

"On the particular day we were to bomb Kassel, I recall flying back after dropping our payload over Kassel and receiving word that we were hit with a big 20-mm shell in the fuel tank. The fact anyone was talking about it was a miracle because a 20-mm in the tank generally meant our time had come to kiss the world goodby. After landing back in England, flight captain Bohn went to ask our crew chief for the shell in the tank to keep as a souvenir. Marsden told Bohn to come back on the following day.

"When Bohn came back, Marsden told Bohn he did not have the choice of *one* shell, but *eleven* which had been found in the fuel tank. Bohn was shocked and speechless, he inquired as to how this could be when one shell alone in the fuel tank meant the end of the trail. Marsden, equally amazed, began to give the details Captain Bohn.

"It appeared that when the tank was taken out for inspection there was the rattling of more than one shell in the tank. The shells were taken out and taken to the armorers for inspection and removal of the explosives, a very dangerous job—except in this case. They opened each of the shell and found that they did not contain any explosive charges. They were clean as a whistle and as harmless. Empty? Not all of them. One contained a carefully rolled piece of paper scribbled in Czech. The intelligence captain scoured the base for a man who could read Czech and finding such a man gave him the paper to read. He replied that it said, 'This is all we can do for you now.'

"As you can well imagine, the men Hitler enslaved from his captured provinces were hog tied and forced to work to support his war machine. For a captured people forced to work in a Nazi ammunition factory, their little note 'This is all we can do for you now' was more than enough."

One can surmise that this was an accident, or admit it was a miracle, as all aboard the B-17 later confessed. One shell could be luck, eleven shells is the direct hand of God's divine protection. This is one of those-amazing-hand-God stories that without documentation one would find suspicious, and hard to believe. I did do the necessary research to verify the story reading through Elmer Bendiner's book *The Fall of Fortresses.*

What I found more amazing is that Mr. Bendiner does not seem to make any mention of having any faith in Christ, nor attribute the salvation of the *Tondelayo* and all aboard to any other factor than a miracle. He does recognize the miraculous nature of the event, but does not investigate it to the point that it would lead him to faith in Christ. In the majority of accounts within this book you are reading, they are performed by the hand of God on behalf of a professing believer. One would almost expect Christians to see the divine intervention of God in their lives. The Bible is full of accounts where God has intervened to save, protect, and deliver His own people called by His name. I chose this account in order to show a side of God that is often over looked, and that is the aspect of God's divine mercy on all of humanity.

The Bible says, *"The Lord is...not willing that any should perish, but that all should come to repentance" (2 Peter 3:9).* All to often God is accused by faithless people of being a God of wrath ready to meet out some juicy divine punishment on behalf of unbelieving sinners. This view of God is completely false and a lie from the pit of hell. God showers mercy and forgiveness on undeserving humanity, and has done so since Adam and Eve violated His command and sinned. No sinner will ever stand before the Almighty God and accuse Him of being unfair and unjust.

When Mr. Bendiner and the entire flight crew stand before God's throne in judgement they will have no excuses to offer for their unbelief in the face of God's extended mercy and protection. Sinners may never fully know how many times God's hand of mercy was extended throughout their lives in order to woe them toward seeking His face and forgiveness. God beckons us, but does not force us to receive His pardon for sin through Christ's death on the Cross. Even at the cross God's mercy was extended to the one thief who cried, "remember me."

For sinners who have not traced those so called "lucky" escapes to the throne of God, and remain in unbelief despite the divine intervention of God, it will be very serious for them on judgement day. They will weep and wail knowing they were so close to God and never received his forgiveness, while it stared them right in the face. I think it fascinating that Mr. Bendiner and the flight crew received a the note from the Czech's, "This is all we can do for you now," when on the other hand God sent His "note" of love to mankind in the giving of His son Jesus Christ to die on the cross. God's note reads "This is all I can do for you forever."

"The Lord is merciful and gracious, slow to anger, and plenteous in mercy. He will not always chide; neither will he keep his anger forever. He has not dealt with us after our sins, nor rewarded us according to our iniquities. For as the heavens are high above the earth, so great is his mercy towards them that fear Him. As far as the east is from the west so far hath he removed our transgressions from us" (Psalm 103:8-12).

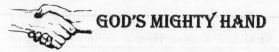

MIRACLE AT THE BULGE 1944 A.D.

By 1944, Germany—ever diligent to invent weapons of destruction in an attempt to win World War II—began to use V-1 and V-2 rocket bombs. These bombs were an early form of today's guided missiles. The V-1s, launched from bases in Nazi-occupied France, and the V-2s, launched from the Netherlands, were effectively reaching England. These missiles killed thousands of English civilians, motivating the Allied forces to step up advances into Germany under the American General George S. Patton, Jr.

General Patton concentrated his soldiers east of the Rhine River. They were desperately attempting to penetrate the German defenses protecting their homeland. The Germans battled like tigers and tried everything in their power to keep the Allied advance back, but it was to no avail. The Allies entered Germany in September, crossing the German border east of Aachen. The American soldiers were about to see the mighty hand of God perform a miracle that would eventually lead to the surrender and complete defeat of the German army.

The cold, wet, freezing season which arrived in late fall and early winter gave the Germans an advantage in keeping the American soldiers at bay. On December 16, 1944, the Nazis launched a furious counterattack in the Ardennes Forest. While overcast skies grounded Allied planes, twenty-four German divisions drove a bulge (hence the name of the battle) sixty miles wide and forty-five miles deep into the American lines. Part of this success was gained by a specially trained German unit wearing American uniforms and driving captured American vehicles. The Germans took advantage of their opportunity to launch a surprise counterattack before the American units could call an air strike.

The biggest problem for the Americans was the bad weather.

An advance air strike was impossible, with visibility not more that a few yards. The Battle of the Bulge had placed the Americans in a desperate position.

During this seemingly hopeless situation, General Patton silently sought out God's mighty hand of power to grant just four days of favorable weather. During four days of sunshine, reconnaissance could pinpoint the targets for the artillery, and fighter-bombers could find and bomb the enemy lines under General Von Rundstedt's command. Four days of sunshine would also dry up the hindering mud, allowing trucks carrying ammunition, supplies, and rations to reach the forward lines. Four days of good weather would permit Patton's ambulances to speed the wounded to hospitals. Such weather also would enable his artillery and tanks to maneuver once more.

Inspired with a plan, General Patton picked up his phone and called his Third Army Chaplain, James H. O'Neill. "This is Patton," he said. "Do you have a prayer for good weather? We must do something about these rains if we are to win this war." Chaplain O'Neill, a man devoted to prayer, was prepared for such a request. "I will search among my prayer devotional books to see what has been written on weather prayers," he assured the General. "I'll report within the hour."

But his books on prayer contained no formal "weather" prayer the chaplain thought might be acceptable to Patton. Therefore, he sat down and typed his own Spirit-led prayer direct from his heart:

"Almighty and most merciful Father, we humbly beseech Thee, of Thy great goodness, to restrain these rains with which we have to contend. Grant us fair weather for battle. Graciously hearken to us as soldiers who call upon Thee, that armed with power, we may advance victory to victory, and crush the oppression and wickedness of our enemies, and establish Thy justice among men and nations. Amen."

Chaplain O'Neill, wisely added a personal Christmas message from General Patton to each officer and soldier in the Third United States Army. After considerable thought and prayer the chaplain wrote:

"To each officer and soldier in the Third United States Army, I wish a Merry Christmas. I have full confidence in your courage, devotion to duty, and skill in battle. We march in our might to complete victory. May God's blessings rest upon each of you on this Christmas Day. G. S. Patton, Jr., Lieutenant Commander, Third United States Army."

The chaplain immediately crossed the quadrangle of the old French military barracks and reported to General Patton. The General scanned the prayer and ordered, "Have 250,000 copies printed, and see to it that every man in the Third Army gets one."

"Very well, Sir," the chaplain replied. This was putting feet to the prayer, and this pleased the chaplain in a great way!

The size of the order amazed the chaplain. After a moment's hesitation, he called the General's attention to the personal greeting on the reverse side, hoping that he had voiced the General's sentiment. "Very good," the General said, with a smile of approval. He signed the card and returned it.

After the war, Chaplain O'Neill wrote the following account of his conversation with General Patton that night:

"Chaplain," the General said, "sit down for a moment. I want to talk to you about this business of prayer."

Patton rose and walked to the high window, where he stared out at the ceaseless rain. For several seconds, he rubbed his face in his hands in thoughtful meditation. He stood there silently for what seemed a long time.

He was six-foot two, solid in stature, and, as always, impeccably dressed in full military "spit and polish." But there was something in his stance conveying the inner power of the man. This was a sacred moment etched in the memory of Chaplain O'Neill, something he thought about long after the war was over.

Sitting there observing that powerful physique, Chaplain O'Neill had time to recall the thoughtfulness of this man who felt a great responsibility for the welfare of the men under his command. How he was known to take time in the heat of action to discuss new methods to prevent trench feet. How he would personally order that dry socks be sent forward daily, with the rations, to the troops on the line. How he would kneel in the mud to care for a wounded soldier, administering medicine and waiting until the ambulance came.

"Chaplain, I am a strong believer in prayer," the General said at last. "In war there is always an unknown between the military planning and the operations. That unknown spells the difference between defeat or victory, success or failure. It is the reaction of the actors to the ordeal when it actually comes. Some people call that 'getting the breaks.' I call it God's will. God has His part or margin in everything. That is where prayer comes in.

"Up to now, God has been very good to us in the Third Army. We have never retreated. We have suffered no defeats, no famine, no epidemics. This is because a lot of people back home have been praying for us. We were 'lucky' in Africa, in Sicily, and in Italy, simply because people prayed. But we have to be responsible, and pray for ourselves too."

O'Neill recalled that Patton declared that men should pray no matter where they were, in church or out of it. If they did not pray, sooner or later they would crack up. "We've got to get not only the chaplains, but every man in the Third Army to pray," Patton said. "We must continue to ask God to stop these rains. These rains are the margin that holds defeat or victory. If we all pray... it will be like plugging in on a current whose source is in Heaven. I believe that prayer completes that circuit. It is the source of tapping into God's power."

Immediately following Chaplain O'Neill's meeting with General Patton, 250,000 copies of Patton's call to prayer were distributed among all the fighting men in the Third Army, officers and soldiers alike. No sooner had the distribution been made than the need for prayer became even more pressing.

General Von Rundstedt's Nazi forces crept out of the Schnee Eiffel Forest on December 16 to the complete surprise of the few American divisions on the Luxembourg frontier. Heavy rains, thick fogs, and swirling ground mists cloaked the enemy's movements and muffled the sound of their approach.

Shrouded in those mists and shielded from view above by lowering clouds, the jubilant Nazi forces pressed relentlessly forward. The few divisions of General Patton's Third Army on the Luxembourg front—with their visibility reduced to just a few yards, and all sounds muffled by snow, mud, and heavy mists—found it hard to fight an enemy they could neither see nor hear.

And the weather did not look as if it were going to change. The best meteorologists in the world were employed by the army to get accurate forecasts of the weather. As General Patton had said, "The weather often means the margin between defeat or victory."

For the Allies, the weather reports continued to be bleak. The forecasters informed the American Command that no break in conditions was possible. The weather would continue as it was, indefinitely: "Cold, rain, and snow; ceiling 100 feet; visibility 300 feet."

These circumstances were the stage on which the mighty hand of God would appear, just as in the days of Israel of old. The Third Army turned from east to north on December 19 to counter the Nazi thrusts, and then the prayed-for miracle happened. By noon on December 20, the clouds began to thin and two hours later the sun broke through.

Every American soldier on the front knew what that meant, and a mighty shout went up along a hundred-mile stretch of the Allied line. Throughout the Third Army, the cry was, "A miracle! A miracle!"

Patton's reconnaissance planes quickly sped forward to map enemy positions, and by three o'clock, English and American fighter bombers streaked to the attack. Soon the troops in the forward positions were cheered by the sight of wave after wave of supporting planes and by the sound of bombs crashing along the advancing Nazi units. In the closest enemy positions, they could hear the rat-a-tat-tat of the machine guns as their air support strafed the enemy lines. As wave after wave of Allied planes thundered over their heads, shaking the snow and ice off the treetops, the soldiers cheered lustily and made ready to follow their tanks into the fray.

The fighter bombers kept up the attack until dark, and in one day they accounted for 361 Nazi planes shot down. At nightfall, the "Black Widow" night-fighters took over. Their radar equipment found the Nazi supply columns, and their machine guns strafed them in the total darkness.

The next day dawned bright and clear, and the huge American Flying Fortress and Liberator bombers from the British air bases began chalking their vapor trails across the sky as they attacked the Nazi rear areas. It was Christmas week, and the miraculous weather, appearing out of nowhere, continued for eight straight days.

Trucks, tanks, artillery, and ambulances pulled out of ruts and moved forward on the sun-dried roads. General Hugh Gaffey's Fourth Armored Division began to gather speed and fought its way to within sight of French city of Bastogne on the second day of fair weather. On the third day, they defeated the last opposition and rumbled into the city. Immediately, twenty-two ambulances were assigned to evacuate the wounded and were given road priority. Forty truckloads of supplies also followed General Gaffey's forces.

Von Rundstedt's daring probes into the U.S. lines, hoping to isolate them from the British forces and to defeat the Allies one at a time, had brought him out of the formidable fortifications of the Siegfried Line and had made him more vulnerable to allied air attacks.

Those prayers and the fact that their commander had requested those prayers had added something immeasurably potent to the Allied army's fighting power. General Patton was right. His Third Army soldiers needed to pray for themselves. And they did—250,000 of them. Their collective prayer added hope and faith to their fighting; giving them a greater confidence that God would hear, heed, and help them. Those prayers had indeed "closed the circuit" between heaven and earth, bringing them power and victory.

After driving the Germans from the Ardennes bulge, the Allied armies advanced into Nazi Germany in 1945. By the end of March, the Americans and British had slashed halfway across Germany. The Nazis also collapsed on other fronts. Budapest fell to the Soviets in February, and Vienna was taken in April. In Italy, Mussolini was caught and shot by partisans on April 28, 1945. The German Reich caved in. Hitler committed suicide. There remained no other choice but unconditional surrender.

It is certainly foolish and thankless to think that God—the Ruler of all the nations, the final and supreme Judge of history—does not sometimes use the forces of nature to work His will with the nations of men. If He worked His wonders in controlling the weather for Israel in the days of the Old Testament, why would He not continue to work wonders today?

Those who still ponder this amazing question can consider once again the historical accounts in this book. They are just as astounding as the day in history when Joshua called the sun to stand still in the sky (Joshua 10:1-15). There is little doubt in light of these and other records of history that the God who answered prayers of faith in times of grave peril still moves His mighty hand today to show His power so that all men may see, believe, and receive salvation by trusting in His Son, Jesus Christ.

May you be like Rahab, who, having heard about the God of the Jews, repented of her sins and trusted in God's provision for salvation. One of major reasons I produced this book is that skeptics would come to believe in God and trust Christ for their salvation.

"By faith the walls of Jericho fell down, after they were compassed about seven days. By faith the harlot Rahab perished not with them that believed not, when she had received the spies with peace" (Hebrews 11:30-31).

GOD'S MIGHTY HAND

BLOOM LIKE A ROSE IN THE JUNGLE 1945 A.D.

Not long ago, I had the opportunity to spend a couple of days with Darlene Deibler Rose while observing a video shoot of her experiences in missionary work during and after World War II. Her life is a testimony to the mighty hand of God in so many ways. This is but a scant look at how God protected her during the difficult early years of her missionary life.

Darlene McIntosh Rose and missionary C. Russell Deibler were married on August 18, 1937. Within the year, they departed for the interior of New Guinea to minister among the newly discovered tribes of the pygmy people called Kapaukus.

What an adventure! Imagine going to live where crocodiles, venomous snakes, and cannibal tribes roam! Think of living where huge pack rats the size of small dogs would ramble through your primitive dwelling every night! Where you would have no indoor plumbing, water heaters, or any modern kitchen conveniences! Such was Darlene's new home. The only thing that would possess a pretty, young, healthy, and above all, Godly woman to go to a place like this could be the love of Christ and of her husband.

Her peaceful, missionary-centered world came to an abrupt end when Japan invaded New Guinea in 1942. During the latter part of January, the Dutch police came to Benteng Tinggi from Malino to inform the mission outpost that a ship lay at anchor on the south coast and would evacuate all foreigners who wished to leave before the dreaded Japanese came to kill, steal, and destroy the land and its people.

With the horrors and dangers of war, especially to young girls and women, one can imagine the concern Darlene now faced. With a way to escape, it seemed that this was a God-send. However, Dr. Jaffray, a missionary there for over thirty years, gathered the whole outpost together to seek the Lord's will.

Darlene Rose gives this account in her book, *Evidence Not Seen:*

As we gathered for prayer, Dr. Jaffray said, "I want to counsel not to discuss this decision that must be made with each other—not even husband and wife. Go to your knees and say, 'Lord, what do You want me to do? Shall I go or shall I stay?' This is extremely vital, because then, no matter what happens in months or possibly years that lie ahead, you will know you are exactly where God wants you to be. If He leads you to leave, you'll never feel that you were a coward and fled. If you are led to stay, no matter what happens you can look up and say, you intended for me to be right here."

When the truck arrived on Friday to take them to the ship, there was not a person among us who felt led to leave. As Dr. Jaffray had said, "God does not work in confusion, a wife against a husband or vice versa, in a matter that concerns both of you. This is but a confirmation to hearts of His directive."

About three days later, news arrived that the ship had been torpedoed and sunk. There were no known survivors. Then I knew God had said, "Don't go."

It is imperative that we know the voice of the Shepherd and learn to follow Him when He speaks. We must be obedient, no matter what He says to us; it may even mean our life.

Spared of immediate death, Darlene would soon find an even more difficult road to travel in God's sovereign plan, without her husband, but with God as her guide.

On March 5, 1942, the Japanese soldiers finally arrived at the primitive jungle mission outpost. These filthy soldiers in faded, tattered uniforms from months of jungle warfare, rounded up the missionaries at bayonet point.

These "shock troops" were the most dreaded of the Japanese soldiers. So cruel were these soldiers that in a matter of moments,

Darlene's husband was inhumanely beaten on his hands for no provocation on his part. The Japanese told the missionaries that they were prisoners of war and were not to have any contact with anyone outside of the outpost, or they would all be shot. Then they departed.

After a few weeks, the Japanese returned to take the men to an island prison camp. Darlene ran to her primitive home to gather a few necessary things to pack for her husband. Sad to say, by the time she finished the quick packing, her husband, along with the other men fit for slave labor, had been loaded onto the back of the army truck.

Darlene barely had enough time to say goodbye. Fighting tears in order not to give the Japanese the satisfaction of seeing her weakness, she handed Russell his Bible while he leaned over, and very tenderly and quietly said, "Remember one thing, Dear: God said that He would never leave us nor forsake us." She never saw him again. The Japanese worked him to death.

Darlene was privileged to see another instance of the mighty hand of God at work during those difficult war years while living at their mission in New Guinea. She records it as follows in her book:

> One night my rest was disturbed by what I thought were rats. I could hear them moving around the living room, in the dining room, and along the halls. I tried to ignore them with a promise: "I'll get you tomorrow." But when I heard a book fall to the floor, that did it. I jumped up, giving Margaret's [a fellow missionary] bed a shake, and called, "Margaret, grab your robe. We'll light the lamps and have another go at the rats. I've been hearing them from one end of the house to the other."
>
> A hall ran the full length of the house. Our bedrooms and the kitchen opened off it with the living/dining room on one end and a bathroom on the other. When I pulled the bedroom door open, in the dim light of a little night lamp I saw someone swish past me. I thought it was Dr. Jaffray

and was perplexed at his strange behavior in the middle of the night. When I stepped out into the hall to get a better look, I found myself face to face with a native Boegis bandit.

He was wearing a black sarong that he swooped up over his shoulder to free his machete. With one fluid movement, the knife was extricated from his belt and held up in striking position. I'm really quite a coward, and why I rushed at him, I have no idea. Perhaps it was the element of surprise, but he was a bigger coward than I, for he turned and fled down the hall, through the bathroom, across the porch, and down over the mountainside with me hot on his heels until I saw others emerge from the jungle. He yelled something in their language, and together they fled. I stopped dead. "Lord," I whispered, "what a stupid thing for me to do!" Immediately He answered, "The angel of the Lord encampeth round about them that fear Him, and delivereth them."

I went back to the house and reached to pull shut the door that was standing wide open. There was no doorknob, no lock or key; instead, I pulled the door toward me to find a porthole carved in the door by the intruder with his long knife.

Dr. and Mrs. Jaffray were now awake and had joined Margaret. "What happened?" Dr. Jaffray asked, much shaken by the noise and sight of the damaged door. "We had bandits! They must have been here for hours. I thought they were rats!" A tour of inspection proved that tablecloths and other linens were missing, books had been pulled from the shelves and searched, probably by someone expecting to find money hidden in them—and I had thought they were rats!

The next long months turned into years and were spent at a Japanese concentration camp where she endured deplorable conditions and inhumane treatment. One day she was abruptly summoned to withstand interrogation by the dreaded Japanese police. The Japanese, convinced that she was a spy, sent her to a worse prison camp. This camp was so bad that a dear missionary girl friend who was also incarcerated in this infamous prison lost her sanity.

Darlene faced months of torture mentally and physically. She was approaching death from starvation and disease. Her only hope was to commit herself to the mighty hand of God.

Once, from the window of her cell, she viewed a Japanese soldier carrying a bunch of bananas. She found herself crying out to God that if it were possible, would He please send her just one banana. This might be done by a guard who could smuggle a banana to her. But realizing this could cost the guard his life, she repented of her request.

Only God could have worked out the details of what happened next. Within moments of her prayer of repentance there was the sound of keys in her prison door. The door opened and she expected to be taken for more torture. But to her surprise, there stood her former camp commander who had come to visit her.

He was shocked to see her in such poor condition. Moved by God he ordered dozens of bananas to be brought to her. Needless to say she cried like a baby to witness the kindness of the Lord in answering her request for just one banana. God was more than able to bring just one. He is God, and he proved to her that He is *"able to do exceeding abundantly above all that we ask or think, according to the power that worketh in us" (Ephesians 3:20).* Darlene lived to see many instances of God's delivering power throughout her years in confinement.

On September 19, 1945, seventeen days after the peace treaty ending the war had been signed aboard the battleship *USS Missouri* in Tokyo Bay, Darlene's emaciated, eighty-pound frame was set free from her military prison. Imprisonment— combined with beriberi, malaria, and dysentery—had left her frail and debilitated. But it also manifested numerous events that displayed the mighty hand of God's grace and power in troubled times. Summing up her experiences in God's care while imprisoned, Darlene said, "Sometimes the Lord takes us through the fire to make us shine brighter through Him, to break us and mold us into

His image, for His glory."

Darlene Rose goes on to tell that after the war, when she returned to the island, she was speaking to the gardener whom she suspected was one of the bandits the night of the robbery. He admitted he was, and that he was very sorry.

She said she had thought they had heard them outside the house several nights after their first robbery and they feared a second attempt. The gardener again confided this was the case. She asked him why they had not reentered the unlocked door. He said, "Because of those people you had there, those people in white who stood about the house!" Darlene recognized that the Lord had sent His angelic host for protection.

" Be merciful unto me, O God, be merciful unto me: for my soul trusteth in thee: yea, in the shadow of thy wings will I make my refuge, until these calamities be overpast. I will cry unto God most high; unto God that performeth all things for me. He shall send from heaven, and save me from the reproach of him that would swallow me up. Selah. God shall send forth his mercy and his truth. My soul is among lions: and I lie even among them that are set on fire, even the sons of men, whose teeth are spears and arrows, and their tongue a sharp sword. Be thou exalted, O God, above the heavens; let thy glory be above all the earth. They have prepared a net for my steps; my soul is bowed down: they have digged a pit before me, into the midst whereof they are fallen themselves. My heart is fixed, O God, my heart is fixed: I will sing and give praise. Awake up, my glory; awake, psaltery and harp: I myself will awake early. I will praise thee, O Lord, among the people: I will sing unto thee among the nations. For thy mercy is great unto the heavens, and thy truth unto the clouds. Be thou exalted, O God, above the heavens: let thy glory be above all the earth" (Psalm 57:1-11).

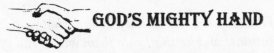 **GOD'S MIGHTY HAND**

KOREAN CONFLICT 1950-1953 A.D.

Wars are usually classified as major or minor. However, from a Providential perspective there is no such thing as a minor war. Every war is major when lives are involved. Although God's mighty hand is often not overtly visible, in the eternal pattern of events, every single conflict has a greater purpose. Without a doubt, God is heavily involved. And make no mistake, this world will never experience lasting peace apart from the Prince of Peace Himself, Jesus Christ. Every event that has transpired throughout the ages, and every one that ever will transpire, serves the same major purpose: the redemption of humanity, and the establishment of the Kingdom of Christ here on earth.

As a matter of fact, the second coming of Christ is so important that there are more Bible prophecies regarding it than the total number that were fulfilled at Jesus' first coming. It is clear that God is bringing all mankind to the place where everyone will have to admit and submit to the Kingdom of Christ and His rule. Only under this rule will there be real peace. How do we know? The Bible declares:

"And there shall come forth a rod out of the stem of Jesse [Christ], and a Branch shall grow out of his roots: And the spirit of the LORD shall rest upon him, the spirit of wisdom and understanding, the spirit of counsel and might, the spirit of knowledge and of the fear of the LORD; And shall make him of quick understanding in the fear of the LORD: and he shall not judge after the sight of his eyes, neither reprove after the hearing of his ears: But with righteousness shall he judge the poor, and reprove with equity for the meek of the earth: and he shall smite the earth with the rod of his mouth, and with the breath of his lips shall he slay the wicked. And righteousness shall be the girdle of his loins, and faithfulness the girdle of his reins" (Isaiah 11:15).

"And out of his mouth goeth a sharp sword, that with it he should smite the nations: and he shall rule them with a rod of iron: and he treadeth the winepress of the fierceness and wrath of Almighty God" (Revelation 19:15).

In comparison to World War II, a truly major war, the Korean Conflict seems minor. Yet significant events transpired that changed the course of world history and led to the Korean Conflict. Let's look at how the mighty hand of God was at work during the Korean Conflict.

The roots of the Korean Conflict are deeply embedded in history. For centuries, Korea's three powerful neighbors, China, Japan, and the Soviet Union, all vied for control of its territory. By 1910, Japan had established a military supremacy that controlled Korea until its defeat in World War II. Seven days before the Japanese surrender, the Soviet Union declared war on Japan in order to drive the Japanese from Korea. By agreement, the Soviets accepted the surrender of all Japanese forces in Korea north of the 38th parallel, while the United States accepted the surrender of the military units south of the 38th parallel. Immediately, the Soviet Union sealed off the 38th-parallel border. Then they set up an interim civil government for the nine million Koreans of the north, which contained most of Korea's industry. The government was run by Soviet-trained communist officials.

After World War II, the United States maintained a military presence in the southern portion of Korea. The South Koreans were content to be left alone and subsist on agriculture as they had done for years on end; they were not completely satisfied with such a large military presence in their country. As a result, a United States-Soviet commission was established to make plans for the reunification of Korea under a free government. Unfortunately, it failed. In 1947, the United States took the problem before the newly formed United Nations, which voted that free elections under its supervision should be held throughout Korea in order to establish a single independent free government. But the Soviet Union refused to permit the United Nations

Election Commission to enter the north with voting privileges for the North Koreans. Therefore elections were held only in the south, where a National Assembly and a newly elected president, Syngman Rhee, were chosen. The new democracy was named "The Republic of Korea." The conflict continued until the Soviet government invaded South Korea in an attempt to take control of the entire country. This led to the Korean Conflict.

After three costly years of war, which could have very well led to World War III, a peace treaty was signed. On July 27, 1953, South Korea was granted the land south of the 38th parallel.

Just after World War II, Japan lost control not only of Korea, but also of Taiwan. With Japan out of the picture, the communist government of China made plans to invade the island of Taiwan. Had they succeeded, they would not have had to deal with a military response from the United States. The unexpected assault upon Korea in 1950 by the Russian communist government providentially changed China's plans. America responded by stepping up its military force in the Orient.

Seemingly insignificant Asian wars and factions? Yes, but through it all God's mighty hand orchestrated amazing deeds.

First, God used atheistic communism to destroy five thousand years of gross Oriental paganism. Wherever Communism takes control, religion is crushed, both for the bad if it is Christianity, and for the good if it is paganism. The difference is that Christianity can never really be eradicated as paganism can. Again and again we have seen that Christians under persecution simply move underground and grow stronger, while paganism, a religion of self-works, fails to thrive. It cost the lives of millions of saints, but just like the Roman purge of the first and second centuries, the true Church grew and was strengthen beyond anyone's imagination. Generally, false religion carries no long-lasting convictions, and definitely it has no divine protection. And so it is destroyed during persecution—at least temporarily until Satan can rebuild another form of false religion. For example, in Russia the strong hand of communism kept false religions at bay, but try as they may, the communists could never stop true Christianity. In the end, Communism failed, and when it did, Christians came out from under cover, alive and well. Amazingly, God used Communism to destroy paganism and allow Christianity to grow!

Secondly, from the 1920s to the 1930s, a mighty revival of the Spirit of God shook Asia. Many missionaries went to evangelize Asian countries with eternal results. Yes, Communism stopped the evangelism, but again the Church remained alive and well. Today in China, there are millions of "born-again" Christians. Furthermore, God's mighty hand has allowed a beachhead for Christianity to flourish, albeit underground. Taiwan and South Korea have provided free governments that have kindly condoned Christian missionary endeavors among their people. This has allowed a place of refuge for the Church of Jesus Christ to grow and to continue to evangelize Asia, right under the nose of Communism.

Certainly, this is a simplified view of the Asian conflict that has taken generations to develop, yet sometimes it is in an overview that we can best see God's hand at work. The quick, big picture keeps us from getting bogged down and losing the overall picture. God is interested in the salvation of the world. He loves the Asian people, and He has consistently provided places of rest for those who love freedom in the midst of Communism. For those who do not now know Christ's love and His plan of salvation, God has provided a haven for truth in the underground Chinese church, and in the above ground Korean and Taiwanese church.

"God so loved the world that He gave His only begotten Son...." (John 3:16).

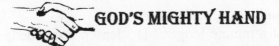

THE DOCTOR WHO LIVED TO SAVE OTHERS
WAS HIMSELF SAVED 1952 A.D.

It was one of those sultry, humid days which seemed as if it would never end. He was traveling from one battlefield to another in the two and one-half-ton army half-track. Dr. Robert Jensen was trying to get some desperately needed rest, having worked for days on end with almost no sleep. But emergency medical aid, gory business that it was, could not wait. Dr. Jensen, a committed Christian, took special care to do all in his God-given power to relieve the suffering of the U.S. soldiers fighting for the South Korean cause.

Dr. Jensen's half-track led a convoy of bedraggled vehicles down muddy roads between the rice paddies. Jensen sat on a gas can in the rear of the vehicle, keeping a sharp eye out for a good place to set up a field hospital. This was no small challenge in the mire and muck of dirty, damp rice fields. "Med school never really prepares a doctor for all this," he thought to himself.

While he prayed daily for guidance and medical skill, Dr. Jensen was fully aware that he was exposed to all the dangers of war. Armed with a medical bag instead of a gun, he would all too often be so preoccupied with helping the wounded that his own life was in danger.

On one occasion while Communist Chinese troops rapidly advanced, army helicopters were evacuating men and supplies as fast as they could. Dr. Jensen was so intensely busy tending to the wounded that he took no notice, and before he knew it, nearly all the soldiers formerly guarding his medical compound were gone. All who remained with him were the most severely wounded and the dying.

A flustered copilot ordered, "Dr. Jensen, get in the chopper now; the Chinese are almost here!" Oblivious to the warning, Jensen intensely continued working on his patient, like a nuclear scientist hot on the trail of a new discovery.

"Yeah, yeah, just a minute longer," Dr. Jensen responded, completely preoccupied with his work.

The minute came and went. All the patients were loaded onto the waiting chopper. Still the only ones left at this crucial eleventh hour of rescue were Dr. Jensen and his patient.

In desperation, the copilot ran up to the doctor and forcefully took charge, "Dr. Jensen, you must leave now!"

"Why?" Dr. Jensen asked. "I'm not quite done; I need another minute."

"You don't have another minute! Look up and see for yourself," the copilot exclaimed. "Those bodies running this way are the enemy, and the bullets will soon be swarming as thick as bees!"

With no other choice, he grabbed the resolute doctor and his medical bag, and ordered the cot to be carried into the chopper. Just as they were lifting off the ground, bullets started flying everywhere. The guidance and protection for which Dr. Jensen had been praying must have been granted, for the bullets missed the huge army chopper as they sped away.

On another occasion, Dr. Jensen hastily evacuated a field hospital in favor of a more suitable medical environment in a nearby village. After setting up temporary medical facilities in a small house, Dr. Jensen began to tend to the wounded as fast as he was humanly able. Wounded soldiers were being brought in to the doctor and his assistants all night. Constant prayer for the Lord's divine assistance ushered from his lips as he continually worked on patients.

Since he was working so feverishly, Dr. Jensen hardly took notice of the all-night barrage of enemy fire. Bombs fell so close that his temporary hospital would rock and shake. Totally focused on saving lives, Dr. Jensen worked through the night.

By dawn the next morning, the fighting had ceased. This brought a lull in the traffic of medics transporting the wounded and dying to this temporary facility. Weary from round-the-clock emergency work, he could not believe his eyes as he gazed out the shattered window. His amazement grew as he walked outside and surveyed the damage. The village was almost completely destroyed by enemy artillery and bombs. Providentially, one of the few remaining buildings left standing was none other than the one occupied by Dr. Jensen for this life-saving vigil. God's mighty hand of protection and guidance had prevailed once again to save Dr. Jensen and those who were under his care.

During non-combative times of unexpected peril, God was faithful to shield Dr. Jensen from impending disasters. Once, while reflecting on some of the past providential events, and giving thanks to the Lord for His protection, he spotted a perfect site for the next field hospital while rounding a bend in the narrow road near a river. He quickly but gently nudged the driver on the shoulder and said in a loud voice over the noise of the convoy, "Turn off the road here, I will set up the field hospital over there under the bridge."

The driver hardly had time to respond. He jerked the half-track to the right and advanced to the bridge. The convoy proceeded on to the left, continuing forward toward the battlefield. The new lead half-track drove over a mine which had been placed in the road by the enemy, and the vehicle was tragically blown up. Dr. Jensen looked back as he heard the explosion, and saw what ought to have been his truck had he not been led to instruct the driver to turn off the road at that very moment. Regrettably, there were no survivors on that other truck, but thankfully, the mighty hand of God had spared his life yet another time.

At the time of the interview conducted for the writing of this book, Dr. Jensen and his wife, Rosemary, have been living in San Antonio, Texas, serving the Lord in their respective ways. Both serve as leaders of Bible Study Fellowship International. Dr. Jensen is also president of a program called Rafiki. He and his research team have developed an inexpensive method of testing for HIV. This is a tremendous blessing, as other tests previously in use were very costly.

The Lord knows our future, and places His hand of protection on His children for future deeds that accomplish His work here on earth. It is a comfort to know that the Lord's hand of protection is on our lives, and that we need not fear in the midst of danger. Dr. Jensen was spared on numerous occasions by God's mighty hand in accordance with His will and His sovereign plans.

" Are not two sparrows sold for a farthing? and one of them shall not fall on the ground without your Father. But the very hairs of your head are all numbered. Fear ye not therefore, ye are of more value than many sparrows" (Matthew 10:29-31).

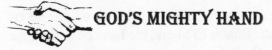 **GOD'S MIGHTY HAND**

STILL THE CHOSEN PEOPLE 1967 A. D.

On May 15, 1967 the armies of Egypt, Transjordan (now Jordan), Syria, Lebanon, and Iraq joined Palestinian and other Arab guerrillas who had been fighting Jewish forces since November 1947. The civil war now became an international conflict, the first Arab-Israeli War. It became known as the War of Independence for Israel. The Arabs failed to prevent establishment of a Jewish state, and the war ended with four un-arranged armistice agreements between Israel and Egypt, Lebanon, Jordan, and Syria. The frontiers defined in the armistice agreements remained until they were altered by Israel's conquests during the Six-Day War in 1967. In 1967, Egypt, Syria and other Arab countries, armed and supported by Russia, declared their intentions of destroying Israel.

By closing the Straits of Tiran at the mouth of the Gulf of Aqaba, Egypt cut off Israel's shipping to and from her southern port of Eliat. Since Egypt had long denied Israel shipping access to the Suez Canal, her closing of the Straits of Tiran was considered by Israel to be an act of aggression.

When diplomatic efforts in the United Nations failed to lift Egypt's blockade, war was inevitable. Israel, with merely 2½ million inhabitants, was faced by a coalition of Arab nations with a combined population of between 100 and 200 million people! Outnumbered forty to one, Israel was at the mercy of God's mighty hand. If Israel ceased to exist, then Christ could not come to set up His Kingdom. You can well imagine who is behind all schemes to displace and destroy Israel: Satan!

When Egyptian tanks rolled across the Sinai Desert, the Israelis mobilized their civilian army. As soon as the firing began, the Israeli Air Force darted into the air, took a circuitous route to the enemy airfields, and destroyed the Arab airplanes and airfields. At the same time, they bombed hundreds of tanks as well. On the ground, Israel moved like lightning across the desert in Israeli tanks to capture Sharm El Shcik, the fort controlling the Straits of Tiran and the Gulf of Aqaba. Complete and unexpected victories on all fronts left the world stunned.

Without God, it would have been impossible for tiny Israel to defeat such a force as came against them. The Bible tells where the sources of strength come from, and how a smaller number can gain victory. *"And I will give peace in the land, and ye shall lie down, and none shall make you afraid: and I will rid evil beasts out of the land, neither shall the sword go through your land. And ye shall chase your enemies, and they shall fall before you by the sword. And five of you shall chase an hundred, and an hundred of you shall put ten thousand to flight: and your enemies shall fall before you by the sword. For I will have respect unto you, and make you fruitful, and multiply you, and establish my covenant with you"* *(Leviticus 26:6-9).* As Israel fought, God worked the victory.

K. Carter, in her out-of-print book *Hand on the Helm,* records God's intervention as follows: "In one instance, an Israeli tank force, halted by a sudden sand storm because of zero visibility, had a wait of only twenty minutes for it to blow over. But when it ended as suddenly as it had begun, it had swept the sand off the road ahead, revealing an enemy mine field."

Another time in the Sinai, a radio operator in the lead tank saw a never-explained veil of smoke rise up in front of the unit and called out, "Turn to the left." The entire unit followed the lead tank to the left, except the very last vehicle, a scout car. Blinded by sand at the turn, the driver proceeded straight ahead. There was a sudden explosion as his tank struck a mine. An extensive mine field was discovered, which had been avoided by the mystifying puff of smoke and the warning to turn to the left. The Israelis swiftly captured and occupied the Sinai Desert. Israelis also defeated the Jordanian army to the east, destroying their attacking planes and capturing a large number of Jordanian tanks.

Orthodox Jews would go into battle singing the Psalms and,

like Israel of old, they believed Jehovah would aid them during their conflict with the Arabs. Once, as soldiers were moving from Bethlehem toward Hebron, they noticed a strange appearance at the tomb of Abraham. As Israeli soldiers reported and eyewitnesses attested, "an old man with a flowing beard, dressed all in white, was standing with hands raised heavenward. We shouted to him, 'There's a war on. If you stay out here in the open, you are quite likely to get killed.' When the old man showed no sign of having heard us, our officer sent one of our force to repeat it at close hand, thinking he was hard of hearing. The soldier reached out to grasp the aged man's arm and get his attention, but suddenly the old man disappeared. In awe and wonderment we left."

A cease-fire arrangement was finally agreed upon with Egypt and Jordan, Israel now turned her attention to the Syrian forces, attacking her on the north. She routed them and was making good headway toward the Syrian capital, Damascus, but before another United Nations cease-fire was accepted by both sides, God performed another mighty deed for His chosen people.

Twenty-one Israeli soldiers were defending a village being attacked by five Russian-built tanks and one hundred Syrian troops advancing through a cornfield standing ready for the harvest. The Israeli defenders had only a few old rifles left over from World Wars I and II, and a limited amount of ammunition, including a few flares.

"We'll have to fire the flares and then run for it," the Israeli leader announced when their defeat seemed inevitable. It was foolish to shoot at tanks with bullets, but what else could these lightly armed soldiers do? Just before fleeing the enemy tanks in desperation, the Israeli soldiers shot their flares. Suddenly, the flares ignited the cornfields, and to the soldiers' amazement, the enemy was on the run.

Syrian infantry forces dropped their arms and ammunition as they fled through the flames. One of their tanks turned and retreated out of the cornfield. In attempting to cross a stream to safety, it rolled over on its back and lay there to be captured by the Israeli soldiers. Another tank ran up on a large boulder in the field and hung there with its treads revolving helplessly. The remaining tanks and soldiers made their escape as rapidly as possible.

Many Israeli soldiers returning home from the Middle East battles in the Sinai, Jordan, and Syria jubilantly reported the miraculous events that aided them. Included was the strange report of an Arab mine set off by an Israeli captain's jeep. The explosion killed the driver and seriously wounded the man sitting next to him, but it set off thundering echoes among the canyons and mountain peaks nearby. They said that it sounded like a massive artillery attack, and the enemy retreated in panic from an advantageous, almost inaccessible, position without firing a shot.

The Six-Day War turned into a faith-building experience for many of the Israelites who were trusting in the God of Abraham, Isaac, and Jacob. Outnumbered like Gideon of old, they defeated their enemies forty-to-one.

Providentially during the Israeli-Arab confrontation, Russia gave no direct military assistance or manpower to the Arab nations, although she had armed them and backed their threats against Israel. Why would Russia hesitate in attacking Israel? Perhaps the mighty hand of God was protecting His people for Zion's sake, and His future return to Zion.

Try as they may, Satan and principalities visible and invisible will never be able to uproot Israel from the land in which God planted His chosen people. To do so would be tantamount to saying, there is no God. The fact that Israel continues to defeat her foes proves that there is a God. Fighting Israel is like fighting against God. None can defeat God; none can defeat Israel. Israel is like a visible representation of God on earth. Israel is in unbelief and will be judged by God in His own good time, but meanwhile woe to the nation that tries to remove Israel from her God-given inheritance, the land of Zion.

"Thus saith the LORD against all mine evil neighbors, that touch the inheritance which I have caused my people Israel to inherit; Behold, I will pluck them out of their land, and pluck out

the house of Judah from among them. And it shall come to pass, after that I have plucked them out I will return, and have compassion on them, and will bring them again, every man to his heritage, and every man to his land. And it shall come to pass, if they will diligently learn the ways of my people, to swear by my name, The LORD liveth; as they taught my people to swear by Baal; then shall they be built in the midst of my people" (Jeremiah 12:14-16).

A FLIGHT TO REMEMBER 1967 A.D.

(As Told by Dr. Jim Leininger)

I was excited as I sat in the La Paz, Bolivia, airport. Never before had I been to Bolivia, and soon our flight would take us across the Andes Mountains, to a small jungle village on the border of Brazil. From there we must use our wits to get across the river, clear Brazilian customs, and board another "puddle jumper." After five stops at jungle villages, it would deliver us to Manaus. Just the kind of adventure I loved!

My partner, Dave, and I were second-year medical students, and we had received a grant to tour medical facilities in South America the summer of 1967. We had stopped in Manaus, the capital of the Brazilian state of Amazonas, on the way down months earlier. We were so moved by the poverty and total lack of health care in the Amazon Jungle that we had committed to return and help plan a hospital in Coari, a village 150 miles up the Amazon River from Manaus.

Suppressed just beneath my excitement for adventure and the unknown was a sense of anxiety and foreboding. The Pan Am Airlines agent in Buenos Aires, Argentina, had at first refused to sell us a ticket on this flight. I explained that this was the only flight which would take us across the Andes and Amazon jungle to Manaus. He said he was aware of that but still refused to sell us a ticket. I told him we had promised to return to Manaus to help build a hospital for the children on the Amazon. He said we wouldn't be much help to them if we were dead! Exasperated, I threatened to go to another airline counter and buy the tickets from them. "Señor," he said, "I cannot in good conscience sell you a ticket. Lloyds Bolivian Airlines has the worst safety record in the world! They do not fly *over* the Andes, they fly *between* the mountain peaks. It is a death trap!"

That was rather sobering, so Dave and I took a moment to discuss the matter. After a few minutes we decided we should keep our commitment and take the flight even if it was a little more dangerous. After all, it was a scheduled airline, and what could be so dangerous about flying through the Andes? Besides, we were twenty-three years old, loved adventure, and presumed we were invincible. After our further insistence the agent reluctantly prepared our tickets. "May God be with you," he sighed as he handed us the tickets.

Nervously, I read through a pamphlet entitled, "Interesting Facts About the La Paz Airport" to kill time before the flight. The airport was the world's highest airport, had the world's longest runway, and the altitude was so high that nothing smaller than a DC-9 could get enough altitude to land or take off. Interesting. The announcement for our flight crackled from the ancient loud speaker, and we headed for the airplane. As we stood in line to board the aircraft, I noticed it was a DC-3. Based on what I had just read, I wondered how it had flown up there. I noticed the engines had been modified and "souped up" with exhaust pipes coming out the sides of the extra long engines and sections of the engine cover were missing. I began to wonder what I had gotten us into!

As we taxied out on the runway, it seemed like forever until we got to the end. This certainly was a long runway! As we turned around in the circle at the end of the runway, we could look right down off the edge of the steep mountain we were perched on and see out over miles of peaceful, beautiful mountain peaks. My sense of peace and tranquility was jarred as I saw two men get out of a pickup truck and place large wooden blocks in front of the plane's wheels on either side. "That seems unnecessary, given the immense length of the runway," I conjectured.

The pilot revved up the motors to the max until the whole plane shook like a leaf in a winter's gale. The men had ropes tied to the wood blocks, but still they did not pull them out from the wheels. I thought there must be tremendous pressure on the wood blocks, and it suddenly occurred to my analytical mind that if they didn't pull the blocks at the same time, or if one of the ropes broke, the airplane would immediately spin around and careen off the edge of the mountain only a few feet away.

My mouth was dry, but at a shout, the blocks were pulled and we sped down the runway! Dave and I heaved a sigh of relief! We reached maximum speed very soon but did not take off. "This runway is tremendously long," I thought, "but it's got to end pretty soon." Still we did not take off as we hurtled along. Then to our relief, the pilot popped the flaps all the way down and we were airborne!

Our relief was short-lived because we immediately began losing altitude and bumped back down on the runway, still crashing ahead at full speed. I tightened my already tight seatbelt and thought to myself, "This plane is too heavy to take off!" Every seat was filled, and the open overhead racks were stuffed with everything imaginable, even a covered basket filled with clucking chickens. Again the pilot popped the flaps, and again we were airborne only seconds until bouncing back onto the runway.

"We've got to get off the ground," I thought. "This runway can't be much longer." He popped the flaps a third time, and again we were airborne. Again we began to lose altitude as the runway suddenly ended, and we literally fell hundreds of feet off the edge of the mountain and then soared through the steep canyons of a pass through the Andes. I figured the plane had to have flown up to the airport empty, or nearly so, and that the pilot was just practicing the first two takeoffs to see how much time he had to get off the end of the runway.

After a minute or so, I began to loosen my grip on the armrests, gradually aware of the aching in my forearms. Many of the people on the plane were praying out loud in Spanish and making the sign of the cross repeatedly. At the time I foolishly thought it was somewhat amusing, since the danger had passed, but now I am thankful for their prayers.

The view out the window was spectacular. I grabbed my Super 8 mm camera and began to film a small segment of the grandeur. The sides of the mountains seemed so close that we could almost reach out and touch them. The anxious moments were soon swept away by the unsurpassed beauty. I was irritated that I occasionally had to stop filming briefly as we passed through small clouds. Finally I put my camera down in disgust as the cloud cover was so thick I couldn't even see the end of the wing.

I thought to myself, "If I can't see the wingtip, the pilot couldn't possibly see the mountainsides, and I know this thing doesn't have radar." The words of the Pan Am agent, "Señor, it's a death trap," echoed in my mind as I said, "Dave, we're in trouble." The beads of sweat on his forehead betrayed his full awareness that any second we could crash into a mountainside and fall thousands of feet. There was no chance anyone could survive. Dave, a recent convert to Catholicism, clutched a beautiful oversized decorative clay rosary he had bought at a recent stop.

Suddenly the airplane swerved 90 degrees to the right. I could feel the pull on my seatbelt which was the only thing that kept me in my seat. Everything flew out of the overhead racks and showered the people on the right side of the plane. The chicken basket burst open like a piñiata, with feathers and squawking chickens flying everywhere. The plane righted itself almost immediately, and a tiny four-foot Indian lady, all dressed in black, stood up in the first row, put both hands in the air, and screamed, "Dios Mio, Ayudami!" ("God help me.") Just then the plane banked 90 degrees to the left and the little lady flew through the air like a helpless rag doll and crashed into the wall on the other side of the plane.

Dave panicked, unfastened his seatbelt and tried to climb over me to get out of there! I wrestled him back into his seat, and he put his seatbelt back on. It was none too soon, as the plane jerked back sharply to the right and the little lady in black went flying through the air to the other inside wall. Everyone was screaming and praying. Again Dave tried to escape, and I again forced him back into his seat. He began praying his rosary with such sincerity and speed that the large clay rosary beads were exploding on contact as he thrust them forcefully up the string.

After a few more sharp turns, the clouds suddenly parted and we cruised out of the mountain pass into the lush beauty and serenity of the jungle below. The valley was so peaceful it was almost as if nothing had ever happened. Incredibly, no one was seriously injured or killed. As we came in for the landing on the grass runway, the pilot had to fly low over the runway twice to convince the chickens, pigs, cows, and one stubborn donkey to move aside and allow us to land. Everyone thanked God for His miraculous protection.

The Bible contains several accounts of the tremendous blessing of friendship. For example, Proverbs 27:6, 9-10, 17 says, *"Ointment and perfume rejoice the heart: so doth the sweetness of a man's friend by hearty counsel. . . . Thine own friend, and thy father's friend, forsake not. . . . Faithful are the wounds of a friend; but the kisses of an enemy are deceitful. . . .Iron sharpeneth iron; so a man sharpeneth the countenance of his friend."*

Think of the relationship between Jonathan and David, and between Jesus and Lazarus, Peter, James, and John. Throughout life, a person will have only about five good friends who will remain faithful through thick and thin. It could be deduced, therefore, that friendship is a gift directly from the hand of God, just as the relationship between a husband and a wife is.

From childhood Albrecht Durer desired to paint and wood carve. When he grew up, he left home to study with a great artist. He met a friend who also had this desire, and the two became roommates. Both were poor, and they found it difficult to make a living and study painting at the same time. Albrecht's friend presented a solution to the problem. He offered to work while Albrecht studied; then when his studies were complete and he secured a living from painting, Albrecht would, in turn, support his friend through painting studies. After much persuasion, Albrecht agreed and studied faithfully while his friend toiled long hours to support them both.

The day finally came when Albrecht began to sell his wood carvings, and his friend went back to his art studies, only to find that the hard work had stiffened and twisted his fingers and he could no longer paint with skill. When Albrecht learned what had happened to his faithful friend, he was filled with great sorrow. It so happened one day that he returned home unexpectedly and found his friend in deep agonizing prayer.

Entering unseen, Albrecht was awestruck with the beauty of his friend's hands folded in prayer before him. Inspired by the Lord, he thought, "I can show the world my appreciation for the sacrifice of my faithful friend by painting his hands as I see them now, folded in prayer."

Albrecht Durer's gratitude was captured in his inspired painting, "Praying Hands," which has become world famous. We are blessed by both the beauty of the painting and the beautiful story of gratitude and the brotherhood of friendship.

I am personally grateful for the small inner circle of friends the Lord has given to us. I shudder to think what we would have missed in the way of friendship with Dr. Jim and his precious family had he been killed in a plane crash over the Andes. The blessing the Leiningers have been to us we count as a gift from God's mighty hand. Many of the avenues on which our ministry has gone have been a direct result of having become connected to this man and his family. I count friendships forged by the hand of God to be of inestimable value.

I close with a tribute to the faithful friends the Lord has given me.

I love you not only for what you are, but for what I am when I am with you;
I love you not only for what you have made of yourself, but for what you are making of me;
I love you not for closing your ears to the discords in me, but for adding to the music in me by worshipful listening;

You have done it without a touch, without a word,
without a sign. You have done it just by being yourself.
Perhaps that is what being a friend means, after all.
— Author Unknown

BRIGHTER THAN THE SUN 1968 A.D.

During the 1880s, Southeast Asia was colonized by Europeans who set up plantations and became rich on the labor of the local people. France had a colony in Indochina which included Laos and Vietnam. Following World War II, Communism was established with Stalin as head of the Communist party. He began to acquire a taste for world power. There were four countries that were divided as the result of global Communist strategy: China, Germany, Korea, and Vietnam. By the 1950s, Communistic power reached its arms into Indochina. Bloody battles took place, and the people of Indochina finally gained their independence from European control. A peace conference was held at Geneva, Switzerland, to determine the fate of Indochina. Concluding in July 1954, the conference determined that French rule would be ended in Vietnam and that the country would be temporarily divided politically. Neighboring Laos and Cambodia, comprising the rest of Indochina, were prohibited from making military alliances. Foreign military bases were barred from their territory and from Vietnam. Unfortunately, since the people had not learned the principles of self-government, they were easily taken over by the Communists.

Until formal reunification in 1976, Vietnam was split at the 17th parallel into North Vietnam, with a Communist government, and South Vietnam, with a republican government. By the 1960s, America was heavily involved in the Indochina conflict. As in all conflicts, although not often seen, felt, or known, God's mighty hand was working His purposes. I am convinced that eternity will reveal how much God was involved in the affairs of men and nations. Here is a story that proves the point.

It happened early in 1968. A whole village in South Vietnam experienced a miracle of divine intervention and protection.

Months later, Major Keith Swaggerty described the strange occurrence.

"Under cover of darkness, a Viet Cong soldier, one of a battalion of over a thousand men in the area, came to the village and warned, 'Tomorrow is your day. So, if you are going to get anyone out of the village, get them out now.'

"This Viet Cong battalion had been capturing village after village at will in that vicinity, and the young soldier had come to love and respect the Christians of this small community, even though he was a Viet Cong guerrilla. He was giving them twenty-four hours' notice of the planned attack, risking his life doing so.

"Mayor Swaggerty did not immediately alert the villagers. He knew that the Viet Cong would not attack by daylight, but would come the next night. The next day he called the villagers together and revealed the message he had received. The villagers realized that they were powerless to defeat the stronger force of the Viet Cong guerrillas and said, 'We cannot defeat the Viet Cong by force. We do not have the necessary arms and ammunition.'

"'But,' they decided, 'we believe that Christ can be our defender.' So they agreed that they would turn to Him in prayer. Fervently, they prayed and sang songs of praise and gave thanksgiving throughout the day. And their hearts were encouraged, refreshed, and strengthened.

"When dusk finally came, they could see the Viet Cong moving in the edge of the surrounding trees, getting into position to attack. A strange peace and courage filled the hearts of the villagers, however. They smiled at each other as they still sang, and prayed.

"When complete darkness closed in, the first shots were heard. But as suddenly as the barrage began, it ceased. Not another shot was fired anywhere in the village area. Nothing but silence prevailed the whole night through. Nothing but silence all the next day, and the next.

"A few days later, some of the attacking men were captured by the approaching South Vietnamese forces and were brought into the village.'Why did you halt your attack on our village?' they were asked.

"'As we opened fire,' the Viet Cong prisoners replied excitedly, 'all of a sudden there appeared, all around the village, men clad in shining white. We fired at them but they wouldn't fall. They shone brighter than the sun and we couldn't aim at them. We were terrified and we ran.'"

After the war Keith Swaggerty was sharing this story with a group of Christians in New Zealand. A woman sitting in the audience kept nodding her head. After the talk, she came up and shook Keith's hand.

"I saw you agreeing with me as I told of the village defenders clad all in white," he said. "You seemed to know what was going to happen before I told it. Were you there?"

"No, I wasn't there," she replied. "But I was in Africa when the Mau-Mau uprising took place. And when some of them were attacking our village, we were in prayer and later they reported the same thing .They wouldn't attack because there were these beings all in white, radiant, glowing, and they couldn't break through."

"Then the king of Syria warred against Israel, and took counsel with his servants, saying, In such and such a place shall be my camp. And the man of God sent unto the king of Israel, saying, Beware that thou pass not such a place; for thither the Syrians are come down. And the king of Israel sent to the place which the man of God told him and warned him of, and saved himself there, not once nor twice. Therefore the heart of the king of Syria was sore troubled for this thing; and he called his servants, and said unto them, Will ye not shew me which of us is for the king of Israel? And one of his servants said, None, my lord, O king: but Elisha, the prophet that is in Israel, telleth the king of Israel the words that thou speakest in thy bedchamber. And he said, Go and spy where he is, that I may send and fetch him. And it was told him, saying, Behold, he is in Dothan. Therefore sent he thither horses, and chariots, and a great host: and they came by night, and compassed the city about.

"And when the servant of the man of God was risen early, and gone forth, behold, an host compassed the city both with horses and chariots. And his servant said unto him, Alas, my master! how shall we do? And he answered, Fear not: for they that be with us are more than they that be with them. And Elisha prayed, and said, LORD, I pray thee, open his eyes, that he may see. And the LORD opened the eyes of the young man; and he saw: and, behold, the mountain was full of horses and chariots of fire round about Elisha" (2 Kings 6:8-17).

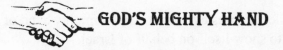 GOD'S MIGHTY HAND

PEACE FOR GALILEE 1982 A.D.

Operation "Peace for Galilee" took place June 6, 1982, a critical battle over the fate of Israel. The war primarily involved the Palestinian Liberation Organization (PLO), under the leadership of Yasser Arafat, and the Syrians.

Since achieving statehood in 1948, Israel has had very limited peace. "Armed to the teeth," Israel is constantly vigilant of surrounding nations trying to destroy them. One of Israel's greatest enemies is the PLO. A long hostility has existed since 1948 between Arabs and Israelites over who would occupy what territorial portions of postwar-deeded land. In the 1960s, Yasser Arafat organized these dissatisfied, homeless Arabs and poisoned their minds through political deception. Organized, trained, and supplied by the Russian government, they pose a threat to the peace and security of Israel. By 1981 the PLO launched several attacks on Israel along the northern border. A successive discharge of artillery, rockets, and countless rounds of gunfire killed and wounded Israeli civilians, while the world looked on without protest. Between July 24, 1981, and June 4, 1982, the PLO launched 290 attacks against Israel. The Israeli government could no longer allow this destructive behavior to continue.

On June 6, 1982, Israel launched a combined land and sea assault against the PLO located in Lebanon. A force of six divisions participated in the invasion, including Israel's navy and air force. The Israeli Mossad, an equivalent to our CIA, informed Israeli leaders that the PLO was well-armed, highly trained, and anticipating the attack. What Israel did not know is how the Syrians and other Arab nations might respond; they soon found out. The Syrian forces were deeply entrenched in Lebanon. They had committed large numbers of infantry, a formidable tank force, armored vehicles, hundreds of the most up-to-date Russian MiG fighter planes, and in the Baca Valley, one of the most impressive ground-to-air missile defenses ever built. God's mighty hand of defense was about to show itself on behalf of Israel.

In an astounding six days, with lightning speed, the Israeli forces advanced sixty miles into Lebanon in the face of severe enemy fire of every possible kind, and across terrain which had been thought impassable. Beirut, the capital of Lebanon, was surrounded by the PLO and placed under siege. The treatment of the Christians living in the city was cruel and inhumane, typical of the PLO. Contrary to the current liberal news media, the PLO is hated even among the majority of Arabs. The liberal media paints Yasser Arafat as a great leader worthy of the Nobel Peace Prize. In reality, to many Arabs who simply want to live in peace, Yasser Arafat is a thorn in their side. He incites rebellion causing the Arabs to be in constant turmoil. Full of deception, he has been classed by those who have followed the character of his life and his philosophy to be in the same league as Hitler and other wicked world tyrants.

When the Israeli soldiers took the city of Beirut, the soldiers were literally welcomed as a liberating army, much as the Americans were treated when they entered Paris during World War II. The threat the PLO posed to Israel was significant. When the Israeli soldiers captured the surrounding areas, they uncovered 413 massive PLO underground munition and storage facilities. In them, they found more than 5,000 tons of ammunition, enough to fill more than 1,500 military trucks. They also found 764 vehicles, including tanks and personnel carriers; 26,900 light weapons; 424 artillery and rocket launchers. There was enough stored equipment to outfit a 30,000 man force, ten times the figure estimated by Israeli intelligence.

By June 8, the Syrians joined the PLO to help exterminate Israel. The Syrians hoped to engage in a quick, decisive, limited war and recapture the Golan Heights, lost to Israel exactly 15 years earlier in the Six-Day War of June 6, 1967. Their involvement in that skirmish had cost them dearly. The Bible proclaims what happens to those who touch Isreal, the apple of God's eye.

Zechariah 2:7-9 says," *Deliver thyself, O Zion, that dwellest with the daughter of Babylon. For thus saith the LORD of hosts; After the glory hath he sent me unto the nations which spoiled you: for he that toucheth you toucheth the apple of his eye. For, behold, I will shake mine hand upon them, and they shall be a spoil to their servants: and ye shall know that the LORD of hosts hath sent me.*"

In five days of fierce fighting, the Syrians lost 385 tanks, including 9 Russian T-72s, thought to be the most powerful tank in the world, and unstoppable. In three days of super-sophisticated aerial dog fights, the Syrians lost 90 planes without a single Israeli plane being downed. Not since World War II have so many planes been engaged in a dog fight in such a brief period of time, and within such a restricted area. In no other battle in aviation history has such a loss been borne entirely by one side.

Remote Piloted Vehicles (RPVs), twelve feet long and mounted with high-magnification cameras, relayed pictures to ground stations and special electronically equipped aircraft. The Syrians could keep no secrets from the Israeli "spy in the sky" reconnaissance. Jamming the Syrian radar screens electronically once they were located, and launching laser-guided missiles from both planes and surface batteries, the "impregnable" Syrian defense system was totally annihilated. This included the 700 anti-aircraft batteries whose purpose was to protect the missiles.

This attack devastated the Russians, for this was their secret system, designed to protect their cities from the United States. Israel had, in effect, shown Russia that their protective system was not what they expected it to be. It was not the most advanced ground-to-air missile defense system in the world. So much for the modern Goliaths in which men put their trust They all fall before God's mighty hand. As a result, on June 11, Syria and the PLO accepted a cease-fire, hastily prepared by Philip Habib, special envoy from the United States.

Once again we see that God's mighty hand brings the best laid plans of men and armies to naught. One would think that the enemies of Israel would take note that in every battle against

Israel they have been defeated. Apparently their satanically inspired hatred has blinded their eyes from what God has promised on behalf of Israel.

"For, lo, I will command, and I will sift the house of Israel among all nations, like as corn is sifted in a sieve, yet shall not the least grain fall upon the earth. All the sinners of my people shall die by the sword, which say, The evil shall not overtake nor prevent us. In that day will I raise up the tabernacle of David that is fallen, and close up the breaches thereof; and I will raise up his ruins, and I will build it as in the days of old: That they may possess the remnant of Edom, and of all the heathen, which are called by my name, saith the LORD that doeth this. Behold, the days come, saith the LORD, that the plowman shall overtake the reaper, and the treader of grapes him that soweth seed; and the mountains shall drop sweet wine, and all the hills shall melt. And I will bring again the captivity of my people of Israel, and they shall build the waste cities, and inhabit them; and they shall plant vineyards, and drink the wine thereof; they shall also make gardens, and eat the fruit of them. And I will plant them upon their land, and they shall no more be pulled up out of their land which I have given them, saith the LORD thy God" (Amos 9:9-15).

GOD'S MIGHTY HAND

GOD KNOWS YOUR PHONE NUMBER 1989 A.D.

D o you believe that God not only loves you, but knows where you are and what you're doing every minute of the day? Evangelist Ken Gaub found this truth in a wonderful way and wrote his story out which I record for you here.

Several years ago I was driving on I-75 near Dayton, Ohio, with my wife and children. We turned off the highway for a rest and refreshment stop.

My wife Barbara and children went into the restaurant. I suddenly felt the need to stretch my legs, so I waved them on ahead saying I'd join them later. I bought a soft drink, and as I walked toward a Dairy Queen, feelings of self-pity engulfed my mind. I loved the Lord and my ministry, but I felt drained, burdened. My cup was empty.

Suddenly the impatient ringing of a telephone nearby jarred me out of my doldrums. It was coming from a phone booth at a service station on the corner. Wasn't anyone going to answer the phone?

Noise from the traffic flowing through the busy intersection must have drowned out the sound, because the service station attendant continued looking after his customers, oblivious to the incessant ringing.

"Why doesn't someone answer that phone?' I muttered. The ringing continued. I began reasoning, "It may be important. What if it's an emergency?"

Curiosity overcame my indifference. I stepped inside the booth and picked up the phone. "Hello," I said casually and took a big sip of my drink.

The operator said,"Long distance call for Ken Gaub."

My eyes widened, and I almost choked on a chunk of ice. Swallowing hard, I said, "You're crazy." Then realizing I shouldn't speak to an operator like that, I added, "This can't be! I was walking down the road, not bothering anyone, and the phone was ringing...."

"Is Ken Gaub there?" the operator interrupted. "I have a long distance call for him."

It took a moment to gain control of my stammering from surprise, but I finally replied, "Yes, he is here." Searching for a possible explanation, I wondered if I could possibly be on Candid Camera. I looked for a hidden camera, trying to smooth my hair. Impatiently, the operator repeated, "I have a long distance call for Ken Gaub, Sir. Is he there?"

Still shaken, perplexed, I asked, "How in the world did you reach me here? I was walking down the road, the pay phone started ringing, and I just answered it on chance. You can't mean me."

"Well," the operator asked, "is Mr. Gaub there, or isn't he?"

"Yes, I am Ken Gaub," I said, finally convinced by the tone of her voice that the call was real.

Then I heard another voice say, "Yes, that's him, operator. That's Ken Gaub."

I listened dumbfounded to a strange voice identify herself. "I'm Millie from Harrisburg, Pennsylvania. You don't know me, Mr. Gaub, but I'm desperate. Please help me."

"What can I do for you?" I asked. She began weeping. Finally she regained control and continued, "I was about to commit suicide, had just finished writing a note, when I began to pray and tell God I really didn't want to do this. Then I suddenly remembered seeing you on television and thought if I could just talk to you, you could help me. I knew that was impossible because I didn't know how to reach you, and I didn't know anyone who could help me find you. Then some numbers came to my mind, and I scribbled them down."

At this point she began weeping again, and I prayed

-344-

silently for wisdom to help her.

She continued. *"I looked at the numbers and thought, 'Wouldn't it be wonderful if I had a miracle from God, and He has given me Ken's phone number?' I decided to try calling it. I can't believe I'm talking to you. Are you in your office in California?"*

I replied, "Ma'am, I don't have an office in California. My office is in Yakima, Washington."

A little surprised, she asked, "Oh, really? Then where are you?"

"Don't you know?" I responded. "You made the call."

She explained, "But I don't even know what area I'm calling. I just dialed the number that I had on this paper."

"Ma'am, you won't believe this, but I'm in a phone booth in Dayton, Ohio."

"Really?" she exclaimed. "Well, what are you doing there?"

I kidded her gently. "Well, I'm answering the phone. It was ringing as I walked by, so I answered it."

Knowing this encounter could only have been arranged by God, I began to counsel the woman. As she told me of her despair and frustration, the presence of the Holy Spirit flooded the phone booth giving me words of wisdom beyond my ability. In a matter of moments, she prayed the sinner's prayer and met the One who would lead her out of her situation into a new life.

I walked away from that telephone booth with an electrifying sense of our Heavenly Father's concern for each of His children. What were the astronomical odds of this happening? With all the millions of phones and innumerable combinations of numbers, only an all-knowing God could have caused that woman to call that number in that phone booth at that moment in time.

Forgetting my drink and nearly bursting with exhilaration, I headed back to my family, wondering if they would believe my story. Maybe I better not tell this, I thought; but I couldn't contain it. "Barb, you won't believe this. God knows where I am!"

"For the eyes of the Lord run to and fro throughout the whole earth, to show himself strong in behalf of them whose heart is perfect towards him...." (1 Chr 16:9).

THE LONG WHITE DRESS 1991 A.D.

"Titiana, now tell me exactly everything you did," the mother said to her three-year-old. "Let's rehearse what happened. Now, I was in the kitchen cooking, and then what did you do?" The three-year-old tried to explain, hoping that she was not in trouble.

Titiana had grown up in a very difficult family situation. Her Godly mother, Australia, met and married a man who proved to be unsuitable. Ramon grew more impatient with Australia the more she grew in her Christian walk; he did not want to have a "Jesus freak" for a wife. As tension mounted, Titiana grew concerned about her parents. What could she do, being just a very little girl?

Her mother had taught her how to pray to Jesus, in Spanish, and to implore Christ to save her papa. But those prayers seemed unanswered, and things grew worse, until the day Ramon moved back to his native country, the Dominican Republic, to live with his mother, Zoraida. Titiana tried to keep joyful, but she missed her papa very much. For what seemed an eternity to a child, she prayed with no results for her father's conversion and return home. In 1991, at age three, she decided to call her father in the Dominican Republic to tell him she loved him so much and wanted him to come back home.

Naturally, she could not know how to punch all those numbers on the phone as she had seen her mother do. But Titiana had the simple faith a child can have in her Savior Jesus. Having seen her mother and some others in church raise their hands during prayers, she approached the phone, raised her hands, and prayed, "Papa Dios, I miss my daddy so much, and I want to call him at Grandmama's, but I do not know how to punch the right numbers. Please help me."

Australia was in the kitchen cooking when she heard her

daughter talking. She surmised that her daughter was playing on the phone as she had done on previous occasions. Young children think the phone is a wonderful toy, especially when an operator will come on and say, "Now hang the phone up." Australia finally left her kitchen duty and asked Titiana what she was doing. Titiana simply said, "Talking to Grandmama Zoraida in the Dominican Republic."

Her mother said, "Sure, sweetheart. Let me have the phone." She expected to hear the operator on the line with a mild rebuke about letting her child play with the phone. Much to her surprise, it was indeed Grandmama, in the Dominican Republic. Australia said, "Hello, Grandmama. It is nice of you to call."

Grandmama said, "Yo no llame; tu me llamaest." ("I did not call; you called.") Australia, thinking her mother-in-law must be well aware of the tension between Ramon and herself, said, "Now, Grandmama, we don't have to play games with each other." Grandmama assured her she did not call, so they concluded Titiana had, but how? She was only three and had not gone to preschool, and she did not know her numbers! Calling overseas with all the complicated numbers is difficult for adults, so how could a three-year-old have called?

Australia then proceeded to go over every detail with her daughter. Titiana told her mother that after she finished praying, she opened her eyes. A man in a "long, white dress" was standing next to her, and he told her to punch the numbers he would say to her. Titiana obeyed, and as the phone lines were connected the man disappeared. She being young and simple in faith thought nothing of the event. It was as if this was a natural response to prayer. Her mother was amazed, since she had not heard any other voice, nor seen anything while in the kitchen.

Australia, being on a very tight budget since her irresponsible husband deserted them, made an account of all long distance calls to compare with the phone statement once a month. When the phone statement came, she expected to pay for the call her daughter made the previous month, but lo and behold, no record of the call was ever listed. It appeared that God's mighty hand placed the call at His expense. This story is testified to be true and was personally given to me by the mother, Austraila while ministering in her church.

Titiana is at the time of this writing eight years old. Her father is still hardened to the Gospel. Titiana would appreciate your prayers for Ramon to be saved and brought back to her mother. She is a brokenhearted young child. Her faith continues strong, and she spends some of her time ministering with her church to the down-and-out of the inner city. The ministry is called "Front Line Ministries." Titiana, the youngest member, goes to encourage others by singing hymns and speaking a kind word to the drunks, addicts, and street people with the good news of salvation that only Christ can bring. My prayer is that God will now save Ramon. Salvation is the most remarkable display of the mighty hand of God. The angels rejoice over the salvation of sinners. Never underestimate the faith of a little child.

"And they brought young children to him, that he should touch them: and his disciples rebuked those that brought them. But when Jesus saw it, he was much displeased, and said unto them, Suffer the little children to come unto me, and forbid them not: for of such is the kingdom of God. Verily I say unto you, Whosoever shall not receive the kingdom of God as a little child, he shall not enter therein. And he took them up in his arms, put his hands upon them, and blessed them" (Mark 10:13-16).

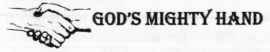

GOING DOWN THE RIVER
FOR THE LAST TIME 1992 A.D.

The hot and muggy month of July in 1992, was proving to be perfect timing for swimming in the Satilla River. At the beginning of the church youth camp-out and swimming party, no one realized that a terrible event would almost claim the life of church counselor Mike Andrews.

The Bible Baptist Church of Brunswick, Georgia, had always had fun times planned for the teen department, and this July 31, was no different. Mike Andrews, Ted Day, and others had spent many days planning a camping trip along the Satilla River which winds down through the South Georgia swamps west of Brunswick. These trips had always been a favorite time for the church teenage boys. Mike's father owned the land where the camping trip was to take place. The boys enjoyed being with their two church counselors, Mike and Ted. Both of these men were excellent examples for the boys.

Mike is a big-framed man, standing 6 feet 2 inches and weighing 260 pounds. There was no fat on him, and the boys really enjoyed wrestling around and trying to pin him. Mike worked at Georgia Pacific, a local pulp mill. His Christian testimony was widely known, and Mike never backed down from telling people what Jesus Christ meant to him. Anyone who thought Christians were sissies never met Mike Andrews.

Ted, like Mike, stands 6 foot 2 inches and weighs 245 pounds. His muscles bulge as a result of working out in the barbell club he owns. His powerful build allows him to witness on a regular basis to young men working out in the barbell club. Thankfully, Ted's devotion to Jesus is greater than his devotion to body building. He was looking forward to this time with the teen boys and the camping trip on the river.

Friday night was a typical camping trip evening with

teenagers. Very few slept, and the campfire stayed big and roaring as the boys fed wood to the fire most of the night. Mike and Ted got as much sleep as they could, considering the pranks the boys had planned. However, after midnight, all finally went to sleep, dreaming of the next day on the river.

Saturday morning started off as any morning you would expect along the beautiful winding river in South Georgia. It was quiet on the morning of August 1, with only the rippling river making a splashing sound as it rounded the turns of the Satilla. The boys awoke first and enjoyed attacking their unsuspecting counselors. In a matter of minutes, all headed over the bluff and into the cool river for a Saturday morning swim. The teen boys ranged from 13 to 18 years old. Typically the older boys didn't want the little ones with them, but Mike and Ted said, "one for all, all for one," and that settled that. After the boys hit the river, the young ones became the objects of attack from the older boys. It was a blast picking them up and throwing them off the bluff, and really, the young boys enjoyed it just as much as the older boys. Boys will be boys, and big boys always like to show off their strength. Everyone was having such a good time that no one had even thought of eating breakfast.

The Satilla River was deep around all the bluffs and made good diving right off the banks. All the teens were having a contest for the best dive. After the best diving events ended, the contest changed to the best belly flops. Everyone could participate in this event as it took no special talent to land flat on the stomach. However, as some found out rather quickly, it does require some strong stomach muscles. Mike had spent his entire life diving off these banks, as his father had owned this land for many years. Mike showed the boys where the deep water was and where the current was either strong or weak. Both Ted and Mike watched with eagle eyes to keep the boys in view. They had been in the pastor's office before the camping trip and received stern warning to keep their eyes on the boys. Pastor Mike Landrum enjoyed the teen camping trips, but always made the counselors understand, he did not want anyone getting hurt. Therefore, every boy was required to wear a life jacket, which proved to be God-ordained. Both counselors fully understood their responsibility and watched all the heads in the river. The youth were having so much fun no one thought of having to watch counselors.

Some of the other adults from the church showed up Saturday morning and also enjoyed watching the teens having a fun time. Ted decided he would show the boys how to dive and immediately made a perfect dive into the river. He came up and swam to the bank. He had no problem making the dive into the deep river. Mike decided to follow Ted and dove approximately in the same spot as Ted.

Mike dove just as Ted had done, but something went wrong. Mike hit something underwater and immediately knew there was something terribly wrong. The pain shot through his body, almost blacking him out. Everything seemed to stop for him. He could not move his head, neck, arms, hands, or legs. He was completely paralyzed. He almost had a peaceful ending as he lay on the bottom of the river, slowly being swept down river by the current. However, Mike somehow got his senses about him and began to struggle, but still could not move a muscle. The current had started to move him down the river and suddenly an uplifting current from nowhere lifted his large frame to the top of the river. His head broke the surface and Mike gasped for a needed breath of air. With all his might he yelled for help. Mike could hear the laughing, and out of the corner of his eye, half covered with water, he could make out the images of the boys and some adults sitting on the riverbank looking at him. Everyone thought that Mike was playing. It was too late as his body slowly sank again to the river bottom.

Again Mike thought he was never to come up again. Still paralyzed, Mike was running out of that last breath and even thought of death. Mike's family began to cross his mind as he had wished he could have told them one last time of his love for them. Would they be okay after his death? All this was going through his mind as he remained silent on the bottom of the river, awaiting to see his Lord he had served these last few years.

Suddenly another swift current lifted him again for another breath, but he again could not get the attention of the people on the bank. Mike sank for the third and probably last time. It was soon to be over.

However, one thirteen-year-old, smaller than the rest, had stayed out of the way of the rough horseplay of the bigger boys. Justin Goodbread had tried to avoid the attacks of the older boys and even had put on a larger military-style life jacket. He hoped that if the bigger boys did get him, the extra large life jacket would help him swim in the river much easier. Suddenly, Justin noticed Mike's body drifting down for the third time, and Justin had a feeling that something was wrong. Justin ran down the bank and dove into the river, life jacket and all, swimming to where he had seen Mike go down. It was the "last time." The current was swift, and Justin had to catch Mike who was also caught up in the current. As Mike went down, Justin got to the point and dove down into the dark river to reach for his counselor. Justin felt a hand underwater and pulled with all his might. His 95 pounds was trying to lift 260 pounds, and even in the water, Justin struggled with all his might to get Mike up to the top. Mike was about to go unconscious when his head broke the surface. There, holding him up, was the littlest boy on the trip. That old military life jacket was keeping both Mike and Justin above water. Justin slowly moved back to shore as more people had realized this was no game and Mike was truly hurt. As Justin laid Mike on the shallow bank, he cradled his head to keep anything from moving. Justin Goodbread had saved his counselor's life. Someone had gone for help and the emergency squad arrived shortly afterwards. Securing his neck in a brace, the squad transported Mike Andrews to the hospital.

After extensive tests, the Savannah hospital detected that he had crushed cervical # 2 vertebra and cracked cervical # 3 and #4 vertebra. Doctors were totally amazed that Mike was still alive. Generally 99 percent of these injuries results in becoming a quadriplegic like famed Joni Eareckson Tada. Mike went into surgery shortly after arriving in Savannah. The vertebras were fused together.

As in all serious accidents, reflection occurs after the fact. It dawned on friends and family how God's superintending hand was present in what seemed to be even minor details. Take for example, the first time Mike came up for a breath of air, had he come up next to an adult, instead of Justin, and been grabbed forcefully as an adult would naturally do, it could have been the very jerk that would have caused him to become paralyzed for life, or worse, dying from severing the spinal cord. Both times Mike needed air he was mysteriously lifted to the surface. The last time Mike went down, he prayed that God would save him from the river. At that moment his arms moved for the first time. As his arm went up over his head, Justin happened to be exactly over the spot where Mike was. Reaching down into a dark river, providentially their hands met and Justin grabbed hold, praying their hands would not slip apart. If Mike's hands had not come up, Justin might have reached and found Mike's head instead. This would have resulted in Mike's being paralyzed or killed.

Justin, of all the boys present had put on the only large military life jacket at the river. It was big enough to carry the weight of a large man. If Justin had not obeyed and had this life jacket on, he would never have been able to hold Mike up in the river. Justin had to swim 60 feet in a swift current, reach his counselor, get him up for air, then swim with the current to get Mike to the bank. Normally, Justin would not have been able to do this alone, much less pulling a 260-pound man. If Justin had switched his hold and grabbed for the neck, this would have resulted in paralysis or death. If anyone had tried to lift Mike out of the river, it would have been fatal.

God daily showed His mighty hand of power while Mike was in the hospital. Miraculously, one week later Mike was released from the hospital to go home. Justin Goodbread's fast reaction saved the life of his church counselor and friend. The Lord used the littlest member of the swimming party to rescue the largest member, so that men would recognize the mighty hand of God.

At the time of this writing, Mike Andrews is studying for the ministry and has nearly recovered the full use of his neck, with the exception of stiffness. Perhaps this is a daily reminder of what God has done for him. It could be said in a humorous way, Mike is a "stiff-necked" Christian, and studying to be a "stiff necked"preacher someday.

Former President George Bush and his wife personally sent Justin Goodbread a letter of commendation for bravery and alertness, which he highly cherishes. Justin continues to be home educated, and is seeking the Lord for further guidance as to his future plans.

"Then they cried unto the LORD in their trouble, and he saved them out of their distresses. He brought them out of darkness and the shadow of death, and brake their bands in sunder. Oh that men would praise the LORD for his goodness, and for his wonderful works to the children of men!" (Psalm 107:13-15).

FOR THE LOVE OF FAMILY 1992 A.D.

Orestes Lorenzo Perez, (Lorenzo to his friends and family) found himself praying in a Catholic chapel in desperation. His prayers to "El Señor" for his family were with deep travail and tears of lament. After being transfixed in the presence of God for some time, Lorenzo was startled to see a woman walk up to him and say, "God has heard your prayers. You will succeed in your mission." As the woman walked away, Lorenzo thought perhaps God was indeed with him in his harebrained idea. After all, how could a total stranger know of his secret mission?

A little background is necessary in order to fully appreciate the mighty hand of God at work once again in the lives of people. Lorenzo was born in 1956, two years before Fidel Castro's guerrilla forces overthrew the Batista regime in Cuba. When Lorenzo was three, his Uncle Orlando brought him a Christmas gift from the United States—a toy airplane. Inspired by the airplane at that early age, Lorenzo began to dream of flying.

His dream eventually led him to be chosen for a scholarship to flight school in the Soviet Union. There he learned to fly a small Czechoslovakian Aero L-29 Delfin two-seat jet trainer. Soon he was flying MiG-21s in Angola, as part of the Cuban forces sent to support the country's Marxist government against the guerrilla armies attempting to overthrow it.

Lorenzo married his wife Victoria in 1976, and they were blessed with two sons. While Lorenzo's military career forced him to endure long separations from his wife, Victoria studied to become a dentist. Their first son, Reyniel, was born in 1981. Four years later the family was sent to the Soviet Union so Lorenzo could attend Officers Training School. Their second son, Alejandro, was born a year later.

When they finally returned to Cuba, Lorenzo was assigned to Santa Clara Air Base, about 165 miles east of Havana. There he found that the only changes in Cuba had been for the worse. Even compared to life in the Soviet Union, which was undergoing the thaw of Mikhail Gorbachev's glasnost, Cuba was unbearably oppressive. Castro, trying to distract the citizens from their internal problems, now kept the country on alert for a United States invasion. "I used to sleep inside the base, three or four nights at a time, because we were told, 'Tomorrow will be the American invasion,'" Lorenzo remembers. "Psychologically, it was terrible."

By this time, he had become deputy base commander. Lorenzo talked with his wife for months about what to do. Finally they both realized he must try to escape Cuba. "We decided that the best way to do it would be for me to fly away," he says. On March 20, 1991, Lorenzo appeared in the Florida skies over Boca Chica Naval Air Station in a MiG-23, circling three times in the noon sun and rocking his wings to signify friendly intentions.

The Cuban government publicly promised that any Cuban with a visa would be allowed to leave the country, which was propaganda common to the dictatorship. Lorenzo hoped the government would want to avoid a scandal by releasing his family since he was a well-known military figure. Yet just in case, he told Victoria on the day he left, "If in a year you are not allowed to leave Cuba, I will be back for you. I don't know how, in a boat, a plane, or swimming, but I will be back for you and the children."

Soon after his arrival in the United States, Lorenzo started a campaign to win back his family. American/Cuban Radio Marti carried his appeals across the Florida Straits to Cuba in hopes of creating political pressure to release his family. Lorenzo then began to travel throughout the United States and the world to seek support from governments that would put pressure on the Cuban government to grant a visa for his family. His travels landed him in New York City, where he denounced the government of his former country at an anti-Castro rally. In Geneva, Switzerland, he asked for the world's help before a United Nations Human Rights Commission. In Madrid, Spain, he chained himself to the gates of Retiro Park and went on a week-long hunger strike. He met with a host of dignitaries, including President George Bush, Mikhail and Raisa Gorbachev, and Coretta Scott King. But it was all to no avail.

Lorenzo began to feel increasingly helpless. He began to have disturbing dreams and visions of his children calling for him. He recalls, "Every night my children were calling me. In fact, I used to sleep a couple of hours and I'd get up scared because I could swear that my children were with me in my room calling for help."

Finally Lorenzo received word that, rather than granting Victoria and the boys visas to join him, the Cuban government planned to cause them to suffer for his defection and never allow them to leave the country. He then realized he would somehow have to rescue them himself. Helicopters and speedboats were out, both were too expensive. The only way he could get to Cuba and back again was with a light airplane. So Lorenzo decided to take flying lessons. Although he had flown over a thousand hours in high-performance jet aircraft, he had never flown piston-engine or light airplanes. He enrolled in a flight school near his new home in northern Virginia, and for six weeks the ex-MiG pilot attended classes with a dozen neophyte aviators as fellow students.

As soon as he obtained his license, Lorenzo started to look for an airplane. Through friends at the Valladares Foundation, a human rights organization founded in 1989 by a former Cuban political prisoner, he learned of a 1961 Cessna 310F with 6,000 hours on it. Painted white with a blue racing stripe and a nose the same turquoise as the water off the Florida Keys, the twin-engine airplane had been manufactured the same year as the Bay of Pigs invasion, and it looked its age. Originally owned by the state of Georgia, it had been in New Mexico for awhile until a man named Ron Murphy purchased it in November 1991. Murphy was willing to sell it for $30,000, and the Valladares Foundation agreed to purchase the airplane for the rescue attempt. Lorenzo was now ready to carry out his scheme. It was at this time that he prayed at the chapel and received God's confirmation of His will, at the beginning of our story.

At around 4 a.m. on December 19, 1992, the manager of the Seaward Motel on Florida's Marathon Key heard the bell ring at the front desk. The manager eyed with suspicion the Hispanic man who checked in under the name of Mr. Garcia. This was southern Florida, where drug smuggling, much of it by air, was a fact of life. Marathon Airport, a small facility that handles mostly Piper Cubs and a handful of corporate jets, was just across Route 1 from the motel. In fact, Lorenzo, alias Mr. Garcia, had just landed there in the twin-engine Cessna 310. He was using a pseudonym in order to carry his dangerous mission to success. When he checked into the Seaward Motel, Lorenzo had not slept for three days. He still could not indulge in sleep: he must summarize the plans for his flight.

Orestes Lorenzo Perez had made headlines the previous year when he defected to the United States by flying a MiG-23 to Florida. Now he was planning a defection in reverse: a flight back to Cuba to rescue his wife and two sons. Every night for the past several months he had been mapping his strategy in his tiny one-bedroom apartment in the Washington, D.C. suburbs. He had purchased a map of Cuba's western coast at a store only two blocks from the White House, and he marked it with equations and sunset times. He hoped his inside knowledge of Cuban air defenses would help him slip through the system.

The next morning he walked back to the airport to check his Cessna. He refueled the two wingtip tanks for what he hoped would be a 200-mile round trip. Several hours before he had arrived in Marathon Key, he had called his wife and, in a carefully planned code, told her when he would be arriving. He would start his flight around sunset, arrive with the last rays of the sun, and escape under a descending curtain of darkness. He needed just enough light to land on a highway, and then darkness to protect him from any Cuban MiG-21s that might pursue him. To arrive at the rendezvous site in Cuba at 5:45 p.m., Lorenzo calculated that he would need to take off at 5:07 p.m. exactly.

Later that morning two friends from the Valladares Foundation met him at the airport. They wanted to take pictures of Lorenzo with his Cessna, and he good-naturedly complied, although he was nervous about creating a scene. Well aware of the prevalence of drug smuggling in the Florida Keys, he didn't want to arouse suspicion by hanging around the airport. He and his friends went for a walk, had lunch at Pizza Hut, and ate ice cream cones.

At 4:00 p.m., Lorenzo returned to the airplane, did a final walk-around check, and then climbed into the cockpit. He was still wearing the running suit, an early Christmas present from friends who had asked him to wear it on the flight. He sat in the cabin repeating everything until 4:50. Then he started the engine. After one more run-through of his checklist, he taxied slowly to the runway. At exactly 5:07 he radioed local air traffic: "Cessna 5819. Departing runway 07."

Lorenzo left the Florida Keys, flying about a thousand feet above the calm, translucent ocean. Far off, he could see a tanker crossing the Florida Straits. Ninety miles away lay Cuba. On his left knee Lorenzo held his flight plan. On his right knee he had strapped his calculator. He had also brought a camera, some soft drinks, and a box of chocolates. To protect himself in the event he was caught, he had left all identification cards at home. As he flew further over the Gulf of Mexico and the water turned darker blue, he shut down the radar transponder, lights, and radio to avoid being detected.

After he had been flying for about 15 minutes, Lorenzo started to descend until he was flying about ten feet above the waves. His altimeter indicated zero. He had a loran (long rang navigation) system to navigate and determine his geographical position. As he approached the 24th parallel, which lies almost halfway between Key West, Florida, and Cuba, he realized that he was ahead of schedule. At Marathon he had obtained figures for wind velocity and direction, but the tailwind was a little stronger than expected.

Lorenzo considered making a 360-degree turn to kill time, but decided against it in case he was already on Cuban radar.

Lorenzo had calculated that once he appeared on Cuban radar, he would have about 15 minutes to pick up his family. He knew it took 20 seconds for the radar to complete a 360-degree sweep. Even if the radar operator were paying close attention, the radar would have to sweep the screen three times before the operator could positively identify Lorenzo's Cessna as an aircraft flying south. But Cuba's P-14 radar didn't provide altitude information: to get that, the operator would have to call a PRV-11 radar operator. This would give Lorenzo at least another minute.

The key to Lorenzo's plan was the clumsy chain of command that would be initiated at this point. An alert would require a time-consuming series of phone calls up the command hierarchy, from a company to a battalion to a brigade to a division. That would buy him a few more minutes as he drew closer to his destination.

He had other advantages. He knew that the island has daily blackouts to save power, so the radar is often shut down. The system's old Russian radar uses tubes instead of transistors, and Cuba's humidity causes them to break down often. He also knew that the people operating the radar were increasingly apathetic. "The situation in Cuba is nobody cares for anything," he says.

In fact, Lorenzo was less concerned that the Cuban air defense system would catch him than he was that his wife and children wouldn't make it to the rendezvous point. Victoria would have a difficult trip. When Lorenzo was checking into the Seaward Motel earlier that morning, his wife had been waking up at her parents' house in Havana, where she had moved with her sons after Lorenzo's defection. To reach the rendezvous spot, she had to travel 70 miles through a country where gasoline was so scarce that Castro had declared 1991 the Year of the Bicycle. Victoria and the boys left at 8 a.m. and, like many around Cuba, caught rides with passing cars. For each ride she paid a hundred pesos—in a country where an engineer made only three times that in a month.

Lorenzo would have liked to meet his family on a highway where he used to land his MiG-21 during military exercises. But the rendezvous would have to take place at a spot that was both accessible to his wife and not likely to arouse the suspicion of anyone keeping her under surveillance. This meant the rescue site had to be somewhere between Havana and Matanzas, where his parents lived.

He knew the Matanzas area well because he used to snorkel nearby. For the rendezvous point, Lorenzo had chosen a new highway that ran from the old coastal highway to a new airport. The only problem was that the site was located near four anti-aircraft missile complexes. But Lorenzo knew that authorities would need Castro's personal okay before shooting down an airplane. Even after Castro had been located and had given the command, it would still take a minimum of three minutes to warm up the radar if it had been shut off during a blackout. Lorenzo also knew that the missiles' range was only 15 miles. He hoped that by the time the missiles were ready to fire, he would be well on his way back to Florida.

Not far past the 24th parallel, Lorenzo saw Matanzas materialize on the horizon. First he saw the hills that loom over the city, then the buildings and the 400-foot-high bridge that spans the Canimar River. As he approached the bridge he began to climb. His wife was supposed to be waiting about a mile east of the bridge, where the road curves around a hill. Lorenzo was flying so low, however, that the hill blocked his view of the rendezvous site. He banked around the hill at about 20 feet and finally spotted the rendezvous place. But he still didn't see Victoria. He had only a single chance to land, so he reduced speed and dropped the landing gear.

He was approaching to land on the two-lane highway when he saw his wife on his left. As he had instructed, she and the children were wearing brightly colored clothes so he could spot them quickly. It had been twenty-one months since he had last seen them, and now there they were on the side of a road, wearing fluorescent orange T-shirts and caps. Below him, a small car was moving in the same direction as the airplane. Several hundred yards ahead of it a truck was approaching. Behind that a bus was trying to pass. Lorenzo planned to fly over the car and land in the highway between the car and the oncoming truck when he noticed a large rock in the middle of the road.

He didn't have room for a proper landing, but he knew there wasn't time for a second approach. He overflew the car, raised the left wing to pass the rock, then touched down. When the Cessna came to a stop, Lorenzo found himself staring directly at the truck's driver, who sat clutching his steering wheel, his eyes wide and mouth open.

Victoria didn't see her husband until the airplane was almost on the ground. She and the children had their backs turned to the Cessna as it approached and couldn't hear it because of the traffic on the highway. Now they ran toward the airplane, Victoria gripping her sons' hands.

While his family was running to him, Lorenzo turned the Cessna around and then made another 90-degree turn to the left to keep the propellers away from his family. He opened the door on the starboard side and they scrambled up into the cockpit: Reyniel, Alejandro, and finally his wife. Alejandro was barefoot because he had lost both his shoes while running. "Papa! Papa!" the children cried as they tried to hug their father. But Lorenzo had to concentrate, and he sternly ordered them to be quiet and sit in the seats behind him.

His family now aboard, Lorenzo hurried to close the door. Twice he tried, and each time he failed. "Calmate, calmate," his wife said. "Calm down, calm down." On the third try he got the door closed.

With the airplane's flaps set for a short field takeoff, Lorenzo began to accelerate down the highway. As the airspeed indicator showed 60 mph—not fast enough to take off—Lorenzo could see the highway's curve approaching. He pulled the yoke back slowly, and the airplane continued accelerating, gaining speed.

Finally the Cessna cleared the ground. "We did it!" Lorenzo thought, as he retracted the landing gear. In the back seat, Victoria wrapped her arms around the boys. They recited the Lord's Prayer, praising God for His mighty hand of deliverance: *"Padre nuestro que estás en los cielos, santificado sea tu nombre....."*

As he left Cuba, Lorenzo flew over the sea as low as he could. "I had experienced flying at low altitude for the war in Angola," he says. By flying over the water at night at low altitude and low speed, he hoped to be an elusive target for any pursuing MiG, which would have to spot him from above, using radar information from the ground that would be at least three minutes old by the time the pilots received it.

Soon it became too dark for Lorenzo to continue hugging the water safely. He climbed to 200 feet and maintained that altitude until he reached the 24th parallel. There he climbed to 3,000 feet and turned the transponder and lights back on. Victoria and Lorenzo took some pictures with the camera, and Lorenzo remembered to give his children the box of chocolates he had brought. It was dark. No moon or stars were shining, but soon Lorenzo saw the lights of the Keys and U.S. Route 1 with the lights of cars, beautiful lights of a nation that would become their new home. America, "the land of the free and the home of the brave." The Perezes were indeed a brave family, and they were the kind of people America needs most: those who appreciate its God-given blessing.

"Mira, mira," Lorenzo urged his wife as he pointed to the lights. "Look there, look ahead." He called air traffic control, and they assigned him an altitude of 7,000 feet. Originally he had planned to fly to an airport near Miami, but now he was spent, physically and emotionally, and ready to land. "I was so excited," he says. "I wanted to embrace them, and not wait a moment longer after being apart twenty-one months."

At 6:45 p.m. he was back on the ground. From start to finish the rescue flight had taken less than 100 minutes. Those 100 minutes had seemed like an eternity.

"Have not I commanded thee? Be strong and of a good courage; be not afraid, neither be thou dismayed: for the Lord thy God is with thee whithersoever thou goest" (Joshua 1:9).

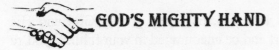# GOD'S MIGHTY HAND

MINISTERING SPIRITS 1996 A.D.

(As told by Pastor Steve Coy)

It was about 7 o'clock Friday morning, September 22, 1996. I was working my way up a local canyon in my 4WD Bronco. I planned to sit at daybreak overlooking the mouth of the canyon in hopes of catching a buck returning to bed from the green meadows below. I scanned the slopes on both sides of me as I neared the area where I would park. I was more intent on looking for deer during the first hints of daylight than on driving, and suddenly found my right rear tire had slipped off the road into a creek hole. I was stuck. I climbed out to put the front hubs in gear, then climbed back in to see if the rig could pull itself out. No go. It spun tires in forward and moved nowhere. I put it in reverse without better results. I climbed out again to look behind the truck to determine if there was any room to reverse the rig out of its present predicament. It didn't look good. Thoughts of the possibility of needing to hike out for help were entering my mind. I re-entered the rig thinking, "Lord, is this all I came up here for, to get stuck?" I went to press the gas pedal once more to try to climb out. Before my foot touched the pedal, the truck lurched forward and out of the hole, somewhat jerking my head back. I quickly touched the gas pedal lightly, and the truck settled safely back on the road. Something or Someone of great strength had pushed me and my truck out of that hole. I sat there somewhat stunned for a moment.

The realization that something supernatural had just occurred in my behalf began to flood my soul. Tears came to my eyes and I whispered, "Thank you, Lord." I sat for two minutes overwhelmed by the goodness of God in my behalf. I share this testimony publicly not to bring attention to myself, for I am nothing special, and certainly one of the least of the servants of the Lord. I share it that you, too, may glorify God and His goodness in your heart and be encouraged in your faith. If you're one who still wonders if God is real, this verse came to my mind and made Him very real to me on that early September morning:

"Are they not all ministering spirits, (angels) sent forth to minister for them who are the heirs of salvation?" (Hebrews 1:14)

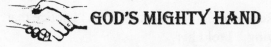

A CHRISTMAS SURPRISE 1997 A.D.

I conclude God's Mighty Hand (Providential Occurrences in World History) Volume I by writing of a personal experience that shows how the hand of God works in our lives. After my story you will find several blank pages for you to write those times God's mighty hand became evident to you. This exercise is important for you and your heritage to remember the goodness of God on your behalf. This book was packed with many wonderful testimonies which might make your experiences seem insignificant. Do not let that deter you from writing of your experiences. To the world they may seem slight, but to you they are assurances of God's care and watchfulness. The story you are about to read tells of a turning point in my faith and trust in the Lord. I would not trade anything in the world for what the Lord taught us through this event many years ago. You also have such testimonies. Write them down—who knows but what someone may someday benefit from your story.

If you believe your story would be one that should be printed in *God's Mighty Hand (Providential Occurrences in World History) Volume 2,* or if you know of a story that shows the mighty hand of God in the life of another, please submit it along with your name, address, and phone number to allow me to contact you if I have any questions.

Excerpt taken from *The Little Bear Story (A Retarded Gopher Trapper).* Available upon request in writing.

"Now, let me go back to tell you of how the Lord provided for my family during the time I didn't have a job. While I was on one of my prayer walks (this has been my typical manner of prayer for over the past twenty-five years), the Lord prompted me to go up to a stranger's door and knock to ask if I could mow the lawn. I obeyed. When I knocked, an elderly lady answered. "I notice that your lawn needs mowing," I told her.

"I am a widow, and I don't have any money to pay you," she said.

"You don't need to pay me. I'll gladly do it as a Christian act of love and charity."

She was overcome with surprise and consented to my labor of love. She was so appreciative that, from time to time, she came outside to thank me and offered me a glass of lemonade.

I finished the job, so I knocked on her door and told her, "Good-bye."

As I started to leave, she said, "I want to give you a donation for helping me." I tried to talk her out of doing so, but she insisted that I receive the money as *"unto the Lord."*

I left humbled and grateful to the Lord for leading me there and for His provision. God's provision was always exactly what was needed. We learned, first hand, that *"my God shall supply all your need according to His riches in glory by Christ Jesus"* *(Philippians 4:19).*

Another example of God's provision was when I needed leather to sew my buckskin Royal Ranger outfit. There was a wonderful leather shop in town which was run by a Christian couple, the Walters. I often went to the shop to fellowship with the couple and, all the while, I would secretly drool over the leather, wishing I could afford it. During one of my visits, Howard Walter told me that he needed to paint his building, which was a huge two-story structure. I asked him if I could paint it for him free of charge, but he said, "No." I replied, "I don't work for pay but only to do the Lord's service."

Howard's comeback was, "You can work for a donation of part money and part leather."

"You've got a deal!" I was elated. Howard didn't know that I wanted leather to make my outfit, but the Lord did and He was making provision! I borrowed scaffolding and a paint sprayer from the local school district and began painting. About two weeks later, I completed the job and walked home happy as a lark because I had enough leather to make my entire buckskin outfit. For three months I hand-stitched my outfit including all the Indian beadwork. Today, the outfit is worth $1,500. My buckskin outfit has been used as an evangelistic tool in numerous ways throughout the United States. It has been used by God to lead countless numbers of children to Christ as I have woven the Gospel message with a mountain man or Indian theme of one sort or another. Not having a job and pursuing my desire to follow Jesus left me with no choice but to live a life of faith. Living the life of faith can be scary and, at the same time, exhilarating. I wouldn't trade those years for "all the tea in China."

God granted us another remarkable answer to prayer. One Christmas season, Marilyn expressed to me in private that she longed for a roast beef for our Christmas meal. Now, this may seem strange to some, but for Marilyn it was perfectly normal as she is from Scottish descent. As turkeys are a part of the typical American tradition, so roast beef is of the typical Scottish tradition. As a husband, I wanted to please my wife and provide her every need and desire whenever possible. I contemplated her desire, but a roast was so much more expensive than a turkey. I was doubtful that I could buy a turkey much less a roast beef. My faith was little in regard to such a request. In passing, I silently mentioned my wife's request to the Lord. *"Casting all your care upon him; for he careth for you" (I Peter 5:7).* I asked the Lord to lead me and I left my request at His feet and went about my merry way, thinking, "A Christmas turkey would be blessing enough as there are times when we don't have enough money to know even where our next carton of milk is going to come from."

It may not have been expected, but the Lord always provided our needs and sometimes our desires too. What amazed me was that the Lord never provided in the same way twice. In His infinite wisdom and abundance, He always guided and provided in a unique way. During one of those times when we were wondering what our next meal would be, I came home and found outside our front door a bag of three freshly skinned chickens that the Lord had prompted someone to place there anonymously.

Christmas was fast approaching and I had resigned to forgo getting anything but yams to eat for our Christmas meal. However, two days before Christmas, we were summoned to the door by a knock. When we opened the door, we saw Mr. Leo Phillips who was the father of our dear friend Steve Phillips, the boat builder. Mr. Phillips said, "Merry Christmas, Wheelers! The Lord has prompted my wife, Dodie, and me to bring over a Christmas turkey to thank you for your service in our church." We were blessed and grateful beyond words. A big hug sufficed as we were too choked up to say much of anything else. Now, at least, we could add turkey to our Christmas dinner. The thought of having only yams for dinner didn't sound all that great.

The next day, on Christmas Eve, we heard another knock at the door. This time, we found Steve Phillips, himself, standing out in the cold with a brown bag. As Steve stepped into our living room, he wasn't aware that his dad had been over the day before with a turkey, and we weren't about to tell him since we were in such dire need. Both Marilyn and I were thinking that we could have the second turkey for our New Year's dinner, so I said, "Steve, thank you so very much-we love turkey. It's so good and the leftovers make great enchiladas and tacos. Praise God."

Steve said, "Wait a minute! Don't get your hopes up too high because, while I was fixing to pick up a turkey, Carol and I decided perhaps we should get you a ham."

By this time, my mind was reeling with excitement. I thought to myself, "We can have Mr. Phillips' turkey for Christmas and Steve's ham for New Year's dinner. We won't have to eat so much turkey and get sick of having turkey for both holidays."

Steve continued talking and then said, "We're really sorry, but for some strange reason we didn't feel led to get you the traditional turkey or the ham. Instead, we got you a six-pound roast."

We had tried to conceal our tears from Mr. Phillips, Steve's dad, but we were now unable to hold back our tears of gratitude. In Steve's presence, our tears streamed forward as we experienced God's love and overwhelming assurance of His care and provision. We hadn't told a single person on the face of the earth about Marilyn's desire for a Christmas roast; yet, God knew and, in His love and mercy, He provided.

God has provided so many things for us over the years since then. However, next to our gift of salvation, the Christmas roast has been the greatest blessing that He has given us. That roast caused us to be encouraged and built up in our faith and knowledge of God, our Father, as our eternal provider. I can't get over the fact that God heard our private conversation and responded without our having to toil in prayer about it. God cared for my wife and wanted to bless her.

" *Therefore I say unto you, Take no thought for your life, what ye shall eat, or what ye shall drink; nor yet for your body, what ye shall put on. Is not the life more than meat, and the body than raiment? Behold the fowls of the air: for they sow not, neither do they reap nor gather into barns; yet your heavenly Father feedeth them. Are ye not much better than they? Wherefore, if God so clothe the grass of the field, which today is cast into the oven, shall He not much more clothe you , O ye of little faith? Therefore take no thought saying What shall we eat? or, what shall we drink? or, Wherewithal shall we be clothed.... For your Father knoweth that that ye have need of these things. But seek ye first the kingdom of God, and His righteousness; and all these things shall be added unto you*" (Matthew 6:25-33).

RECOMMENDED READING AND MINISTRIES

I wrote this book to be more of an inspirational volume designed to magnify God's hand in history, than a scholarly thesis. Therefore I did not include a bibliography. The majority of books I used to gather the story line came from our personal library of out-of-print books. If there are specific stories you would like information on, write Mantle Ministries and we will try to supply you with the information you are seeking.

For your further study I have listed available ministries, like ourselves, that specialize in Providential history that magnify the mighty hand of God in world events. Most of the ministries below are also available for speaking engagements and have catalogs of their excellent materials to enhance your knowledge of Providential history.

Rev. Peter Marshall, speaker and author
81 Finlay Road
Orleans, MA 02653
Phone: (508) 255-7705

Rev. Marshall Foster, speaker and author
Mayflower Institute
2159 Speck Lane
Newbury Park, CA 91320
Phone: (805) 499-2044

Dr. Paul Jehle, speaker and author
Heritage Institute
P.O. Box 1353
Sagamore Beach, MA 02562
Phone: (508) 888-1889

David Barton, speaker and author
Wallbuilders
P.O. Box 397
Aledo, TX 76008
Phone: (817) 441-6044

Jim Rose, speaker and author
American Christian History Institute
P.O. Box 648
Palo Cedro, CA 96073
Phone: (916) 547-3535

Steven McDowell, speaker and author
Providence Foundation
P.O. Box 6759
Charlottesville, VA 22906
Phone: (804) 978-4535

Evangelist Richard "Little Bear" Wheeler
speaker, author and publisher
Mantle Ministries
228 Still Ridge
Bulverde, TX 78163
Phone: (830) 438-3777

Write for free catalog of other Mantle Ministries materials
Visit our home page http://www.mantlemin.com
E-mail mantle3377@aol.com

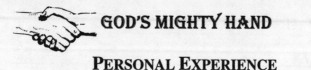

GOD'S MIGHTY HAND

PERSONAL EXPERIENCE   A.D.